Horatio Oliver Ladd

The Story of New Mexico

Horatio Oliver Ladd

The Story of New Mexico

ISBN/EAN: 9783742809841

Manufactured in Europe, USA, Canada, Australia, Japa

Cover: Foto ©ninafisch / pixelio.de

Manufactured and distributed by brebook publishing software (www.brebook.com)

Horatio Oliver Ladd

The Story of New Mexico

THE STORY OF THE STATES

THE STORY OF NEW MEXICO

BY

HORATIO O. LADD

BOSTON
D LOTHROP COMPANY
WASHINGTON OPPOSITE BROMFIELD STREET

COPYRIGHT, 1891,
BY
D. LOTHROP COMPANY.

TO THE

PIONEERS OF NEW MEXICO,

OF WHATEVER RACE, AGE, FAITH OR OCCUPATION,
THIS STORY OF THEIR ADVENTURES, PERILS, TOILS AND SUFFERINGS
IS RESPECTFULLY DEDICATED
BY ONE WHO HAS EMULATED THEIR DEVOTION, SHARED THEIR LABORS
AND CHERISHED THEIR FAITH IN THE FUTURE PROS-
PERITY OF THIS GREAT TERRITORY.

PREFACE.

DURING a residence at Santa Fé, N. M., in the years 1880-90, my duties in planting educational institutions for the American, Mexican and Indian populations, led me to extensive travel among them, and also in behalf of these institutions to the prominent centers of the East. Many opportunities were thus afforded among these strange scenes and experiences, to gather the material for this story of adventure, Indian life and warfare, and of the modern development of New Mexico.

I am greatly indebted not only to prominent libraries in this country but also to J. P. Whitney, Esq., of Boston, whose valuable collection of books on New Mexico was kindly furnished for my use.

Especially, also, do I gratefully acknowledge the friendly aid of Mr. A. de F. Bandelier, of Santa Fé, whose noted archeological publications and unpublished manuscripts were placed at my disposal, after his thorough investigations and transcriptions from the Franciscan Mission and Mexican archives had left no desirable authority for the search of less favored students.

I have also been enabled to make careful use of the official reports of the United States War Department, and the Ethnological and Indian Bureaus at Washington. I have thus examined over seventy volumes and pamphlets in several languages to verify the statements which this history contains. I therefore believe that they will be confirmed by the best authorities, however questioned through the prejudice of party, church or nationality. To avoid this has been the constant desire and effort of

THE AUTHOR.

NEW YORK, February 1, 1891.

CONTENTS.

Period I. to 1536.

CHAPTER I.

ANTIQUITY OF NEW MEXICO, THE ORIGIN AND CONDITION OF ITS FIRST PEOPLES . . . 1

Period II. Spanish Discoveries. 1536 to 1591.

CHAPTER II.

NICA . . . 19

CHAPTER III.

CORONADO'S MARCH AND INVASION . . . 36

CHAPTER IV.

CORONADO'S CONQUESTS . . . 50

CHAPTER V.

CONQUERORS BY THE CROSS . . . 73

CHAPTER VI.

EXPLORERS — ESPEJO, CASTANO . . . 85

CONTENTS.

Period III. Spanish Colonization. 1598 to 1680.

CHAPTER VII.

ONATE . . 101

Period IV. Rebellion and Native Independence. 1680 to 1692.

CHAPTER VIII.

OTERMIN, CRUZATE TO VARGAS   125

Period V. Spanish Rule. 1692 to 1821.

CHAPTER IX.

CAMPAIGNS OF VARGAS AND HIS SUCCESSORS   147

CHAPTER X.

A CENTURY UNDER SPAIN — 1700 to 1800 .   167

Period VI. New Mexico Under the Mexican Confederation. 1821 to 1846.

CHAPTER XI.

ANCIENT DWELLINGS OF NEW MEXICO 173

CHAPTER XII.

THE PUEBLO INDIANS , , , , 198 .

CONTENTS.

CHAPTER XIII.
RELIGIOUS CUSTOMS AND GENERAL CONDITION OF THE PEOPLE IN 1837-40 . 222

CHAPTER XIV.
AMERICAN EXPEDITIONS — ARMIJO 234

Period VII. American Occupation. 1846 to 1862.

CHAPTER XV.
THE COUNTRY AND PEOPLE . . 255

CHAPTER XVI.
NEW MEXICO IN THE WAR OF 1846-47 270

CHAPTER XVII.
CONSPIRACY AND REVOLT . 283

Period VIII. New Mexico in the Civil War. 1862 to 1868.

CHAPTER XVIII.
THE CONFEDERATE INVASION . 297

CHAPTER XIX.
ENGAGEMENTS AT APACHE CANON AND PIGEON'S RANCH — RETREAT OF THE CONFEDERATES . . 316

Period IX. American Rule. 1865 to 1878.

CHAPTER XX.
NAVAJO AND APACHE WARS 333

CONTENTS.

CHAPTER XXI.
SUBJUGATION OF THE NAVAJOES AND CHIEF VICTORIA . 353

CHAPTER XXII.
CONQUEST OF THE CHIRICAHUAS BY GEN. CROOK . . 370

CHAPTER XXIII.
THE CAMPAIGNS OF GEN. MILES . . 390

Period X. American Development. 1879 to 1890.

CHAPTER XXIV.
RAILROADS AND CIVILIZATION 405

CHAPTER XXV.
RELIGION AND PUBLIC EDUCATION . 410

CHAPTER XXVI.
IRRIGATION IN NEW MEXICO . 425

CHAPTER XXVII.
CLAIMS TO STATEHOOD 435

THE CHRONOLOGICAL STORY . . 455
BOOKS RELATING TO NEW MEXICO 463
INDEX . . . 467

ILLUSTRATIONS.

		PAGE.
Coronado's march	*Frontispiece.*	
A home in the cliffs		2
Utensils of the stone age		5
An ancient pueblo restored		9
The country of the Cliff Dwellers		13
A Moqui village		23
In an old pueblo		31
The ancient Navajo		39
View of the Cibola country		45
Old Spanish palace — Santa Fé		55
"Roamed immense herds of buffaloes"		63
A Spanish friar		75
"The Black Robe is dead"		81
A Navajo blanket weaver		89
The Pueblo of Zuñi		95
Pueblo Una Vida, Chaco Cañon		105
A Zuñi interior		113
A Zuñi pueblo restored		131
Death to the Spanish		139
An old Santa Fé Christmas Eve		151
Governors of Zuñi		159
Old New Mexican houses		179
Zuñi clay baskets		189
An Indian idol		205
Pueblo basket work		215
The hour of vespers		225
An adobe house		229

ILLUSTRATIONS.

The pueblo of Santo Domingo	237
A hostile pueblo	245
"The most tremendous chasms and gorges on the continent".	259
A trading company	265
A New Mexican ranch	273
Along the line of march	279
Ringing the church bells at Santa Fé	285
A young pueblo hunter	289
On the line of battle	301
Leaving the lines . . .	309
After the surrender	321
Santa Fé looking north	327
Navajo Indian with silver ornaments . .	337
Apache Indian boy . . .	345
Kit Carson	357
On the Santa Fé trail . .	365
A Chiricahua camp	377
"The rough country cut up with ravines and cañons"	385
Captain Lawton's Attack	393
A New Mexican fireplace	399
Founding a town in an irrigation district, Eddy	407
Victoria the Apache	415
Apache boys, two weeks at school . . .	421
Head-gate irrigating canal in the Pecos Valley	429
State capitol, Santa Fé	439
A field of New Mexico sugar-cane . . .	447

THE STORY OF NEW MEXICO.

PERIOD I. TO 1536.

THE STORY OF NEW MEXICO.

CHAPTER I.

ANTIQUITY OF NEW MEXICO, THE ORIGIN AND CONDITION OF ITS FIRST PEOPLES.

NEW MEXICO is very old. It was the pathway of migrating races within a few centuries of the beginning of the Christian Era. It has been the abode of nations according to Humbolt since the year 600 A.D. Peoples kindred in their remote ancestry with the mound-builders, from the same regions of the Northwest, occupied the lofty mesas and tremendous gorges of New Mexico as they slowly spread southward. Fallen walls, half buried by sand-storms in many desolate places of this country of the Southwest, testify of the lives and activities of a population of many thousands when the Knights of the Middle Ages were leading multitudes on crusades to the Holy Land. Caves and cliffs and the smooth faces of submarine volcanic fissures still preserve the stories of their ancestors and the symbols of their superstitious faith.

A HOME IN THE CLIFFS.

The romance of a prehistoric past broods over this wonderful country. Nearer to us are the incursions of savage and marauding nations, ravaging among the relics of semi-cultured peoples. Even the Spanish conquest and rule over New Mexico and its quite numerous population make a strange story to our youth who associate only Gosnold, the Cartiers, John Smith, and the Pilgrims with dim ideas of the Norsemen, in their impressions of the earliest American history.

There are two theories worthy of consideration, by which to account for the first inhabitants of New Mexico. They may have sprung into existence on this continent, a truly aboriginal race; or they

ANTIQUITY OF NEW MEXICO. 3

came from Asia. It will require much more scientific research than has yet been given to American antiquities, to make the first theory credible, and to overcome the more probable evidence of the Mongolian origin of this people. Their strong likeness in physical traits, customs, religious ideas and industrial relics, to the North-eastern Asiatic nations, to the Alaskan tribes, and also to the civilization of Mexico, Central America and Peru, links the earliest people of New Mexico to the old world human types.

It is now generally believed that one of the three branches of the Mongolian race turned from Central Asia northward. A subordinate branch from this took an easterly direction, and peopled North-eastern Asia, afterwards crossed Behring's strait and passed into America.

Crossing this Strait would have been comparatively easy. It is accomplished now when frozen over in winter. The headlands of America are visible from the Asiatic side. Passages are frequently made by the Esquimaux traders in summer. There is an island in the Strait on which they live, distant fifty miles from Asia, but one hundred and twenty from America. The narrowest width is but forty-five miles. There may once have been land communication. This is made probable by the relics of the hairy mammoth on both sides of the strait. The lower shore of Alaska could have been populated by way of Kamscatka and the Aleutian Islands. The distance is but four hundred and ninty-one miles, broken into shorter stretches of water by island groups. Then the people streamed eastward, south ward, and along the Pacific coast. Through the lake regions they reached southward to the country of the Carolina States. Northward they touched Greenland, where the Esquimaux lived; and in the South-west they moved from near the boundary of Utah across the plateaus of Arizona and New Mexico. Contemporaneously with the mounds and earthworks of the lake regions and Mississippi Valley, the cliff houses and seven cities of Cibola and numerous Pueblos were rising in the cañons and broad valleys of this region beyond the Rocky Mountains.

There have been three periods of aboriginal history in America. The most recent just precedes and for a while follows its discovery by Europeans. This is called the historical period. Beyond this is the longer period of the mound builders, the ancestors of the Indian races. Still more remote is that which embraces the coexistence of man with extinct species of animals, or the age of the mammoth and reindeer in Europe The accidental proximity of human remains with those of extinct animals near the Mississippi, is the inconclusive evidence upon which this age of man in America chiefly rests.

The original population of New Mexico has been included in the second historical period. In the mounds of the Mississippi Valley were the rude models of wonderful structures far to the South. In similar works of earth and stone in the wilds of Colorado, Utah and New Mexico, the weapons, ornaments and utensils discovered resemble in shape, material and symbols those of the mound-builders.

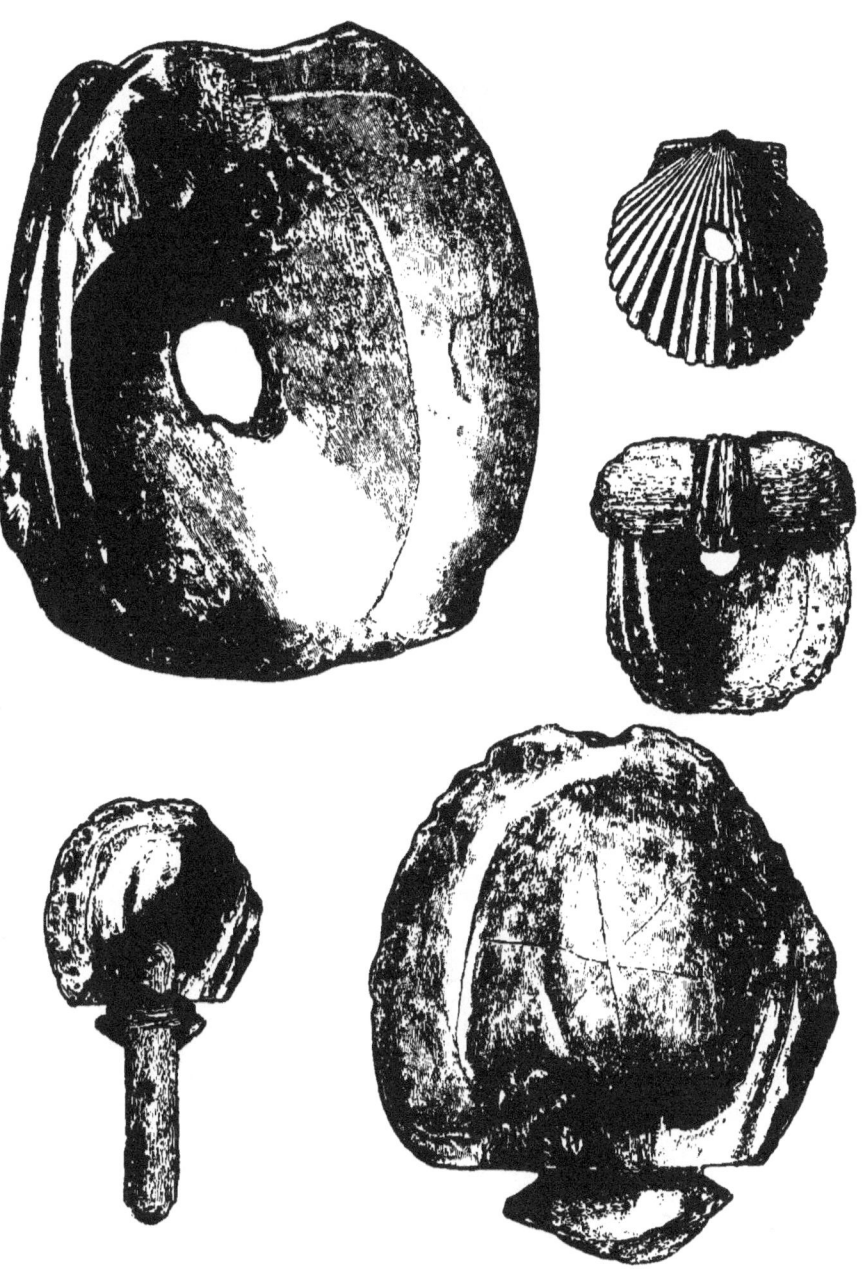

UTENSILS OF THE STONE AGE.

The most ancient are untensils of the stone age. A few pieces of copper in a native state are found, only hammered but not fused into shape for use, as in the historical period. The burial mounds of the Rocky Mountain regions contain evidences of the same customs of burial. There are traces of fire, of bones and vessels of stone and pottery, which contained the food prepared for the departed, or the remains of animals used in sacrifices and funeral feasts mingled with the skeletons of human victims.

The dwelling places of these peoples in the Southwest are indicated by the fragments of pottery on the surface of the soil and washed out of ruins heaped with drifted sands and molds of forest growths. Though their tools, ornaments and utensils do not seem to have improved in long periods of time, those discovered among the ruins of the ancient Mexican civilization and in Yucatan, and those examined by the first Europeans on that soil are nearly equal in texture and finish to the products of corresponding centuries of European history. The oldest people of New Mexico were skilled in agriculture and sowed the land with corn, cotton and other seeds, and raised fruits to supply their necessities. They at first erected numerous buildings detached from one another and irregularly grouped, and afterward large communal buildings, in which several hundreds of people could dwell protected against their enemies. Then came the barbarous Athabaskans, who covered with their incursions the country of New Mexico, Arizona, California and the northern half of Mexico from the Gulf to the

Pacific. This great predatory race occupied the regions from Hudson's Bay to the Rocky Mountains, and moved south over the remains of the partially civilized races left through those great periods of time which rolled over this Continent.

The traces of these different peoples in New Mexico are discerned in languages, customs, products of industry and traits of character, but the marks which distinguish them — roving in habit and warring against one another — are often obscure.

"No attention is paid as yet to the fact that the religious creeds of the Indians over the whole American continent were moulded on the same pattern, that their social organization was fundamentally the same among the Cherokees, the Pueblos of New Mexico, the Mexicans and the Peruvians, that the system of government of the Iroquois differed from that of the Mexicans but very little, and that the same principles pervade aboriginal architecture from one Arctic circle to the other, varying only in degree and not in kind. It is constantly overlooked that the fact of a certain class of buildings being of stone and another group of wood, does not necessarily imply a superiority of the builders of the former over the builders of the latter, and that the long-house of the Iroquois shows as much mechanical skill, if not more, as the honey-combs in which the New Mexican Indians still live in part — that the carved dwellings of the North-west coast denote an advance in art not behind that of aboriginal Yucatan."*

* A. de F. Bandelier's Paper before N. Y. Hist. Society. Feb. 3, 1885.

AN ANCIENT PUEBLO RESTORED.

In the region of New Mexico, Arizona, Colorado and Utah are left the descendants of five great families, into which the more recent populations, from the time of the Spanish Conquests to the present time, are divided. These are the Shoshonian, Keresan, Zuñian, Tanonan and Athabaskan stocks. To the first four belong the Moqui and Pueblo tribes; to the latter the fierce and powerful tribes of the Navajoes and Apaches.

The Pueblo Indians, especially the Zuñis, trace their ancestry to the North-west. Thither their souls will return according to the folk lore of this people. The Shoshones and the Athabaskans also assert their original homes to have been on the Columbia and in the North-west. The sedentary or Pueblo tribes came South to the Rio Grande before the roving peoples. They moved below this river when thus pressed by the incursions of the savages. The ruins in that region were their abode. The Pimas of Arizona, whose organization and rites prove their kinship to the Pueblo tribes of New Mexico, claim an origin upon the soil in which they reside, with the tradition of a disastrous flood, from which only one man was saved.

"Everything conduces to the belief that the population of South-eastern Utah, South-western Colorado, Northern Arizona and Northern New Mexico, drifted into the country from the North-west at various times and with differing forms of culture."

The sedentary tribes at one time ranged over fully three-fourths of New Mexico. The lines of easterly occupation run several miles south-east of

Las Vegas, at an average distance of thirty to fifty miles west of the river Pecos.

Prof. A. de F. Bandelier has traced an unbroken chain of remains of permanent aboriginal structures from the North, forty degrees latitude to the thirty-second parallel. "These ruins have thence been followed through southern New Mexico to latitude thirty degrees, in northern Chihuahua — thence along the Pacific slope to Sonora. And after a break in the extension to Sinoloa, where the existence of ancient villages is certain, and from Sinoloa, there are ample traces of a continuous flow southward, giving ground for the belief that the American aborigines have been sedentary at short distances from each other along the whole line. The detached family house is in theory susceptible of an evolution ultimately resulting in the architecture of central and southern Mexico; and the changes which it has undergone in Arizona seem to indicate a first step in that line.

"The compact architecture typified in the Communal, many storied agglomeration of cells called the 'Pueblo house,' reaches its southern limit along the Rio Grande at San Marcial. There the Spaniards found the first villages in 1580, 1582 and 1598. Below that point the detached-house type, in clusters, occupies the river banks at intervals, as far south as Dona Ana probably, certainly to Fort Selden, or latitude thirty-two degrees, thirty minutes north. It is confined to the river bottom or its immediate approaches. East and west of it the barrenness of the country forbade permanent abode

VIEW OF THE COUNTRY OF THE CLIFF DWELLERS.

ANTIQUITY OF NEW MEXICO. 15

to the land-tilling aborigines. I have no proof as yet of the existence of ruins farther down the great stream."

The great number of ruins scattered through New Mexico does not necessarily indicate a large population. The traditions of the Zuñis and Piruas show that they were occupied successively, but that both the large Communal and the detached family house were in use simultaneously in different sections, the people being forced by incursions of wandering tribes or of their neighboring Pueblo tribes, to seek protection in the larger type of houses, which is also the latest style of dwelling of the natives.

Their devolpment from savage to sedentary tribes was very gradual, and equally unnoticeable was the disappearance of the sedentary tribes, moving away before the wild tribes, who roamed over their former abodes.

Yet the highest social development attained by these aboriginal tribes was that of a very simple organization, rude architecture, limited arts and industries of a tribe or tribal confederacy, and in the largest Pueblo associations, as of Pecos and of the Chaco or of the Animas, not more than two thousand were sheltered and protected in the Communal houses.*

* A. de F. Bandelier.

PERIOD II.

SPANISH DISCOVERIES.

1536 TO 1591.

CHAPTER II.

NICA.

THE earliest European history of America gave room for the wildest flights of fancy. Vast realms of the New World were waiting to be discovered. Wealth untold would reward the brave and hardy explorers of regions that unknown races had occupied for centuries, while the civilized and enlightened kingdoms of Europe did not dream of their existence.

Foremost in the spirit of adventure and the greed of gold were the Spaniards, to whom Columbus had opened a century of marvellous discovery and conquest. Twenty years after the last expedition of this man, who had swung wide the gates of the New

World to mankind, and inflamed the pride of the Spanish nation by his matchless achievement, Pizarro and Cortez aroused to the highest point their ambition, and the lust for gold and power was calling the noble and the mountaineer and the peasant to the perils of exploring unknown lands, and of subduing peoples as numerous as the subjects of the European kingdoms.

After Cortez had conquered the Aztec empire and established his ill-gotten power in Mexico, he went back to Spain to receive the honors of the court and the rewards of his king for such great acquisitions of military glory and domain to the honor of the Spanish crown. In 1530 Cortez returned from Spain with new power and a new title—"The Marquis of the Valley." In his absence, Nuño Guzman had been President of New Spain, and acting with intense enmity to Cortez, had confiscated and wasted the property of Cortez and abused his friends.

Guzman had, however, received information that stirred his ambition to make the first expedition to that land of gold which became famous for adventure during the next sixty years. There came to him the story of the Seven Cities of Gold before the marvelous reports of Cabeza de Vaca and his companions had reached Mexico. This story led to the Spanish discovery and invasion of New Mexico. The idle tales of an obscure Indian led thousands of eager Spaniards, with their Indian allies, to perilous journeying, strange discoveries and miserable deaths. He was Guzman's servant, and the son of a trader, who had been wont to make expeditions into the far interior, obtaining gold and silver from the natives for his feathered wares. The boy had accompanied his father and described towns built of lofty houses and peoples who worked much in precious metals. This land was forty days' travel north of Guzman's country, across a desert and between two oceans. Legends of seven cities in the West, of far earlier date, became confused with these later stories in the minds of the eager Spaniards. Guzman determined to hazard the great expense and danger of an expedition numbering four hundred Spaniards and twenty thousand natives on these unconfirmed stories of the land of the Seven Cities not very far off. Many rich Spaniards left large properties and many slaves behind them in Mexico to join this exploring army. Guzman marched from the City of Mexico with an imposing retinue, but his expedition could proceed no farther than the province of Culiacan and the Yakqui river. Fearing the wrath of Cortez, he therefore colonized this province and sought his fortune in this new country. But the fame of the Seven Cities remained like the Norseman's tales of the vine-clad shores of America, which again drew venturous crafts into the stormy ocean, and roused the thoughtful soul of Columbus to face the scorn and then win the admiration of the world.

Francisco Vasquez Coronado, a brave and princely man, eight years later succeeded Guzman as Governor of Culiacan. Don Antonio de Mendoza was Viceroy of all New Spain, and had received with curious interest the startling account of Vaca and his companions. It seemed to verify the myths whose golden hues were attracting many eyes. They, too, spoke of great and powerful cities which they had seen, or of which they had heard, with houses four or five stories high. The Viceroy communicated to Coronado their reports, and roused him to grasp the prizes of discovery and conquest in a territory neighboring to his province. Vaca and his two Spanish comrades had returned to Spain. The negro Estevanico, who had accompanied them, alone could be used to guide a military expedition into the strange land.

"Before, however, an expedition was started the Viceroy cautiously determined to reconnoiter the country, with smaller preparations, less risk of lives and minor expenditure. No better scouts could the Spanish administrator secure than missionaries of the church. They were wont to risk everything to penetrate everywhere, regardless of danger. For one who perished many were eager to follow. Such men could be implicitly trusted; they harbored no after-thought beyond the crown of martyrdom, which was their most glorious reward."*

In 1538 two friars, Pedro Madal and Juan de la Asuncion traveled so far north that they reached the Gila river, which they could not cross, but they were thus the first to discover Arizona. Mendoza, with clear insight into his character and qualifications, now selected Marcos of Nice, whose experience in Peru, Quito and Guatemala, and for several years in Mexico had specially fitted him for these

*A. de F. Bandelier.

A MOQUI VILLAGE.

difficult northern explorations. The negro Estevanico, and several Pima Indians, who had followed Vaca, and had been taught Spanish for interpreters, were given as guides and companions to Fray Marcos. This Franciscan monk was instructed by the Viceroy to travel with the greatest possible safety. to avoid conflicts with the peoples, to take note of their country, climate, soil and productions, and bring back, if possible, samples of their industries, fruits, grains and metals. The negro was commanded to give implicit obedience to the friar, on penalty of serious punishments for disregard of his instructions. Onorato, a lay Franciscan brother, was added as a companion, but on account of sickness could proceed no farther than Petatlan with him.

The company set forth on their journey Friday, March 7th, 1539, from the town of St. Michael in Culiacan. Their route for the first five days crossed a desert, then northward into the valley of the Sonora, and after five days entered another arid land; then followed the river San Pedro to near the junction of the Gila and entered a barren plain, beyond which was the town of Cibola, which having reached after accomplishing a distance of three hundred leagues, they returned to report to Mendoza at Mexico. Reading the Friars' own story of this remarkable journey, with something of the eager credulity of the Spaniards, whom he beguiled to follow his steps for conquest, we shall not wonder at its power to lead them to disappointment, despair and death. It was a substantially true narration, except that the covetous hearts of the countrymen exaggerated the riches of gold and silver that the natives whom he met, ignorantly reported to exist in the countries he described. Mendoza said of Niça, that "God had shut up the gates of this marvelous country to all those who by strength of human force have gone about to attempt this enterprize, and hath revealed it to a poor and barefooted friar." *

The early stages of their journey were marked by great kindness and hospitality from the inhabitants. Leaving Petatlan, they traveled near the coast, in the thinly settled country of the Yaqui people. Beyond the first desert Niça discovered that the Spaniards were unknown, and their white faces were regarded with astonishment. The inhabitants desired to touch Niça's garments in their reverence, and loaded him and his companions with provisions. To all his inquiries regarding the seven cities of gold, Niça could obtain no satisfactory replies. When in the center of the present State of Sonora, at Vacupa, the modern Matape, he received such assurances of large towns rich with gold and turquoises, from the people, who began to perceive what he most desired to know, that he hoped to find another kingdom like Montezuma's in the country beyond. He dispatched the negro to the north and east, instructing him to journey for one hundred and fifty miles, and if he should learn of populous, rich and extensive countries, to go no farther, but report by token of a white cross the size of a hand's length or proportionately larger, the extent of

* W. W. H. Davis' Conquest of New Mexico.

the country. On Passion Sunday (April 5th), Estevanico set forth, and before Easter Sunday had dawned (April 19th), an Indian brought back to Niça a cross as high as a man, and the story that thirty days' march from where the negro remained, the first town of a country called Cibola was to be found. An Indian accompanied the messenger, who said he had been there, and that there were seven cities in the first province under one sovereign. Their houses were built of stone, masonry and timbers, they were two and three stories high, the house of the king had four well arranged floors, and the gateways of the chief men were ornamented with turquoises laid in the wood. The people of Cibola were clad in gowns of cotton reaching to the feet, with broad sleeves, girt with curiously wrought turquoise belts, and over these were coats of leather ornamented with precious stones. Beyond the first province of Cibola, were three others called Marata, Acus and Totonteac.

Marcos de Niça in two days left Vacupa, passing through the Opala country in the valley of the Sonora river. Here were populous villages and a country abounding in food. The people were dressed in cotton and leathern mantles, and adorned with turquoises in the ears and nostrils. They offered him gifts of hides, beautiful drinking vessels, and food of quails, maize and pine nuts, and when the route lay through the desert, they sent forward food for his company to supply their wants. The gray woolen garments of the friar attracted their attention. They declared that the people of Totonteae wore clothing of a similar material made of the hair of a little beast. The Moquis still wear a cloth or blanket woven from fine strips of the skin of the jack rabbit.

Estevanico the negro, instead of waiting, increased the distance between himself and the monk, sending urgent messages back that he should hasten forward. The friar kept constantly to the north. For five days he passed through the well watered valley of the San Pedro, with fertile soil highly cultivated, and with a large population. Some of the villages were more than a mile in length. They belonged to the Sobaypuris, a branch of the Northern Pimas, in South-eastern Arizona. A fugitive from Cibola in one of these villages, of light complexion and rather more intelligence than the people around him, favorably impressed Niça with the consistent account he gave of the cities and provinces beyond the great desert. It was here that he received the last messages from the negro guide at a village estimated by Marcos as three hundred and twelve miles from Vacupa. The Indians were anxious to accompany the monk to Cibola, and detained him for three or four days in preparations of food and other things for crossing the desert. From the large number who were ready to attend him, he selected thirty who seemed to be principal men, while a number of others carried provisions.

On the ninth of May they entered the desert; the next day crossed the Gila river, traveling over a well-beaten road, by the side of which were convenient stopping places, where provisions and shelter were prepared. It seemed to be the main road to Cibola, where lodging places and signs of fire kindled by travelers were frequent. On the second of June, 1539, Niça relates that he was "met by an Indian, son of one of the chiefs who accompanied me, and who had followed Estevánico, the negro. His face was all dejected and his body covered with perspiration; his whole exterior betokened great sadness. He announced the death of the guide and companion of Marcos."*

Estevanico had passed this desert with three hundred Indians, and having entered the country beyond, with a great display of importance, he had received a great many gifts of turquoises, provisions and clothing, and beautiful women for slaves. He affected a kind of triumphal march through the country, having a great gourd decorated with red and white feathers and a string of bells, carried before him as a symbol of peace. His messengers sent forward to Cibola were prohibited by the magistrate from entering the town. This greatly alarmed his attendants, but Estevanico went bravely forward to the gates of the city. Here he was made a prisoner and plundered of all the turquoises he had brought, and he was put without food under a strict guard. In a council of old men the next day, he was asked why he came into the country. He told them that he preceded two white men learned in divine things which they would tell the people of Cibola. Their king, a mighty prince, had sent them to explore the country. The decision of the council

*A. de F. Bandelier.

was that his story was false. Estevanico was a black man, but professed to come from a country of white people. He was arrogant in his manner and demands and did not act like a messenger of peace.

After four days Estevanico was condemned to be put to death, and being taken toward the town, he attempted to escape, but was shot with arrows, and in a conflict which immediately arose between the inhabitants of the town and his followers, only three escaped, two of whom were wounded and the third was the bearer of these alarming tidings to Niça. The Spanish historian, Casteneda, says, that "sixty out of the three hundred who had accompanied the negro, shared his fate."

The friar was astounded at the fate of his guide, but could not be dissuaded from his purpose of reaching Cibola. His Indian companions refused to go farther. He learned that they were intending to put him to death, on account of the disasters which had overtaken their people with Estevanico. Niça divided among them all the articles for trade and gift which were still in his possession, and temporarily quieted their anger. But he was a resolute man, and though a priest he had all the courage of a warrior. With undaunted heart he declared that he would see Cibola, whatever the dangers he must meet. Two of the chiefs at length decided to go with him; and with a few other Indians, he immediately resumed his journey. Soon they met the two wounded companions of Estevanico in a terrible plight, and again his courage triumphed over the fears of his Indians. They came in sight of Cibola, built in a plain on the

IN AN OLD PUEBLO.

slope of a hill of round shape. Niça ascended a mountain to view the city, whose fame had filled the imaginations of Spaniards with glowing pictures of grandeur and royal magnificence. He beheld the houses built in order as the Indians had told him, "all made of stone, with flat roofs and divers stories."

"Niça's account of the town states that its size was more considerable than Mexico.* But how large was Mexico in 1539? The Indian settlement had been destroyed in 1521; its ruins, even, were obliterated. The Spanish town sprang up in 1524, and it is questionable whether in 1539 it had many more than one thousand inhabitants. A many storied Indian Pueblo always looks, from the distance, twice as large as it really is, and even if Mexico had two thousand souls, the comparison, far from being exaggerated, was very proper and truthful indeed."

The friar was tempted several times to go into the town, but considering the danger that if he should be killed the knowledge of the country might be lost, he, faithful to the instructions of the Viceroy, refrained from the needless risking of his life and defeat of the mission entrusted to him. He therefore limited himself to the act of taking formal possession of the seven cities, the kingdoms of Totonteac, Acus and Marata in the name of Don Antonio de Mendoza, Viceroy and Captain-General of New Spain, for his majesty the Emperor. Raising a heap of stones upon the mountain and surmounting it with a cross, the province of Cibola

*A. de F. Bandelier.

became by this act, "The New Kingdom of Saint Francis." A priest's conquests are the least expensive of blood and treasure.

The most faithful ethnological researches by those thoroughly qualified explorers and historians, Messrs. A. de F. Bandelier and F. H. Cushing, have without doubt determined that the town of Cibola of the sixteenth century was the Zuñi town Caquineco, which lies in a niche of the southern slope of the great mesa of Zuñi and is plainly visible from the south side only.

Niça did not stay long to dream of other worlds to conquer. From the mountain top he turned to regard the realities of his situation, and with "more fear than victuals," as he says, he hastened to rejoin the Indians whom he had left two days' journey behind him. He re-crossed the great desert and painfully encountered the Sobaypuris, who were filled with grief on account of the loss of their relatives in the retinue of Estevanico. He felt that there was no safety until, by a rapid flight through the second desert, he found himself again among the Opalas. Then the monk turned aside from his direct route to explore the great plain on the east, where were "seven villages, of reasonable size and tolerably distant, a handsome and very fresh-looking valley, and a very pretty town whence much smoke arose." These were towns in Southern Sonora inhabited by people who knew and used gold.

Taking possession of this country by planting two crosses, this loyal friar now made great haste to return and make report of his discoveries; and having arrived in Compestella, he became at once the hero of the hour. The story of his adventures aroused Coronado to intense interest, and gave the necessary impetus to a great military expedition, which forms the most romantic chapter in the history of New Mexico. The official report of Marcos de Niça was made on nine sheets of paper and given to the Viceroy September 2, 1539.

CHAPTER III.

CORONADO'S MARCH AND INVASION.

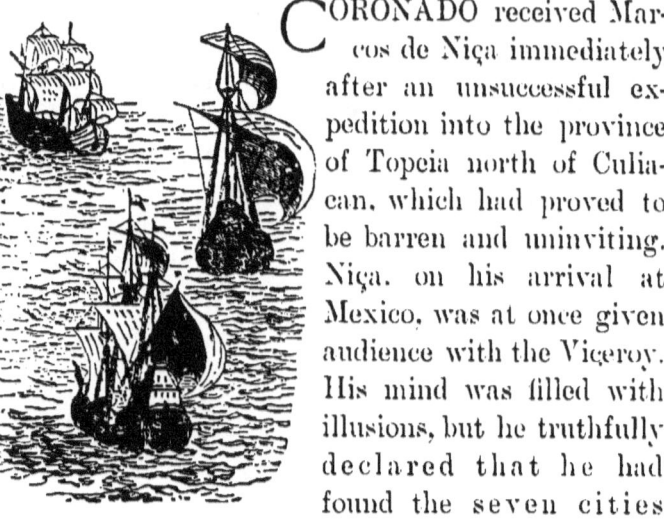

CORONADO received Marcos de Niça immediately after an unsuccessful expedition into the province of Topeia north of Culiacan, which had proved to be barren and uninviting. Niça, on his arrival at Mexico, was at once given audience with the Viceroy. His mind was filled with illusions, but he truthfully declared that he had found the seven cities which Nuñez de Guzman had sought in vain. He told his story in the pulpits, which added to it the authority of the church.

It was repeated in neighboring towns, with no loss of wonders. The pulpit in those days performed the office of the press. The authority of both the Viceroy and the church speedily made successful the effort to raise an army to conquer these regions. Four hundred Spaniards and eight hundred Indians volunteered for the expedition to Cibola. Mendoza invested seventy thousand pesos (dollars), an immense sum at that time, in this enterprize. He appointed as Captain-General, Coronado, whose qualifications as provincial governor and whose patronage of Niça, inspired great confidence. His conduct of this expedition confirmed the character ascribed to him, as, "a good gentleman and a wise, prudent and able man." He left behind him in New Spain not only a fortune, but a lovely wife, and was indeed as proud as he was careful of the brilliant retinue of gentlemen who composed the expedition, fully sharing the privations and toils which their adventures imposed on them all. Coronado's letters and official report to Mendoza give reliable information of the events and discoveries which are so honorably associated with his name. And Casteneda, a man of education and ability, though a common soldier of the expedition, in an account written after his return to Culiacan, supplements and confirms the official statements of his General, with interesting descriptions and details in manuscript preserved in the Lenox library in New York, and first published in French by Ternaux Campans in 1838.

Coronado chose from among the distinguished cavaliers of his little army Don Pedro de Tobar for standard bearer, and Lopes de Samaniego as colonel, and for captains, Trislan de Arellano, Pedro de Guevara, Garcia Lopez de Cardenas, Rodrigo Maldonado Diego Lopez and Diego Guterrez. Mendoza designed in the service of this expedition to find relief from the numerous titled youths who crowded upon attendance at his court, and whose ambitions and passions were a peril to his power. The troops were lodged and fed by people of rank, and when fully organized were ordered to rendezvous at Compestella, on the Pacific Coast. Soon after New Year's Day, 1840, they were there reviewed by the Viceroy. After Mass was celebrated he addressed them with most encouraging words. Their expedition was to add to the national glory and to their personal fortunes. It would be of incalculable service to the King, who would reward them with lavish bounties and favors on their return. The Viceroy appealed to their devotion to the Christian religion which they would carry to a heathen country and establish among a great people. The soldiers took oath of entire obedience to their General, the officers were acknowledged anew before the whole army, and the next day after the Viceroy's arrival, the march was begun. Great numbers of noblemen and other people assembled to witness the passing of the army. It was headed by the Viceroy for two days, adding by his presence to the intense enthusiasm which prevailed among the troops and the populace, who shouted to each other in the ardor of anticipated triumph in the conquest of rich nations.

There were fifteen hundred men with a thousand horses in the procession as they marched out of the city with trumpets sounding, glistening banners, armors flashing in the morning sunlight, and the brilliant colors of the dress of Spanish cavaliers.

THE ANCIENT NAVAJO.

Five thousand sheep and one hundred and fifty cows of Spanish breed, for the new settlements, were driven before the army.

After two or three days of easy marching, they entered upon a wild and mountainous country. The baggage, loaded insecurely on pack-horses, fell off, and after many vain attempts to transport it, much was thrown away by the discouraged soldiers. The gentlemen who had expected a holiday excursion became their own mule drivers and servants, performing the most menial duties, and their hardships increased with every mile. The army, greatly exhausted, reached Chemetla, where their provisions failed. Coronado's march was designed to be along the sea-shore, and two vessels loaded with provisions and baggage had been dispatched from Natividad under Pedro Alarçon to join the expedition at the head of the Gulf of California, with supplies for the troops, but no junction was ever made. At Chemetla Colonel Samaniego was killed by the Indians, upon whom summary punishment was inflicted, and the village in which he was surprised, destroyed, with all its inhabitants. The lack of food, the unexpected hardships at the beginning of the long march, and the savage character of the inhabitants of this province, caused some to be discouraged, and the return to Chemetla of a detachment sent by Coronado toward Cibola when Niça went to Mexico, still further dispirited the troops. Their report, though they had not crossed the great desert, was in great contrast to the glowing accounts of Niça. The friar at once, with unabated zeal repeated his stories of wonderful cities, rich countries, green valleys and broad rivers beyond the desert. He believed that all who should enter this country would return rich in possessions. The soldiers' spirits were somewhat revived by the monk's confident words, and proceeding on their march. they arrived near Culiacan on Easter Eve. This was the last Spanish settlement six hundred miles from the City of Mexico.

The citizens welcomed their Governor and his army on the day after Easter with special honors. A sham battle was fought, in which the Spanish troops entered the city in triumph. They were freely received into the houses, where was left much of the army baggage which could no longer be transported. While recruiting the army here for a month Coronado attempted to stimulate his men by artifice. A soldier declared that he had been tempted by the devil in a vision to kill Coronado and even promised his wife if he should succeed in the attempt. Marcos de Niça, in an eloquent sermon, declared that this was on account of the wonderful discoveries for the glory of the Christian faith that Coronado should make, and this injurious interpretation was sent back to be repeated with many additions for the comfort of the soldiers' friends in Mexico. Truxillo, the soldier, was ordered to leave the army.

Coronado's impatient spirit could not wait for his army. He took with him fifty cavaliers, a few infantry soldiers, a number of special friends, and all the monks eager for the conquests of the cross, and departed for Cibola, leaving the army in command of Arellano to follow in fifteen days. Coronado made good progress, till one of the priests broke his thigh, and was sent back to Culiacan. The Indians of the country were friendly, remembering Niça, over whose course they were marching. In a distance of six hundred miles they took in Petatlan, Cinaloa, the Yakami river, Sonora, thence to the Nixpa river, then descending the San Pedro for two days, which runs in a northerly direction, they skirted Mount Graham and reached the Gila river, near which they found some remarkable views, and soon after entered the ruins of Chichilticale. This place had been extolled by Niça in his narrative to Coronado, who, finding that it dwindled down in his own sight to a pueblo in ruins and roofless, was filled with forebodings as to what might prove bitter disappointment of cherished hopes of discovery. Neither the country nor the inhabitants, in their wretched condition, gave him any encouragement.

But Coronado would not wait for his army. The populous part of the country had been passed. The edge of the great desert was at hand. Coronado pushed forward into it, and for fifteen days the company traveled through this depopulated region of the present Apache reservation. The red and muddy waters of the Vermejo (Zuñi) river met their joyful sight, after monotonous stretches of sand and sage brush and cactus, had been wearily passed. Here they found an abundance of fish like the mullets of Spain, and the first Indians of the Cibola country were discovered. The Spaniards heard the first war whoop in an attack by night made upon them when only twenty miles from Cibola. The next day their eager eyes beheld one of the seven cities, which corresponds to the Havicu of the present day, though not the one which Niça had first seen. The soldiers, however, broke out in curses upon the friar. Their golden fancies were dispelled.

Before them was a village containing not more than two hundred warriors. It was situated high upon a rock. The approach to it was by narrow and steep winding steps. The warriors were drawn up in battle a short distance before the town, and showed signs of bitter hostility, brandishing their weapons with threatening gestures. Coronado ordered them, through an interpreter, to surrender. They again wildly brandished their weapons, and uttered loud cries of defiance.

The starving condition of his men allowed no delay in the assault, and Coronado ordered his horsemen to dismount, and himself led the attack upon the gates, where a scaling ladder was visible The cross bowmen could not keep the Indians from the walls by their arrows, and they hurled showers of stones upon their assailants. Coronado, conspicuous by his shining armor, was struck down by one of these missiles, and he nearly lost his life at the outset of his adventures in this strange country. Alvarado and Cardenas threw themselves before him, receiving the shower of stones which followed his fall, and carried him bruised and exhausted from the field. The Spaniards gave the besieged no rest, and the Indians in dismay saw them steadily advancing up the height. In an hour they had captured

VIEW OF THE CIBOLA COUNTRY.

the town, and the subjugation of the Pueblos to long years of Spanish rule had begun. The place contained many provisions, and the troops rested on their victory. None of them were fatally injured in the assault.

Meanwhile the army had resumed its march upon the route pursued by Coronado, but advanced no farther than the river Gila, where they awaited instructions from the General. These came by the middle of October. Niça accompanied the bearers of these dispatches, who also were on their way to the Viceroy with Coronado's report of the expedition. They had not found at Cibola, the fairy cities, kingdoms nor palaces of their dreams. Marcos would have been crushed under the maledictions of the soldiers had he remained with the army.

Arellano had founded a city, where the soldiers unfit for the march were ordered to remain under the command of Melchior Diaz, while the army proceeded to Cibola, where the troops were received by Coronado into comfortable winter quarters.

The seven cities of the province of Cibola were favorably situated in a valley. The most populous was named Maçaque. Some of its houses were six and seven stories high; most of them were four stories high, ascended by ladders from terrace to terrace. Coronado reported to Mendoza that the town from which he wrote had about five hundred houses. The people wore cotton mantles, with furs and skins for winter covering, but generally went nearly naked in summer. They daily received instruction from priests selected from the aged men. The climate was variable, often cold, with occasional rain, and they provided themselves with fire-wood from cedars growing twelve or fifteen miles distant. They had no fruit trees, but their fields bore excellent grass and maize, which they ground more finely than did the natives of Mexico. The wild beasts of the country were bears, mountain lions, wild sheep and goats, deer, and elk of great size, whose skins the people tanned and painted for clothing and ornament and also embroidered. They were industrious, disposed to peace, and neither given to drunkenness nor cannibalism. They buried their dead with the implements of their occupations. They were fond of music and sang in unison with those who played on flutes. Their worship, received from tradition, was mostly toward the waters, for by them their corn was made to grow, and their lives were thus preserved. Their women were well treated and were clad in tunics of cotton and mantles of finely-dressed deer skins, passing over the shoulder, fastened at the neck and falling under the other arm. Their hair behind the ear, was fashioned like a wheel and resembled the handle of a cup. Turquoises hung from the ears and were used as necklaces and girdles. A man had but one wife and lived single after her death. Their weapons were bows, spears, stone hatchets and shields of hides.

The people of Cibola withdrew their families to the mountains, and were at first unwilling to communicate to Coronado the information he desired concerning the neighboring provinces. They, however, were induced to send messengers to distant towns and invite them to a conference with the strangers. Few responded to the invitation. But the Cibolans declared their willingness to submit to the laws of the Spaniards and to have their children instructed in their religion. They also said that fifty years before it had been prophesied that a people like the Spaniards should come from the south and subdue their country. Had the fame of the landing of Columbus at San Salvador fifty years before, been borne across the gulf and over the plains as a prophecy of the future rulers of this land?

CHAPTER IV.

CORONADO'S CONQUESTS.

WHILE the army were recruiting at Cibola, Coronado decided to explore the country of Tusayan, of which he had received remarkable reports. It had seven towns now called the villages of Moqui, which are about one hundred and twenty-five miles distant from Zuñi. Coronado entrusted the expedition to Don Pedro de Tobar, one of his most skillful and reliable captains. With a small number of mounted soldiers, he rapidly and secretly accomplished the march, not only to the province but to the walls of the first village, without being discovered. Arriving there at night, the Spaniards encamped before the town without being observed. The Indians beheld them the next day with astonishment and superstitious fear of their horses, which they had never seen before, but sounding an alarm, they gathered with their accustomed bravery, to repel the new enemy. The Spanish interpreter sought to assure them of friendly intentions. The Indians commanded the troops not to cross a certain line, and one of them attempting to do this, was immediately driven back. Friar Juan de Padilla, who accompanied the expedition, was so enraged at the resistance thus offered to the Spanish soldier, that he exclaimed, "In truth I do not understand why we have come here." Thus encouraged by a priest, the Spaniards, ever ready for a conflict, rushed forward and drove the Indians to their houses, killing many of them in the onset. The Moquis now sought for peace, and offered gifts of turquoises and poultry, and the whole province yielded at once, the chief men of other villages coming to invite the Spaniards to visit them.

Tobar reported to Coronado his easy conquest, and the location of an immense river of which he had learned, still farther to the west, which greatly excited the interest of his General, who immediately began preparations to explore it. A small party of twelve men were put under command of Captain Garçia Lopez de Cardenas, and in a journey of twenty days through a desert region, they came to the great river Colorado of the west, or Tizon, as it was then named. Its banks were of incredible height. It seemed not more than a yard wide, while they thus looking down upon it, were apparently elevated several miles in the air. The Indian guides declared that this river was a mile and a half broad. The party for three days went along the banks seeking a way by which to descend to the stream. The captain with three men attempted the descent in one place, but could accomplish only one-third the distance. The walls of this river have a height of from 3000 to 6000 feet for a distance of three hundred miles. The river bed is from 1000 to 1200 feet above the sea, and its cliffs rise a mile above the stream.

The honor of the discovery of the Colorado belongs first to Fernando Alarçon, who commanded the two ships of Coronado's Expedition that set sail from Natividad. Unable to communicate in any way with the army he sailed to the extremity of the Gulf of California, proving that the land on the west was a peninsula, and by shallops he entered the great river and explored it for two hundred and fifty miles. Leaving letters fifty miles from the mouth of the river, which were afterward found by another expedition under Melchior Diaz, sent out to the coast to search for the ships while the army was in Sonora. Alarçon returned to report to the Viceroy the arrival of Coronado at Cibola, of which he had heard through the Indians of Sonora.

While these expeditions to the west were being made, and even before the arrival of the army at Cibola, the presence of the Spaniards had been made known far to the east, and there came to Cibola people from the province of Cicuyè (or Cicuie), about one hundred and eighty-five miles distant. They brought gifts of tanned skins, shields and hemlets and hides of buffaloes. With them was a cacique, a young man, who received the name of "Bigotes" from the soldiers, on account of wearing a moustache. They described their country as abounding in buffalo. When they were about to return, Coronado ordered Captain Fernando d'Alvarado to take with him twenty men, to return with them to their home and report within eighty days.

From this party we have the first description of the cliff dwellings so numerous among the ruins of New Mexico. In five days they reached Acuco, the modern Acoma. It was situated so high upon a rock that it could not be reached by an arquebus shot, and its approach on all sides was very precipitous. A single path led to the top, entered by a stairway cut into the rock. It was of moderate width for two hundred steps, then became very narrow for a hundred steps more; and the last ascent was made for a considerable distance by placing the toes into holes in the side of the rock, and clinging to the cliff with the hands at imminent danger of falling. At the top was a quantity of stones to be rolled down on any one venturing to assail this position with hostile intent. Below was a space for the cultivation of corn and arrangements for its storage. There were also natural reservoirs for holding water from rains and melted snows on the cliff. This village contained two hundred warriors, who could attack and rob their neighbors with impunity.

Alvarado sought a conference with the inhabitants, but they drew lines upon the ground, beyond which the Spaniards approaching the town were forbidden to pass. The soldiers were angry at their insolence and demanded permission to attack the town. When they were seen to be preparing for the assault, the people were alarmed at their boldness, and sued for peace, bringing offerings of bread, deer skins, peñon nuts, seeds, flour and corn.

A march of three days farther to the East brought the party to the province of Tiguex, where the presence of Bigotes, the Cicuyè chief, secured the kind reception of the people. This province consisted of twelve villages and was situated on a great river, the Rio Grande. It was the modern Bernalillo, and the abundance of food, the comfortable buildings and mild climate, made it so desirable for winter quarters, that Alvarado in his report, urged its choice for that purpose on Coronado. Alvarado now pushed forward five days longer to Cicuyè. Here in a fine country, in the midst of mountains, and beside a small stream filled with trout, he found a strongly-fortified town, with houses four stories high and well supplied with food. The identity of this place with the ancient Pecos, after the careful researches and personal exploration of Prof. A. de F. Bandelier, though so long disputed, cannot longer be questioned. The inhabitants gave the Spaniards a cordial welcome, saluting them with drums and flutes and other marks of respect, and presenting them with cotton cloths, turquoises, food and other gifts. Pecos is now in ruins, having been deserted by its inhabitants, reduced by wars and sickness to a handful of people, who moved to the pueblo of Jemez. It was the most populous of all the pueblos visited by Coronado's men. The Montezuma myth was located here, a product, however, of the nineteenth century.

While encamped at Cicuyè for several days, a new

OLD SPANISH PALACE, SANTA FÉ.

and exciting chapter of romance was rehearsed to the Spaniards from the lips of a mendacious Indian, who became the evil genius of Coronado, but whose words revived the gilded visions that had cheered the wanderings of the Spaniards till they vanished under the skies of Cibola, and beneath the walls of its narrow streets.

It does not exaggerate the intelligence or shrewdness of the primitive inhabitants of New Mexico to attribute to them the scheme of alluring the Spaniards by a false guide to distant regions, where they would be lost or slain, and the country rid of their dangerous presence. This Indian, called "the Turk," had wandered far from his own house. He was a native of Florida, which had recently been explored by De Soto, but the name of Florida covered the whole region from the Atlantic to the Mississippi. He had been a slave in the country of Quivera, whence he had fled, to become a prisoner here. The Indian was apt in arousing the curiosity of the Spaniards, whose hopes he stimulated anew. He gave the appearance of veracity to his statements, by describing the vast herds of buffalo roaming on the plains between Cicuyè and his country. Alvarado proceeded to the borders of the plains where the bison could be seen, and then quickly returned with the Turk to carry the news to Coronado.

Having approved of the recommendation of Tiguex for winter quarters, Coronado had already sent forward Cardenas to prepare them. Unacquainted with the people who had been so hospitable to his comrades, this captain arrogantly demanded their houses, and would permit them to take nothing but their clothing away from their homes. Incensed at such treatment, they became exiles to another pueblo. Coronado, with a guard of thirty men, had left Cibola, where the main army had meanwhile arrived, and leaving orders for them to follow in twenty days, he reached Tiguex by way of a province of eight towns, probably of the Piros on the Rio Grande, where the people were friendly. Alvarado awaited the arrival of his General at Tiguex.

The Turk was presented to Coronado, who, sharing the credulity of his captain, became a willing listener to his romantic tales. The imagination of the Spaniard gave shape to what the Turk told with difficulty through interpreters, or in a foreign language with the aid of signs. In Quivera was a river six miles wide, in which fish as large as horses could be found. Their canoes, with twenty oars on each side, were used by the chiefs, who also propelled them by sails and sat in their sterns under a protecting dais. The sovereign chief reposed for his afternoon nap under a huge tree, while above him golden bells were hung in the branches, which tinkled as they waved in the summer breeze. The commonest vessels in this land were made of sculptured silver. The bowls, plates and dishes were of gold. The Turk pretended that golden bracelets had been taken from him at Cicuyè. Alvarado was sent back to recover them. The inhabitants indignantly declared that they had never taken them from the Indian, who was a great liar and deceiving them by his stories. Alvarado enticed the chief

Begotes into his tent, and ordered him to be chained. His people now turned upon the Spaniard with reproaches for such faithless and perfidious acts after the pledges of friendship he had made, and hurled at him a shower of arrows. But the chief was taken to Tiguex and detained by Coronado for six months.

The Spaniards were now acting the part of hostile invaders, kidnapping, imprisoning and robbing the natives, and serious troubles began to arise. Coronado's troops were in need of clothing. His demand from the people of Tiguex brought a supply of three hundred pieces of cotton. The art of weaving was evidently widely diffused in New Mexico. But the people determined to resist further oppression. They barricaded their houses and acted on the defensive. Coronado lay seige to one of their towns. After brave resistance the defenders surrendered, as prisoners of war, and then were ordered to be burned to death. A hundred were massacred in attempting to escape this cruel fate. Through all the country it was known that the Spaniards were faithless to their oaths. The rest of the army arrived from Cibola, and Coronado proclaimed to all the villages peace, but the people replied that their massacred countrymen and imprisoned chief were proofs of Spanish perfidy. To intimidate other towns Coronado besieged Tiguex for fifty days. The Indians lost more than two hundred warriors in gallant resistance to the various attacks of the Spaniards. Their supply of water failed, and sending away their women and children during a truce, they attempted to abandon the town at night. They were discovered, attacked and defeated, while those who reached the river were drowned, or overcome by cold, were captured. The town of Tiguex was occupied by the Spaniards and its inhabitants fled to the mountains. To regain the confidence of the inhabitants of Cicuyè Coronado promised to restore their chief, and thus prepared the way for his expedition to Quivera. In May, 1541, the Rio Grande was sufficiently clear of ice, and the deluded General began again the search for gold and silver in distant lands, while these metals were everywhere about them in the mountains and plains that would yield them to the patient toil of the miner. He had in great measure quieted the hostility of the tribes that were upon the route between the present Benalillo and Pecos. The powerful nation of the Tanos with ten villages lay somewhat to the north of the trail over which the people of the Pecos and lower Rio Grande had their friendly communication. They held the mountain regions from the Sandia to the Santa Fé ranges, and were unfriendly to the Pecos tribes. They were, however, generally reduced to submission before the expedition to Quivera was begun.* Coronado was at Benalillo, master of a depopulated province, his army encamped among the ruins of three villages, none of which were at peace. The conduct of the Spaniards at Tiguex was an unjustifiable crime. So the government later on punished Garcia Lopes de Cardenas, but retribution began for Coronado even during the

* A. de F. Bandelier. History of Colonization of New Mexico Mss.

unjust war against the Tiguas. Bad news reached him from Sonora. Melchior Diaz was dead. Alcarez, his successor at Suya, had just departed with his command, which had risen against him. Coronado sent Don Pedro de Tobar to San Hieronimo to repress the insurrection. Meanwhile, he himself, blinded by the tales of the Turk, prepared his unfortunate expedition in search of Quivera.

Taking the route to Pecos, Coronado restored Bigotes, then chief to this people, who provided food for the whole army and gave to Coronado a young native of Quivera, named Xabe, for a guide. His story of Quivera confirmed that of the Turk, except that the gold and silver were not so common nor abundant as represented. The Turk, however, reaffirmed his statements, and the Spaniards crossed the plains in full belief of the existence of the golden city. It is said by one of their chroniclers that "the Spaniards were so avaricious of gold that they would go into the infernal regions to obtain it."

Leaving Pecos (or Cicuyè), the army crossed the Pecos, farther on the Mora river, then entered and passed through the southern spurs of the Raton mountains, and a four days' march brought them again to the Canadien river, swollen at this season by melting snows, over which they built a bridge. Thence they came to habitations of Indians called Querechos, and the wandering tribes of Indians whom they met, and who belonged to the Apache nation, in collusion with the Turk, confirmed his account of Quivera. The direction of their march was north-east. The great plains which stretched between the Rocky mountains and the Missouri, opened before them. These were covered with tall grass, in which roamed immense herds of buffoloes that were hunted with enthusiasm by the Spaniards. But the stories of the Turk were now greatly questioned. Coronado was in great perplexity amid conflicting rumors. He dispatched Captain Maldonado in the direction of Quivera with his company, who came upon a village of Indians who had seen Cabera de Vaca. The country was populous, the people dwelt in huts and cultivated the ground. They informed the Spaniards, however, that Quivera was still toward the north.

The army had now marched thirty-six days and 850 miles from Benalillo, when their provisions failed. Coronado determined to continue the search for Quivera with thirty picked men, and Diego Lopez, second in command. Notwithstanding the remonstrances of the army, he ordered it to return. But taking the Teyans as guides and the Turk loaded with chains and the other Indian guide in his company, the General set out in another direction for Quivera. In forty-eight days, in latitude forty degrees, he reached this province, after crossing a great river. It consisted of a series of towns and villages, extending for many miles on small streams running into this great river. The people were less civilized and their houses less imposing than the inhabitants of Cibola. Instead of having stores of silver and gold, they knew not what they were. Their cacique greatly prized even a copper plate which he wore on his breast. Their comforts of

"...ROAMED IMMENSE HERDS OF BUFFALOES."

living were few. The country was beautiful and watered with streams of water. Prunes, grapes and flax grew wild in the valleys, but the people lived in houses of straw of circular shape, with thatched roofs.

Coronado in his bitter disappointment questioned the Turk as to his motives for deceiving him. He confessed his lies about the vast riches of Quivera, and that the people of Cicuyè had induced him to lure the Spaniards far out upon the plains, where their horses would perish and they would become an easy prey to the Indians, or returning exhausted, would be destroyed by the injured people of New Mexico. The enraged soldiers strangled the Turk at Quivera as a reward of his treachery, and Sopete, the other Indian guide, whose more truthful statements the Turk had denied, took great satisfaction in his death.

Coronado had been led into the Cañons of the Canadien, where he had left his army. In forty-eight days he passed through the Indian Territory and Kansas, and on the tenth of June, 1541, found "Quivera, mouth of the Arkansas river, in the North-eastern part of the State of Kansas, of the American Union."*

The Spanish General had but entered the borders of that vast country of the East, which stretched from the Missouri to the Atlantic and which was to constitute the magnificent domain of the Republic of the United States. "God reserved its discovery to others. He only permitted us," says Casteneda, "to

* Bandelier.

boast of being the first who had any knowledge of it. May the Lord's will be done." Three-quarters of a century afterward the colonists of Virginia landed at Jamestown, and the Pilgrims first trod the shores of Plymouth.

While Coronado was thus indefatigably searching for Quivera, the army under command of Arellano, after fifteen days' recruiting in their camp on the plains of the Indian Territory, began their return march. They took a more southerly direction over a perfectly level country, passed lakes of fresh and salt water, and several tribes of Querechos and Teyan Indians. Arriving at the Pecos river, nearly ninety miles below the point of their first crossing, they followed it up to Cicuyè. Its inhabitants refused to entertain the Spaniards or supply them with provisions, and they pushed on to Tiguex, where they arrived about the middle of July, 1541, after a march of twenty-five days.

Coronado having received the submission of the inhabitants of Quivera to the emperor Charles V. as their rightful master, directed a great cross to be erected at the farthest point of his exploration of the town. It bore the inscription, "Francesco Vasquez de Coronado, commander of an expedition, arrived at this place." The populous provinces said to exist beyond Quivera were left unexplored. In a few days he returned with his escort by a more direct and easier route, through the South-western part of Kansas to Cicuyè, which he reached in forty days and continued his march to Tiguex before the month of November.

Who were the Quiverans? The disputes as to the locality of Quivera have not sufficiently taken into consideration the habits of this people. "They were not," says Bandelier, "a nation of fixed habitation, for 'they changed their country with the buffaloes.' Quivera was then the name of a wandering tribe. It is natural that it changed place with this tribe. So we have found it in eastern Kansas in 1541; it reappears in the east of New Mexico in 1583; in the north and north-east in 1599. Finally, in 1630, the Quiveras are spoken of as being on the eastern boundary of New Mexico in the thirty-fourth degree of latitude. The name, as a name of a tribe, disappeared after the end of the seventeenth century."

"What became of this tribe? The word Quivera tells us nothing as to that. But in 1626 we find a synonym of Quivera. This synonym is Tindaw. It is, moreover, well ascertained that, at the beginning of the seventeenth century, the Quiveras were neighbors and enemies of the 'Escansaques.' Now the Escansaques are the Kansas, and in 1719, one of their principal villages was that of Quirireches. . . . The Tinthow, or Tindaw (described by Father Hennepen in 1683 as a tribe of the prairies living far to the south a part of the year) are the Sioux Tetons, a branch of the powerful, wandering tribe which became the terror of the plains in the eighteenth and nineteenth centuries. It is then probable that the Quiveras belonged to the Dacota. Following here and there the buffalo, they touched at several points the borders of New Mexico, and disappeared as the country became the possession of the Spaniards, either returning to the north, or joining themselves to the tribes which bore another name."

While preparations for wintering were made at Tiguex by Arellano, and several settlements visited and pacified along the upper and lower valley of the Rio Grande, Alvarado went with forty men to Cicuyè in search of Coronado. There he was attacked for four days and the people of this town were severely punished by the Spaniards, who killed two of their chiefs. Alvarado awaited the return of Coronado at Pecos, hearing of his approach.

Coronado's report of Quivera brought terrible disappointment to his soldiers. He, however, revived their hopes by plans of a great expedition into the same country the next spring, and busied himself in reconciling the inhabitants of the surrounding country to the presence of the Spaniards. He endeared himself to his soldiers, by providing new clothing and other comforts for them out of the supplies gathered from the Indians, and in reorganizing the army for the spring campaign. Coronado believed that Quivera was only the frontier of a superior and populous country toward the east. In his report to his majesty, Charles V., he thus describes it:

"The province of Quivera is 3230 miles from Mexico. The place I have reached is forty degrees of latitude. The earth is the best possible for all kinds of productions of Spain, for while it is very strong and black, it is very well watered by brooks, springs and rivers. I found prunes like those of Spain, also some excellent grapes and mulberries." Jaramillo, who accompanied Coronado to Quivera, says of it: "This region has a superb appearance and such that I have not seen better in all Spain, neither in Italy, nor France, nor in any other country where I have been in the service of your majesty. It satisfied me completely. I presume that it is very fertile and favorable to the cultivation of all kinds of fruits."*

The soldiers, cheered by such representations, shared in the adventurous spirit of their General and welcomed the orders given to his army to prepare for their march to Quivera, still hoping for the good fortune which the earlier Spanish expeditions had experienced in Mexico. They were destined again to disappointment. But it was to come now through the superstition or failing courage of Coronado, their generous and faithful leader. A serious accident disabled him for several weeks. In the celebration of one of their festivals, he was indulging in a feat of horsemanship with one of his officers, Don Pedro Mandelado, with whom he was running at a ring. Mounted on an excellent horse, but with a weak saddle girth, which had been substituted for the usual one that needed repair, the girth broke in midcourse, unhorsing the rider. He fell near Don Pedro, whose horse sprung over his prostrate body and kicked him in the head. Coronado narrowly escaped death.

While confined by his injuries, a fresh arrival of troops from San Hieronimo under Don Pedro de Tobar, had added to the discontent of the soldiers,

* Davis' Conquest of New Mexico.

"They came with their noses in the air, hoping to find the General already in the rich country of which the Turk had spoken, and were not pleased to meet Coronado in Tiguex." Letters from home brought by Tobar, turned the thoughts of the troops to their families. Cardenas, one of Coronado's bravest captains, obtained leave of absence, to take possession of an inheritance which had fallen to him in Spain, and returned with others who wearied of their hardships, and desired to establish themselves in Mexico. The sympathy of the army was, however, mostly with Coronado, and their cordial feelings were aroused at his misfortune.

But a superstitious dread of death took possession of the General in his sickness, and reminded of a prophecy of a certain mathematician of Salamanca, that while he should be the lord of a certain country, he should have a fall that would cause his death. He wished to be near his lovely wife and children, and his mind, freed from the constant demands of an active campaign, yielded to the depressions caused by his disappointments. To divert the minds of the soldiers from the new campaign, he feigned himself to be seriously ill. Then he declared his loss of confidence in the richness of the country, and its small value for distribution to the soldiers for settlement. They began to desire some better reward. A council of officers approved of issuing orders immediately to prepare for the march homeward. But after more deliberation, officers and men, petitioned that sixty soldiers might be left to hold the country till reinforcements should arrive, and that he should appoint a new commander, to prosecute further conquests. This petition was refused, and in the beginning of April, 1542, the army set out to return to Mexico.

Two missionaries, full of zeal for the conversion of this great country to the Christian faith, wished to remain. Fray Juan de Padilla, with a Portugese, a negro, and some Mexican Indians proceeded to Quivera, where the friar was killed, and the Portugese was imprisoned for ten months, but afterward escaped to Mexico. Fray Juan de la Cruz also remained at Bernalillo.

Luis, a lay brother of devoted life, remained at Cicuyè. A few Mexicans also stayed at Cibola. The rest of the army crossed the desert, and safely arrived at Chichilticale, where reinforcements were received. The Indians were hostile between Chichilticale and Culiacan, and harassed their march. But in his own province Coronado lost control of the army. With such as he could collect, he continued the march to Compestella, and on account of frequent desertions, he arrived in Mexico with not more than a hundred men of the splendidly equipped expedition with which he had undertaken the Conquest of the Seven Cities of Gold.

Coronado was coldly received by the Viceroy, who had ordered him not only to explore but to remain in the country, and was displeased at the results and conduct of the expedition. An investigation was demanded of his course, and withdrawing from Mexico, he returned to Culiacan. From the government of this province he was soon deposed, in 1548, and he died in obscurity.

Coronado had one of the grandest opportunities ever offered to an explorer of new lands.

He might have carried the banner of Spain beyond the Mississippi to the Alleghanys, and established the undisputed claim of his Emperor to the most magnificent country in the world.

> "Of thine own untried sword afraid,
> Not daring to be wholly great,
> Thou offer'st for thine idle blade
> The coward's facile plea of Fate!"

CHAPTER V.

CONQUERORS BY THE CROSS.

FOR nearly forty years the land of the Seven Cities was left undisturbed by the martial tramp of Spanish invaders, and unsought by the adventurous spirits of this remarkable people, who were bringing back rich rewards of their enterprize in penetrating the new lands of Central and South America. There were not yet any settlements of European Colonies on the Atlantic coast; neither had the civilization of northern Europe begun its slow march through the interior, westward to the Mississippi valley.

Four friars had joined their fortunes with Coronado's expedition. Fray Marcos had exposed his life for it, and been obliged to return to Mexico, under the ill favor and indignation of the army. The incessant movements of the army had left no repose for religious work, and the hostile and cruel conduct of the soldiers toward the inhabitants had prejudiced their minds against the religion of such invaders. Nevertheless, when disappointed in the secular profits and material gain of the expedition, its commander had turned his face homeward, the pious men saw their opportunity to win the souls of the heathen to salvation. The last words of the Franciscan brother Luis to the soldiers at Cicuyè were that he believed the old men of the tribe would soon put him to death, though he was treated kindly by the others.

The spirit of Luis was in the other Franciscan brethren. Fray Juan de la Cruz stayed at Tiguex. He had won the respect of the whole army by his modest and irreproachable conduct, so that Coronado ordered them always to uncover their heads when his name was mentioned. The difficulties of his position and relations to the natives at Tiguex, were too manifest to make his decision to remain with them other than heroic. They could not understand his language, nor could he speak to them in their own, yet he was left by those who had been aggressors, for whose conduct he was made responsible, to teach them a religion whose rites seemed only to be magic. The good effects of magic to the Indian were accepted with natural distrust, the evil effects were to be overcome only by death of the actor. "He could hope for no other result than martyrdom. 'It is believed that he died, shot by an

A SPANISH FRIAR.

arrow,' says an author of the seventeenth century, indicating the probable end of his career. He disappeared at Tiguex, and his name has left not even a trace."

It is certain, also, that Fray Juan de Padilla died a violent death at the hands of the people of Quivera. by whom at first he was kindly received with his companions, "a martyr to his religious zeal, and a victim of his lack of knowledge of Indian character, in the north-west part of the state of Kansas in our day, and probably in the course of the year 1582.* They are no more heard of." Such is the funeral oration, simple but pathetic even in its simplicity, of those two old monks, Fray Juan de la Cruz and Fray Luis remaining alone in the new country, content with finishing their days here, it matters not how, be it only in the service of their master. and for the honor and glory of his name.

Coronado's expedition was well nigh forgotten among the people of Mexico, but the reports of the country and inhabitants of New Mexico, which were gathered by Spanish miners in Santa Barbara, in Chihuahua, aroused the enthusiasm of Fray Augustine Rodrigues, or Ruis, a missionary of the Franciscan order. Moved with a zeal of charity and a desire to save souls, he enlisted two other brethren of the order, Fray Francisco Lopez and Juan de Santa Maria in a mission to these distant peoples. Obtaining the consent of the Superior of the order, and the authority of the Viceroy, Don Lorenzo Suarez de Mendoza, with an order for a military escort

* Bandelier. History of Colonization of New Mexico Mss.

of twenty men, in the Spring of the year 1581, they undertook the perilous journey to New Mexico. They had as companions, eight Spanish soldiers, each with an Indian servant, six Indians and a Mexican, making twenty-three persons in all. The Spaniards were armed from head to foot in coats of mail, and their horses also. The commander of the troops was Francisco Sanchez Chamuscado. They set out from the valley of San Bartolonia in Southern Chihuahua, the sixth of June, 1581. The soldiers were mounted and the priests on foot. It was the season of great heat and also of rain. The journey was very arduous for these soldiers in their heavy armor, and the priests dragging themselves along in the hot sands. They descended the Conchos river to its junction with the Rio Grande de Norte, and ascending that river, their route of six hundred miles is easily traced. They travelled for thirty-one days among the Conchos, tribes of the naked Chicemecks, who had only roots and tunas (cactus fruit) for their food. Then ascending the Rio Grande to within the present borders of New Mexico they found an agricultural people, living in a village with forty-five houses two and three stories high, and having an abundance of corn and other vegetables. They were also clothed in cotton garments. There were several similar villages on both sides of the river. This province, which the Spaniards called San Felipe, marked the lowest point of habitation of the pueblo or sedentary peoples of New Mexico. This people were in fact the Piros, and their villages were near San Marcial. The missionaries still ascended the river, following its many turns for about one hundred and fifty miles. They entered the country of the Tiguas, passed Isletta, and found themselves among the Queres peoples, in a town of four or five hundred houses two and three stories in height, where they heard also of other populous places. This was clearly San Domingo. From this point they went still farther to a village near the Cieneguilla, called Ta-tze, afterwards known as San Marcos. This belonged to the numerous and fierce nation of the Tanos, whose violence they could not prudently meet with their small military escort, and they determined to retrace their steps and sojourn at the village of Puara. This was opposite Bernalillo and contained eight or nine hundred souls.* Its ruins are still visible, in the neighborhood of several other extinct villages, where these missionaries began their heroic work in the midst of this strange people of the Tiguas. Forty years before them, the troops of Cardenas had wantonly attacked and outraged this people. Here also, Fray Juan de la Cruz had sacrificed his life in trying to save their souls. But like children, these Indians had forgotten Coronado. They were disposed to try these new-comers, and quickly to free themselves from their presence if they did not suit them.

But the courage of the soldiers now failed them. The inhabitants surrounded them in such numbers that should they become hostile, resistance would be vain. These troops determined at once to return

* A. de F. Bandelier. History of Colonization of New Mexico Mss.

to the mines, from which they had departed with the missionaries. Three Indian boys and a Mexican were faithful to the priests, who cheerfully remained to instruct these tribes in the Christian religion. Wishing to see more of the country before his return, Chamuscado, who was both prudent and courageous in his conduct of the missionaries, went as far west as the Zuñi villages, and also received information there of the Moqui towns. Even at Cibola he makes no mention of souvenirs of Coronado. He also explored the villages beyond the Sandias near the salt lakes, which are now the Chilili suburbs of Bernalillo, and departed from Pruara shortly after or during January, 1582. Chamuscado never reached the Santa Barbara mines. He died on the journey ninety miles north, near the present railway station, Concho.

In the month of July, 1582, not six months after the departure of the soldiers from Pruara, ten Indian servants who had remained in the country suddenly appeared at Santa Barbara and reported that the three missionaries had been slain by the Indians one after the other, and then three Indian servants had met the same fate.

Filled with a zeal for their work which was fatal to its continuance, the three friars had separated after the departure of the soldiers, and sought each a field of labor among different nations.

"Fray Augustine was an old man, the other two younger and full of life. Fray Juan de Santa Maria desired to convert the powerful tribe of the Tanos, who held the province near the buffalo coun-

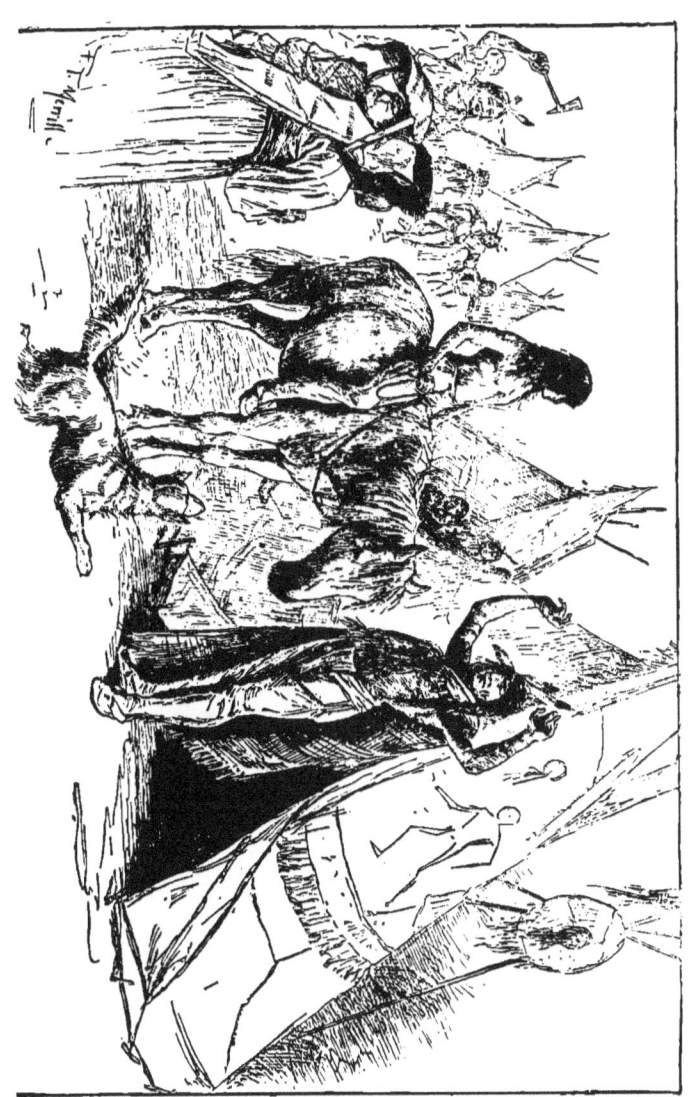

try and containing the turquoise veins, which made them of great commercial importance to the other tribes. They were unfriendly to the Tiguas. Their country embraced the numerous Santa Fe and Gallesteo villages, and the Cerrillos mountains."

Maria was convinced that the field was too difficult for him alone, and he determined to return to Chihuahua to obtain aid. He marked out a route by the stars, claiming to have such a knowledge as would surely direct him by a shorter route than the Rio Grande. He took some Tanos Indians for guides by the way of San Pedro, on the mountains bordering the country of the Tiguas. This imprudence cost him his life. As he slept at the foot of a tree, these Indians crushed his head with a great stone.

Rodrigues and Lopez remained at Puara. The medicine men of the tribe became jealous of the friars, whose zeal conflicted with their own influence. The priests were not understood in their teachings, and their rites were a cause of fear, rather than reverence. The Indians shot Lopez with arrows one afternoon while on his knees at prayer, and buried his body. Rodrigues was afterwards led to the spot, and gave the remains a Christian burial in the pueblo.

He sadly mourned his companion, and left alone, could only await with patient heroism his own fate. The war captain of the Tiguas was friendly to the old priest, and sent him five miles up the Rio Grande to another pueblo, but the waters of the river soon received his body from the hands of his murderers.

The zeal of the three friars was accepted of God,

and their blood was not shed in vain. In forty-eight years their brother friars of the Franciscan order, had baptized 34,650 Indians and erected in New Mexico forty-three churches.

In fear for these brethren, the Franciscans in Mexico called for an expedition to rescue them, and Antonio Espejo offered his life and fortune to the cause.

This territory has received three names: from its first discoverer Niça, the kingdom of San Francisco; from its first conqueror Coronado, the kingdom of Granado; from these three martyrs, the new kingdom of Mexico. And for three hundred years it has borne the name with which they baptized it in their own life blood.

CHAPTER VI.

EXPLORERS — ESPEJO, CASTANO.

THE hidalgo Don Antonio de Espejo was a gentleman engaged in working the mines at Santa Barbara, in Chihuahua, though he was a native of Cordoba, in Spain, and had resided in Mexico since 1559, possessing a considerable fortune. In the month of March, 1582, he had obtained a commission to make a tour of exploration and commerce in New Mexico. The reports of the tragic end of the friars hastened his preparations, and he set out from Santa Barbara, Nov. 10, 1582, with fourteen Spanish soldiers, a number of Indians, and one hundred and fifteen horses loaded with provisions, weapons of war, and articles for trade. His route was nearly the same as that of the missionaries, following the Rio Grande, and the journey to the

first pueblo, or sedentary people of the Rio Grande, occupied sixty-four days. On the 13th of January, 1583, he reached the same villages of the Piros near San Marcial which Chamuscado had found, and after ascending the river four days, he came to Tiguex. The Piros occupied ten villages, and the Tiguas eight. Puara was one of the villages of the latter province occupied by Coronado, of whom the inhabitants told Espejo, from memory or tradition, saying that white men had visited them, and made war upon them for the loss of forty horses killed by the Indians. At Puara, Espejo made an encampment. The people guilty of the death of the missionaries did not dare long to remain near him, and fled with their families to the mountains, from which they could not be persuaded to return. An abundance of food and fowl was found in this and the neighboring towns.

Among the Piros in the south there was a disposition to barter with the Spaniards. They brought them curious things made of feathers of divers colors, well tanned deer-skins, with which they were clothed, and many mantles of cotton, streaked with blue and white, like those brought from China. They wore boots and shoes with soles of neat leather. The women were carefully attired and their hair well combed. Their weapons were bows and arrows headed with flints, targets of hides, and clubs half a yard long, very thick at the end. They were governed by caciques, whose orders were proclaimed by subordinates and carefully obeyed. They had prayer-places in every house for the worship of idols, and chapels for the worship of the devil, where he was said to rest and refresh himself.

Espejo heard of rich and populous towns to the east and north, and having ascertained the sad fate of the missionaries, he began the explorations which had been his first object in planning the expedition. He was a fearless but prudent man, of much tact in dealing with the Indian character, and avoiding acts of violence towards himself or the peoples among whom he made his explorations. His first adventure was toward the east, among the "Maguas," a people of the Tanos nation, occupying the arid basin of the Gallisteo. He discovered three sources of water south of this basin, which were once frequented by buffaloes, but there was a general lack of provisions in these valleys and he returned to Puara. Thence he went north on the Rio Grande to the first pueblo of the Queres, now obliterated. It was near San Felipe on the left bank of the river. The Queres had five towns. Three had disappeared since Coronado's time. The five that now remain are San Domingo, San Felipe, Cochiti, Santa Ana and Cia. The Queres were kind and friendly to Espejo, as they had been to Coronado. They directed him to five villages two days' journey to the west, of which the principal one was Cia. Its houses were plastered and painted with many colors. Thence he went to Jemez, where there were six villages, and turned south to Acoma. The country here was inhabited by wandering Indians, and the important pueblo of Laguna did not exist at that date of the sixteenth century. The people of Acoma, as also the Piros had done, received Espejo with the honor of dances and festivals, but he happened to arrive at Acoma in the season of the great Snake Dance, now preserved only by the Moquis in their customary feasts. Espejo was deeply interested in the solemnities of the Snake Dance, which is the worship of the spirits of their ancestors. The "Queerchos or Apaches in this region were much disposed to barter with the Spaniards. They were the Navajoes who are first mentioned by the Europeans at this time, though they were and are still the most powerful tribe of the Apache nation," and occupied the mountains north of Acoma, the deep valleys around the Sierra de San Mateo, and in general, the north-west of New Mexico. They were as great a scourge to the pueblo peoples as subsequently to the Spanish colonists.

Espejo pushed on seventy miles west from Acoma in a more venturesome trip to a province of six villages, "which province is called Zuñi and by another name Cibola." "He gave," says Bandelier, "to this group of pueblos also the names of 'Ami' and 'Amé,' and to one of the villages 'Aguico.' We have here, then, not for the first time, the name of Zuñi, but at the same time the first positive statement that Zuñi was Cibola! 'Ami' et 'Amé' recall the 'Camé' of Chamuscado, proving thus indirectly that the latter visited Zuñi, and Aquico it is easy to recognize in the 'Havico' of Fray Geronimo de Zarate Salmeron of 1626, . . . and the ruin of 'Ha-vi-cu' of our day, situated near the hot springs of Zuñi." In Zuñi were still standing the crosses

A NAVAJO BLANKET WEAVER.

erected by Coronado, and three Christian Indians whom he had left here were still living. They had almost forgotten the Spanish tongue, but were fluent in the language of Zuñi, and communicated much information concerning the country to Espejo.

Fray Berardina Beltran, who had accompanied Espejo in the entire expedition, here fell out with his leader and insisted on a return, because they had as yet found neither enough silver or gold. He refused to go farther west, and remained at Zuñi, while Espejo with nine soldiers and one hundred and fifty Indians, entered upon another long journey of eighty miles to the Moqui towns. Receiving messengers from this province, whom he conciliated with gifts, though he had been forbidden to approach, he went forward, and was welcomed three miles from their first town by two thousand of this people bearing quantities of provisions. The cacique with a multitude of his people came forth to greet him, scattering corn-meal on the ground under their horses' feet in token of their pleasure. Espejo, surrounded by multitudes of natives, distributed presents of hats, beads and other articles very acceptable to them. Messages were sent out by the caciques to other towns, and from all parts of the province there came people loaded with presents for the Spaniards, and invited them to their own towns in the valley of Osay, which Chamuscado had also visited.

Espejo still looked toward the west. A great river, a great lake, populous towns and rich mines, of which he constantly heard in that direction, still aroused his ambition. With five or six men to carry the baggage and only four soldiers, he penetrated for one hundred and thirty miles, the present country of Arizona. He did not reach the Rio Colorado, but he found smaller streams, groves of walnut trees, vineyards and much game, and ascended the mountain where were the mines, which showed a broad vein of ore exceedingly rich in silver. "He was in the region of Prescott."* Espejo and his little company returned safely to Zuñi, where his men had been treated with great hospitality by the Zuñis. They promised to plant for them more corn if they would return to them. Espejo, with a part of his company, then departed toward the northeast, but the friar with six soldiers set forth toward New Biscay. Espejo crossed the Rio Grande into a country of the Tubeans, or Hubates. Here were many mines, houses five and six stories high, and the people numerous in numbers, clothed in colored mantles and dressed skins. These were the people of San Marcos, Cienega, San Lasaro, Gallisteo and San Christobal. They were of the nation of the Tanos, and in the northern part of the province, which he had first visited on the southern borders. Without doubt he was there again in the midst of those whom he had called Magnas, in the first visit he had made. But while he then touched the valley of the Gallisteo on its Southern line, this time he had arrived from the East-north-east and entered then the northern boundary, leaving the village of Cua-Po-o-qué, where is now the city of Santa Fé, more than thirty kilometres to the left. From

* History of Colonization of New Mexico Mss.

San Christobal, the most eastern village of the Tanos, Espejo proceeded to the three pueblos of the Tamos, another people who must not be confounded with the Tanos on account of the similarity of pronunciation. These were by a river which Espejo says was not the Rio Grande, and as it was in the country of the buffaloes, twelve days' march from the river Conchos, it could only be the Pecos, and the Tamos were, therefore, the Pecos people. Espejo says the villages were those which Coronado called Cicuique or Cicuyè. Fifteen years after Juan de Oñate called Pecos the "Pueblo," which Espejo had called the province of the "Tamos."*

The Pecos were hostile, and not being permitted to come near their villages, Espejo turned south, following along the river Pecos for six days to the location of Fort Sumner. There immense herds of buffalo covered the plains, through which they traveled for three hundred and fifty miles. Near the mouth of the Pecos river in Texas, they were guided across the country by three Jumanes Indians to the Conchos, whence they arrived at Santa Barbara September 20th, 1583. The expedition had occupied with its wanderings in the north, ten months and two days, and had been accomplished without any conflict with the people, or the loss of a single man, greatly to the credit of the skill and humanity of Espejo and the Spanish soldiers who had accompanied him. Espejo gathered much valuable information, confirming by his observations the accounts which Cabeca de Vaca, Coronado and Chamuscado

* History of Colonization of New Mexico Mss.

had given of the country and people. His estimates of the population of the provinces and pueblos which he visited in New Mexico and Arizona, amount to 253,000 souls. It has seemed unworthy of a history to ascribe such a population to the sedentary or pueblo nations of this region. It did not include the Tiguas on the Rio Grande or the Tiguas and Piros around the salt lakes, nor the Tehuas of Taos, an agricultural population of fifty thousand more. Castenada estimated it at seventy thousand, which he thought should be more or less reduced. Bandelier asserts that Espejo was honestly deceived in his estimates of the population by two things which could not have failed to produce an illusion. He did not thoroughly explore the country, and judged of the villages at a distance or on a short sojourn among them. As he recalled them, they had an exaggerated size, and again, wherever the Spaniards stopped in a village, the people in great crowds surrounded them, led by curiosity as much as distrust, and new crowds came so long as he remained. He multiplied the number of these by the number of villages.

Espejo was exact in other observations, and especially intelligent in his allusions to the mineral resources of the territory. He reported New Mexico to be rich in metals; Coronado believed to the contrary. But Espejo reckoned upon the indications of mines which were to be worked in order to enrich their possessors. Coronado as a conqueror sought for gold and silver in the hands of the Indians.

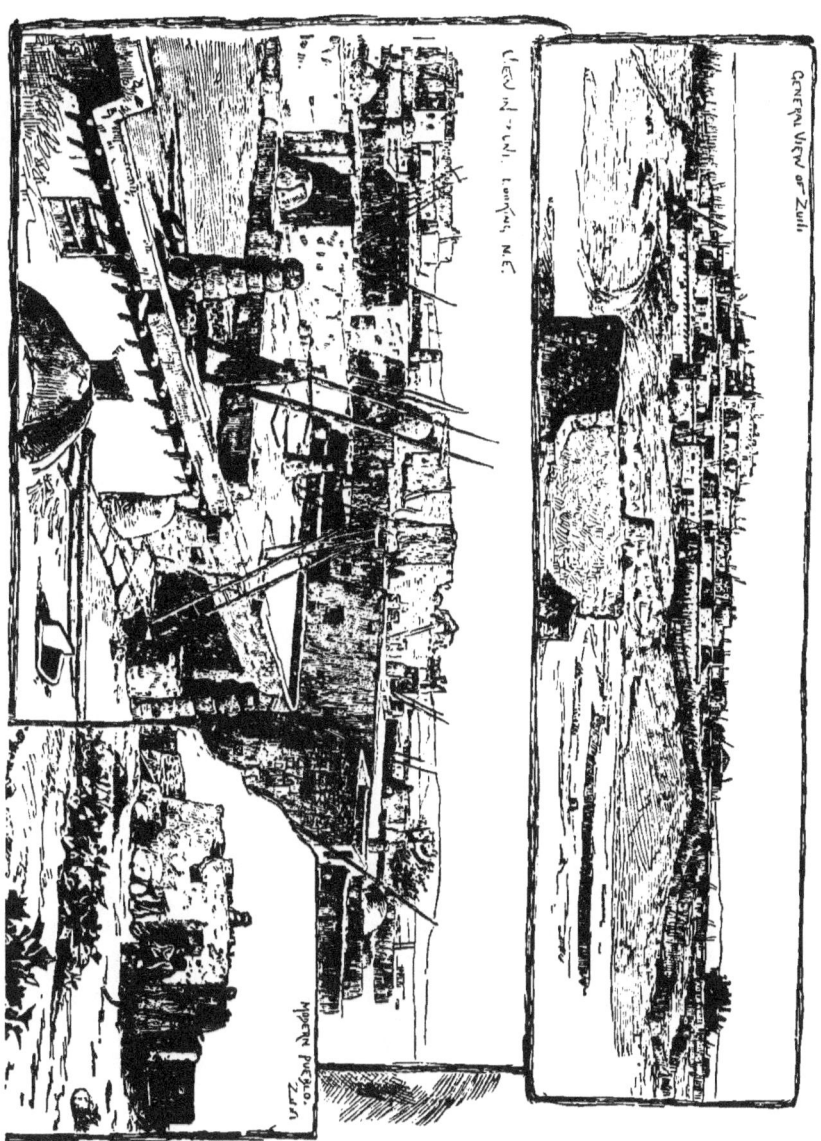

Espejo sought on his return authority to colonize New Mexico with four hundred settlers, of whom one hundred should be married. Similar authority had been asked by Christobal Martin, six months before, also by Francisca de Vargas. All were refused by the government, who mistrusted the reports of this country. Espejo died soon after his return.

Not one of Espejo's companions remained in the country. He founded no town in New Mexico, nor did he ever enter Santa Fé. He formed a great scheme for colonization which he presented to the king, but fortunately for him and his associates it was never executed, on account of his death. In 1589, a contract was made with Juan Baptista de Lomas by which he was permitted to conquer and colonize New Mexico. Though this contract was renewed in 1592, the project was never carried out; still the agreement was regarded in force. The Spanish government had but little faith in the resources of its northern provinces, and refrained from embarrassing itself with their development.

Yet the Captain-General of New Leon, Gasper de Castano de Sosa, by virtue of royal ordinances and his powers as acting Governor, proclaimed in 1590 an expedition to explore the north, and on the 27th of July, with a hundred soldiers, he set forth unconsciously in an unlawful enterprize, which revealed many interesting features of this unknown country. It was very successfully conducted. With supply wagons and oxen, he took a new route up the Pecos valley, discovered the remarkable pueblos in the Cañon Pintado, visited Pecos and the Tanos villages on the Gallisteo and the provinces in the Rio Grande valley as far as Santo Domingo. There he was arrested by a detachment of fifty troops sent after him, for violation of the laws and interference with the rights of Loma under his contract with the government. Castano returned a captive instead of an honored explorer, which his wise conduct of the expedition and remarkable prudence and kindness in treating with the inhabitants of the country, deserved. He was Coronado's equal in courage and fertility of resources, and but for the unfortunate mistake in the inception of his enterprize, which made him in modern terms, a fillibuster, rather than a lawful invader, he would have served most effectively his country and king.

PERIOD III.

SPANISH COLONIZATION.

1598 TO 1680.

CHAPTER VII.

ONATE.

HE results of the expeditions which were well equipped for long adventures, were enough to deter reasonable men from the search for wealth in New Mexico. But it was not long before a party of prospectors for gold and silver mines were led to the northern country by a Portugese captain, Leyva Bonilla, and one of his soldiers, Humana. They were pursuing hostile Indians and were directed to search for Quivera toward the North, by order of the Governor of New Biscay. Bonilla was disobedient to the command of his captain to return, and with eighty men, notwithstanding the refusal of six of his subordinate officers to march under him, pushed out upon the plains. There they disappeared. Not one returned to tell their fate. It was learned from a Mexican Indian, whom Juan de Oñate afterward, in 1599, obtained for a guide at Picuries on a similar expedition to Quivera, that Leyva marched toward the north, leaving the Pueblo villages on his left, and traveling always on the great plains. There he was murdered by Humana, who took command, and in fact reached Quivera north-east of New Mexico near where Coronado had discovered it. On their return, while the Spaniards were asleep, the Indians set fire to the grass of the plains, and the camp was burned and all perished but José, a mulatto girl, and a young Spaniard named Alonzo Sanchez, who were separated from the soldiers.

Two hundred miles to the north-east, in the village of San Juan, on the plains of Colorado or Kansas, Oñate discovered pieces of armour, horseshoes, scraps of iron and the bones of horses. It was proof to Oñate's party that Humana and his men had perished there. Nothing was ever heard of them again. Oñate found the Indian and the woman who survived that disastrous fate.*

Still the story of Quivera occupied the Spaniards. It went to Spain in new and attractive garb. Coronado's sober reports of it were forgotten, or overlooked, and New Mexico was believed to be the only pathway to its riches.

Juan de Oñate is the prominent name in the history of New Mexico for the next twenty years. He

* Bandelier. History of Colonization of New Mexico Mss.

undertook its colonization and settlement in a more systematic way, and was well fitted to give civilization to this country. A resident of Zacatecas, in the richest mineral region of Mexico, and a man of wealth, he sought the honors of nobility which were decreed by the King of Spain to the discoverers or conquerors of new lands. His father had been a lieutenant in Nuño de Guzman's army. His wife's grandfather was one of the four founders of Zacatecas and a principal proprietor in the mines. Oñate offered to equip at his own expense and pay the wages of at least two hundred soldiers. The king was to bear no expense. The proposition was accepted by the Viceroy, Don Luis de Velasco, on the 15th of September, 1595. Oñate was to obtain the title of Adelantado, Governor and Captain-General, and high official titles for his two cousins, and for his young son Cristobal, Oñate, who should accompany him in the dangerous enterprize. On February 28th, 1596, the agreement was approved by the Count de Monterey, and on the 8th of May, Oñate was ordered to suspend his preparations. Not until the 17th of December, 1597, was he able to overcome the obstacles and enemies to his enterprize at court. For two years he maintained two hundred soldiers with all their equipments at his own expense. Then he departed from San Bartolemo, in Chihuahua, to colonize New Mexico, with a company of four hundred, including the families of colonists, and 600 or 700 head of cattle. He was accompanied by eight Franciscan friars and two lay brothers. Ascending the Rio Grande on the 30th of

April, 1598, he entered the present boundaries of the United States territory, and "for the sixth time since 1539, the Spaniards took formal possession of all the Kingdoms and provinces of New Mexico."*

The country was mostly inhabited by wandering Indians below this point. He crossed the Rio Grande at El Paso, on the 4th of May, and on the 27th arrived at the villages of San Marcial, traversing the Jornada del Muerto. Then successively visiting the Piros, Tiguas and Queres, discovering relics of former expeditions, and forming friendly relations with the different peoples, he established his first location between the Chama and the Rio Grande, and founded the first town in the fertile valley thus protected by these rivers. It was called San Gabriel of the Spaniards, now Chameta, and was the first European settlement on new ground in New Mexico. Here the first church was built, which was consecrated with much ceremony. The older towns of Zuñi, Bernalillo, Taos, occupied by Spaniards as early as 1540, antedate this settlement, which never had any importance as a town. The first camp was at San Juan Baptista, the present San Juan. At San Gabriel the Franciscan fathers established their first convent, which was for a long time the centre of their mission work until the importance of Santa Fé as the capital of New Mexico drew their interest and institutions to that town.

Oñate allowed no violence in the treatment of the natives of the different colonies. They quite readily

* A. de F. Bandelier. History of Colonization of New Mexico Mss.

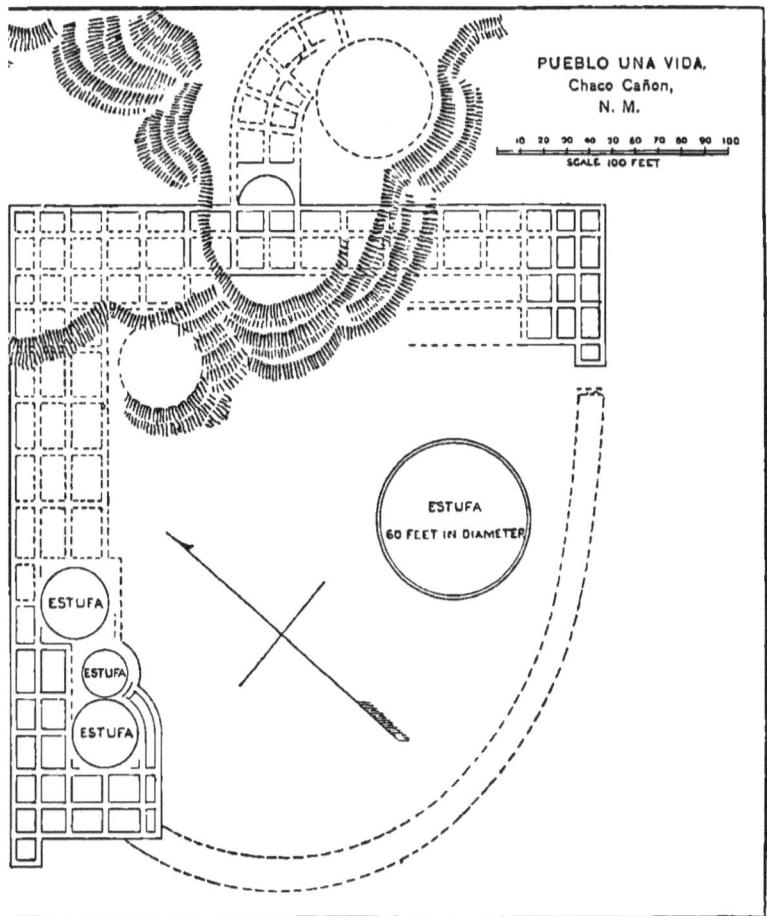

submitted to the authority of the King of Spain, believing generally that they would receive advantages from the new-comers and their religious rites, superior to those of their own government and superstitions. The discoverers were not allowed to take to themselves the name of conquerors, lest it should give countenance to acts of oppression and violence. The tact and friendliness of previous invaders of this country since Coronado's time, had prepared the way for the easy colonization under Oñate. He went from province to province, to establish the authority of Spain in a friendly way over them, and to introduce the religion of the Holy Faith by the priests who accompanied him. A conference of pueblo tribes was held at Santo Domingo the 7th of July, 1598, where they gave in their allegiance to the King. At a second conference the 9th of September, the same year, the religious missions of New Mexico were definitely located, and the chiefs of the missions appointed. There were seven thus commissioned to most dangerous and difficult charges, which included the Apaches, and wandering tribes with the pueblos or sedentary Indians. As these provinces and tribes were often not in friendly relations, and their languages were distinct and learned with great difficulty, it was a superhuman task thus imposed on these priests to reconcile, to convert and to civilize by the Christian religion these idolatrous and warlike people. They could be protected only by the power of the God they served, when they should depart to their separate fields. The natives received them as instructors, prophets and intercessors for things spiritual and material.*

The colonists were at first pleased with the country in which they had settled. Its high elevation, healthful and inspiriting air and fertile soil, were as attractive as the valleys and plateaus of old Spain. The Indians were friendly and aided them in building their houses. There was an abundance of game in the mountains and of fish in the streams, and the soil promised a quick return to its cultivation. Their plantations were soon green with the growing corn, wheat and vegetables. They improved the excellent grazing lands, for the raising of cattle and sheep. The skins of the buffalo, wolves, bears and deer protected them till their flocks yielded wool for their weaving; and they dwelt in peace with the natives. Some were discouraged with the necessary hardships of new settlements and a few returned to Mexico.

But new emigrants came into the country and extended their settlements to the north and east as far as the boundaries of Colorado. The efforts of the friars in the missions were not so prosperous. The missionaries gathered but few converts. They were too much scattered. Their loneliness was painful in the extreme, and they suffered from the destitution and improvidence of the natives. These were unwilling to learn of the missionaries, and the heathen rites, still observed in the neighboring estufas, were far more eagerly sought than the Christian worship.

* Bandelier.

Oñate was unwearied in his efforts to explore the country, and bring into obedience and good will the different tribes. He also sent fifty men far to the east, into the country of the buffaloes, and out upon the plains, in search for Quivera. They found the traces of Humana's expeditions, and met the Apaches, and returned to camp in twenty-two days. They reported as the famous Quivera a series of the Apache wigwams which they had seen, several miles long, united for protection against the herds of buffalo. This led Oñate some years after, between 1601 and 1606, to lead another expedition of eighty soldiers six hundred miles out upon the plains in search of the illusory city of gold. It brought him into conflict with the Esquansaques in defence of the people of the Quiveran tribes, who are said to have made a treaty with the Spaniards. The accounts of this expedition are very obscure and unreliable.

The submission and immediate revolt of the Acoma tribe and the speedy capture of this almost impregnable fortress, was the most remarkable occurrence in the early history of Oñate's colonization. Oñate narrowly escaped the assassination which befell a small company of troops, who, in their search for him had arrived at Acoma, and had been invited to the hospitality of the pueblo. Eleven thus perished in a night. Oñate's prompt punishment of the tribe, in which the fortress was assaulted and burned and great numbers of the Acomas slain, gave from that time all the country into his possession, terrified by the intrepidity of the Spanish troops in thus successfully subduing the strongest defenses and most warlike tribe.

Oñate afterward explored the country eastward of his settlements towards the Canadien, whose great cañon he discovered and called it the Palisado. He claimed to have found evidences that the country of Quivera abounded in gold, and even sent to the king of Spain a captive who, when taken to Mexico, had shown remarkable knowledge of the precious metal and of the manner of refining it. This Indian excited great interest in the City of Mexico at the court.

But when Oñate returned from his explorations of the country of the north-east beyond the plains, he found dissensions and discouragements among the colonists, who had become improvident. Drought followed by famine, overwhelmed the colony. The troops robbed the Indians of their stores of maize. The Indians suffered with the colonists from hunger. The missionaries were starving and almost naked, and abandoned their missions. The settlers, impoverished, disappointed and deceived, in regard to the resources of the country, which at first promised so well, deserted the colony, in 1601, and went to Chihuahua, accompanied by the disheartened missionaries.

Oñate, by vigorous correspondence with the heads of the order in Mexico and Spain, succeeded in securing the return of the Franciscans to their missions, and with them came many of the settlers. The prosperity of the colony gradually returned, and Oñate having received reinforcements of troops, marched westward so far as to follow the great river Colorado to its mouth, in 1604-5.

In this new period of prosperity, in 1605, the capital was transferred to Santa Fé. In 1608 nine priests were at work in New Mexico. Fray Geronimo de Zarate Salmaron, established at Jemez pueblo, had learned the native language and preaching with remarkable success, reported that he baptized and administered the Sacraments to 6566 Indians of that nation, besides many others of the Cia, Santa Ana and other Queres people.

Churches were built which remained as monuments of the zeal of the missionaries. Salmaron's journal of eight years' labor in New Mexico, with accounts of its richness and fertility, stimulated others to like sacrifices.

When the capital was removed to Santa Fé, the town of San Gabriel was completely abandoned and the churches and buildings fell into ruins. The beautiful valley between the Chamita and the cañon of San Ildefonzo was left to the Tehuas, the former proprietors or occupants.

"The Spaniards," says Bandelier, "and the Pueblos were thenceforth without daily communication, except when renewed by journeys for trade. The missions were also by themselves, and the priests had not constantly to mediate between the two races. They could devote themselves exclusively to their work. There was insensibly forming in New Mexico two distinct societies, the Spanish colony and the missions. The first had to protect the others, and the missionaries, in working for the gradual civilization of the Indians, had to render that protection unnecessary. There was on the part of both, rights and duties, prerogatives and obligations. The Governor was bound to succor the missionaries in time of danger. The religionists were bound to minister to the spiritual welfare of the colony as well as to the converts. So long as Oñate remained Governor there were no serious conflicts between the powers which represented under the same flag, the two states, geographically speaking, of which one included the other."*

Oñate returned to Spain, and about 1608, Pedro de Peralta arrived to replace Oñate as Governor. There were grievous differences between him and the representatives of the church. The records of the ecclesiastics are very partisan and violent with regard to him. The Franciscans wished to hold the colonists to the rights pledged to the Indians, and for good reason, for their contact with civilization was an evil so long as it was not moral. On the other side, the Governors thus interpreted their position, as expressed by one of the successors of Peralta: "The colonists (*encomenderos*) of that province have received their grants of land from his majesty and from the Governors, in his royal name, in order that they might dwell in that city of Santa Fé, in order to form there a community and not for another thing except that the Governor should order them conformably to the condition of their grants. The colonists had certain privileges. The king gave them, after Santa Fé had been founded, instead of

* History of Colonization of New Mexico Mss.

salaries, the *encomiendas* of the Indians in the neighborhood."

There were at Santa Fé, belonging to the Tanos, the remains of two ancient pueblos, when the Spaniards came to establish the town site. Tezuque of the Tehuas, ten miles to the north, and Tzi-guma near the Cieneguilla, twelve miles to the south-west, San Marcos, Galisteo, on the south, and Pojuaque on the north, were around the capital. Their inhabitants brought as tribute to the Spaniards of the city, a cotton mantle, and a fanega (two and a half bushels) of corn for each family.

Thus a door was opened to oppression and alienation of the natives by the Spaniards, which increased during the administration from 1608 to 1640. There were, in 1617, but forty-eight colonists and soldiers in Santa Fé. The Spanish population was necessarily very small elsewhere in the Territory. Yet the office of Governor was sought, for its profitable revenues. The Indians had submitted peacefully to Spanish rule because of the advantages which at first seemed to come with it in the arts of civilization, which they readily took up to a certain degree, especially in industrial pursuits. The Spaniards became selfish and greedy. They often abused their easily acquired power over the natives. They had a rare opportunity to raise them by their religion and education to a condition similar to their own. This was the effort of the priests; but the Spaniards often regarded the Indians as vassals or dependent wards of whom they could exact the service of captives rather than of subjects to the King.

Many converts were made to their religion by the priests in twenty years. In 1617, there were 14,000 baptized, and as many more ready for it, and there were eleven churches.* In 1630, all the pueblos were converted except Zuñi,† but the requirements of the Spaniards dispelled their illusions. The Spanish rule did not protect them from their inveterate enemies the Apaches, whose massacres and robberies of the Pueblos were left unavenged. The old traditions of the natives were dishonored: their marriage arrangements interfered with and restraints put upon the license of their heathen practices; their religious dances were forbidden; their estufas deserted and their altars destroyed. They had not the Christian character by which they could easily drop heathen customs, and the medicine men or magicians were jealous of the Spanish opposition to their rites. Their new religion required them to serve priests and masters, and add to the revenues of missions, churches and estates. They could not distinguish between the secular and religious powers over them.

---

* We must find these at Santa Fé, Pecos, Taos, Picuries, Santo Domingo, San Felipo, Sandia. There are four others, whose locations are not known, but they were probably at San Diego de los Jemez. The ruins of that Church in stone are still visible.

San Joseph de los Jemez. The ruins are not visible, but it is certain that the church was extant in 1622.

Santa Cruz de Galisteo.

San Francisco de Nambe. The last two we cannot affirm as a fact, but it seems probable to us that they are among the most ancient edifices of Catholic worship in the country.

Mss. in the Vatican. A. de F. Bandelier.

† Fray Francisco Detrado, the founder of the missions in Zuñi, and Père Martin, were assassinated by the Zuñis in 1630. Fray Antonio Gutierez was poisoned to death by the Moquis in 1633. He founded that mission.

The latter were often interposing for their relief from impositions by the more arbitrary Governors of colonists.

In 1642, Governor Rosas was assassinated on account of a quarrel between the ecclesiastics and the secular judges. This event caused great alarm in Mexico, as if it had come from an insurrection against the royal Government. But while it meant no disloyalty to the King, it was the culmination of much strife between the religionists and officials, and several priests were involved in the violent deeds of the insurgents. None of them were punished, but a colonist, or soldier, was executed for the crime. Immunity from punishment by civil laws was claimed by the religionists, among whom was a disposition, if not a well-defined purpose, to establish a theocratic form of government in the colony.

The increasing restlessness of the natives, the consequent peril and the difficulties of transportation, with the hardships of living in New Mexico, caused the Colony to increase but slowly, and the missions languished. The Indians were continually reminded of the past by their crafty magicians, who appealed to their worst passions and hindered or entirely forbade the youth to learn of the priests. Their frequent losses from Apache raids, their unpunished enemies, and their irksome restraints were regarded as cruel wrongs. Ten different pueblos* were soon

---

*The term pueblo became common during the Spanish occupation of New Mexico — with two significations:
Pueblo — the group of community houses.
Pueblo — the nation occupying them.

secretly united in measures planned to overcome the Spaniards. The natives became insolent and defiant, and their masters became more exacting of obedience and service, and were suspicious of their designs, on account of the frequent warnings of the priests.

In the year 1650, when General Arguello became Governor and Captain-General, forty Indians were whipped, imprisoned and hanged for conspiracy. At this their countrymen seized their arms, but had no concert of action. One Spaniard was killed, but twenty-nine of the conspirators were arrested and imprisoned, and the rest dispersed.

Ten years passed away and the Pueblo Indians became with each effort apparently more helpless. The Teguas nation, and the pueblos of Cochite and Jemez conspired, in 1650, with Apaches as allies, to massacre or drive from the country every Spaniard or priest. The Governor, General Concha, promptly and energetically repressed this movement, at its very inception. On Thursday night of Passion week when the Christians would be assembled in their churches, the assassins were to rush upon them in their devotions. Some Indians who had stolen horses, were overtaken and confessed the design to murder the Spaniards. The Governor, informed of this confession, ferretted out the principal leaders, who with many others were imprisoned. To quell the turbulent spirit of the natives, nine of the prisoners were hung and others sold into slavery for a period of ten years. The rebellion was crushed, and the Indians lived in grief and despair. In 1660, during the administration of Governor Mendezabal, a census of the territory gave twenty-four thousand people of all ages, including the Indians. The Piros and Apaches in the administration of General Villanueva, from 1675 to 1680, joined in a raid upon the Spaniards in which five of the latter were killed. Six of the Indians, who were afterward captured in the Magdalena mountains, were hung, and others imprisoned. In 1675, the Spaniards accused the Teguas Indians of San Ildefonzo of bewitching the friar Andres Duran, who was superior of the convent there. Two persons had been killed there by poison, and as a result of the trial, forty-three Indians were sold into slavery and four more were hung. Seventy Teguas warriors came early one morning to the Governor's rooms with eggs, chickens, tobacco, beans and skins, as a ransom for these their countrymen, who were in confinement. The Governor, alarmed at their demands, consented to their release, and the Indians peacefully retired.* Among those implicated in the San Ildefonzo affair was that most remarkable character, Popé, who at this time made his first appearance. Through his untiring efforts and wonderful strength of character, five years later, the rebellion of 1680 was entirely successful, and his country delivered from its oppressors, after five distinct efforts to combine the pueblos had been made by others, which had been each time defeated by the betrayal of the conspiracy by native informers.

From the administration of Pacheco to that of

* Davis' Conquest of New Mexico.

Otermin. in 1680, there were fourteen Governors, of whom eleven only are known. Special importance attaches to the administration of Don Diego Dionisio de Peñalosa Briziño, who entered upon that office in 1661. He returned to Mexico in 1664. He was in frequent conflict with the religious officials and went so far as to imprison the Commissary of the Holy Office in New Mexico. He also interfered with the commerce of the Pueblos and the Apaches in the missions and forbade the entrance of the Apaches into the Spanish communities, chiefly at Santa Fé, which was the only Spanish town in the territory till 1695. For Peñalosa's treatment of the Commissary, he was tried by the Inquisition in Mexico and severely punished. He made several explorations of the eastern and western borders of New Mexico, but made a false report of a pretended expedition to Quivera. Embittered by his disgrace he entered into treasonable negotiations in England and France for the proposed capture of the rich provinces of Chihuahua from the power of Spain, and the separation of the provinces north of it from Mexico. He died in Paris in 1689.

The vigorous administration of Governor Concha effectually restrained the Pueblos from any important measures to secure their freedom. Still the enslaved and maltreated natives, under fourteen different governors, driven to desperation, formed at last a league in which they sank their tribal jealousies for the sake of liberty and revenge. The Northern tribes were most active in efforts to unite all the nations against a common enemy. The Taos

Indians formed a new conspiracy, and communicating their plans for its execution by symbols on two deer skins, they sent them out to the Indians in all the Christian pueblos as far as the villages of Moqui, inviting them to join in the insurrection. The Moquis refused to unite and the rest deferred their attempt for liberty till they could be assured of success by the certainty that the Spaniards could secure no Indian allies.

PERIOD IV.

REBELLION AND NATIVE INDEPENDENCE.

1680 TO 1692.

CHAPTER VIII.

OTERMIN, CRUZATE TO VARGAS.

THE Spaniards were aroused to a sense of their danger in 1676, by the efforts and devotion of an eminent official of the Franciscan order, Fray Francisco de Ayeta. "He came to New Mexico in the quality of Procurer, and became the Director of the missions in 1674. There was an official reconciliation between the secular authorities and the clergy; all the previous documents containing accusations against the ecclesiastics were publicly burned at Santa Fé. The danger which threatened all, brought both parties together. Ayeta recognized from the first the gravity of the situation, and became the intercessor for the colony to the authorities in Mexico. His declaration of the year 1676, to the Viceroy, is a cry of alarm, a solemn and prophetic warning."

Ayeta proposed immediate relief. He called for an increase of the military force in the province by fifty well-armed soldiers provided with horses. Knowing the exhausted condition of the treasury at Mexico, he offered to transport these at the expense of the Franciscan order. The soldiers were equipped by the Viceroy. A thousand horses were bought and fifty men arrived at Santa Fé in time to shed their blood in a useless defense. But it was too late to save the colony or its twenty-five Indian missions in New Mexico.

Popé now rises to view from the obscurity in which his secret machinations for several years had kept him. He was a native of San Juan, but dwelt in the esoteric circles of the Taos pueblo, where he had acquired a great reputation by his necromancy, and also by secret acts of violence against the Spaniards. He had learned his arts of legerdemain among the Apaches and Navajoes. He had great gifts of eloquence and the elements of character necessary to leadership. With burning words he inflamed the passions of the Indian chiefs and warriors against the Spaniards who had first deceived and then enslaved them. Hidden in an estufa, he and two companions, Zaca and Tacu, received the wise men who came from all the pueblos to be assured of his power and asserted communications with the spirits of the under-world. Their bodies rubbed with phosphorescent substances, glowed in the darkness of the estufa and seemed to break forth into flames at their extremities. The devil, whose worship was much practised by those pueblos, inspired him. Spirits from the lake Cibobé, the happy place of the dead, communicated to him their wish that the pueblos should all unite against their oppressors. The visitors departed and confirmed to their own people in the estufas of distant pueblos the messages of Popé and the authority with which he spoke. Thus Popé labored for four years with his countrymen to unite them. Their minds were therefore prepared for the messengers who bore to them one day in the summer of 1680, swiftly running from tribe to tribe, a rope of palm-leaf tied with knots, giving the number of days before the time fixed for the great uprising, which should sweep their oppressors and the missions from the country. Each day they untied a knot as the time drew near. The conspiracy was kept in profound secrecy from the women. Death was threatened to all who refused to join it, but the plot was everywhere known to the men in the territory. If one was suspected of treachery he was killed. Popé's own son-in-law, the Governor of San Juan, was killed under suspicion of his unfaithfulness to the cause of his country. The Piros nation were not included in the conspiracy.

Such secrecy so well preserved indicated remarkable strength of character, and at the same time a deep sense of rancor against the Spaniards. It seems impossible that so many Christian Indians, greatly attached as many were to the priests and to the Spaniards whom they served, should have kept in their hearts through superstitious dread or patriotic devotion, the knowledge that their friends and masters and religious teachers, were doomed to death.

There were fifteen hundred Spaniards in New Mexico at this time, and at least twenty thousand Pueblo Indians were enlisted in the conspiracy. There were a thousand inhabitants in Santa Fé, half of whom were Mexican Indian servants. There were Spaniards living in every pueblo, five hundred men probably, scattered on farms from Algodones as far north as Taos, and east and west of the Rio Grande valley. The capital had a few soldiers and two small cannons, with but a small quantity of firearms and ammunition for defense, and the Spaniards were wholly unprepared for such a tremendous outburst of wrath.*

---

* SANTA FE IN 1680. "On the south side of the little river, as already stated, there was no town. A few houses occupied by Spanish families had been built among the little huts of the Indian servants. The name 'Analco,' given to the quarters about San Miguel, dated from the past century. The chapel of San Miguel, built after 1636, loomed up over scattered fields and dispersed buildings of small proportions. The town proper stood all on the North side. The town was somewhat larger than it is to-day. It extended further east. Its north side was occupied by the 'Royal Houses,' as the palace was mostly called. San Francisco street was the 'Calle Real,' the principal street of the place. A street intersected it at right angles, passing through the buildings now owned by Gov. Prince, and continued northward along the east side of the Palace. It terminated in a broad trail leading to Tezuque. The Palace had, therefore, a wider façade than the edifice that bears its name to-day, and which occupies only parts of the original site. Another street ran from north to south along the western side of the royal houses, and a fourth one continued west of the main front of that building, so that the town lay really west of the present square, and was divided into three bodies of buildings, one between San Francisco street and the river, another north of that street and south of the military headquarters, and the third (composed

The new moon of August 28 was the appointed time for the outbreak. The priest at Tezuque had been twice warned by faithful Christian Indians before he fled to alarm the Governor, who, two days before, had also been notified from the same pueblo of the impending destruction of the colony. The treachery of the Tezuque Indians was discovered, and the conspirators in whose exulting hearts the flames of passion had been scarcely smothered for so long, leaped to their long-cherished vengeance on the 10th of August.

The Spaniards were terrified at their peril. Governor Otermin took measures to fortify the capital, and messengers were at once despatched to all the Spanish settlements instructing the people to gather in the North at Santa Fé, and in the south at Isleta. The Indians of the different pueblos were also immediately informed by their allies of their betrayal. The messengers of alarm and of wrath crossed each other's paths, speeding on their conflicting errands of mercy and revenge. The same night of the 10th of August, the conspirators began to slay without mercy all Christians within their reach. Priests, women and children fell without distinction before their murderous blows. A few maidens were reserved for wives to the warriors, but the work of extermination went on with unrelenting ferocity.

only of a few dwellings), on the site of headquarters and north of it. The houses were not contiguous. Gardens, nay small fields, surrounded each residence. Santa Fé formed a long triangle tapering gradually to the west, the eastern side of which was marked by the parochial church and its convent. The site of that church, the foundations of which were laid in 1622, is the same now occupied by the cathedral." — BANDELIER.

It was indeed true that the inspiration of this rebellion came from the infernal spirits of evil, for the quiet and peaceable Pueblos were transformed in an hour to cruel fiends.

Two soldiers from Taos bore the first official news of the conspiracy and rising of the Teguas, and the massacre at Santa Clara and La Cañada. In three days the same mournful tidings had come to the capital from the north and south, and the east as far as Pecos, and from Jemez in the west. Eighteen out of the twenty-five priests in the various missions were slain and three hundred and eighty Spaniards, old and young, assassinated and treated with great cruelty, as subsequent information proved. The summons to the settlers was heeded at once. They left their homes and sought the places of rendezvous, but many were overtaken and became victims of the Indians.

From the first news of the revolt, Governor Otermin began to gather the inhabitants of Santa Fé to a place of safety. He chose to fortify the buildings and enclosure on the present site of the Governor's palace. The women and children, the houses, the consecrated ornaments of the church, the valuable possessions of the town, with such provisions as could be collected, were placed within the enclosure. There were two towers at the corners, where the small guns were stationed. The approaches to this plaza were barricaded by the soldiers. The place of defence was badly chosen. From the high ground toward Fort Marcy they were under the inspection of the enemy. They were cut off from

the river which was the main supply of water to the town, except springs near the palace and the Cienega on what is now Palace Avenue. They were in great danger from a siege, to which, in fact, the Indians resorted to conquer them.

The return of detachments sent out to the neighboring towns of Santa Cruz and the Cerrillos, and the recitals of fugitives to the capital, filled the people in the fortifications with horror. The Spaniards had been exterminated as far north as Taos, except a few families who were defending themselves in the valley of Santa Cruz. A few were blockaded at Cerrillos. Six families below San Domingo had escaped to Isleta, and from Albuquerque to Socorro the settlers were fleeing toward El Paso.

The Tanos, Pecos and Queres were reported approaching from the south, having reached Arroyo Hondo on the 13th, and on the morning of the 14th of August, they were seen from the roof of the fortified palace, on the banks of the river by the San Miguel church and spread out on the plain, pillaging the deserted houses of the servants of the Spaniards. They occupied the place which the Governor should have taken for his defense, and there awaited the approach of their allies from the north, protecting themselves in the church and abandoned houses. The Indians were armed with bows, cross-bows, firearms, and swords and lances, and many rode horses which they had taken from the Spaniards.

Otermin sought to parley with the Tanos and induce them to withdraw their warriors before the Teguas should arrive. They vigorously refused any terms of peace and sent to him two crosses, a white one, which signified peace and immediate withdrawal of the Spaniards from the country; a red one, which indicated war and extermination. Otermin chose the red cross, having no confidence in their pretended offer of peace. The Spaniards were surrounded in their fortifications. Within were a thousand people and a great many horses and other animals. The Indians became more numerous every day. The Teguas and northern tribes were coming in over the hills. They occupied, the heights above the town, shut off the stream of water that partly supplied the Spaniards, and determined to reduce them by starvation. Horses and other animals began to suffer and die. The supply of provisions became reduced. Otermin determined to attack the Indians, and made a sortie on the 20th to drive them from the streets in the lower part of the town. They were surprised in the houses, and by eleven o'clock in the morning the Indians were completely scattered. Otermin lost one of his principal officers and a few soldiers, and was himself wounded ten times by the Indian arrows; but his victory was of little importance except in the capture of forty-seven prisoners, and the killing of many Indians. The rest dispersed and left the Spaniards in perplexity. Their foes were very numerous, their provisions had failed. The only way to save their lives from the savages was to escape to El Paso. For the captive Indians were examined before their execution as to the details of the conspiracy, and its details gave little hope for the Spaniards.

They then executed the prisoners in the plaza. A council was called, and in view of the scarcity of provisions and exhausted condition of the soldiers, of whom now not more than a hundred were in effective condition for fighting, it was determined to abandon the town.

The sick and wounded were prepared for the march on the night of the 20th, some valuable baggage packed for transportation, and at sunrise the next morning the whole population entered upon the desperate march of three hundred miles through a country filled with hostile Indians.

The natives were much discouraged at their losses and the death of the prisoners the previous day, and watched the Spaniards from the hills until they were fairly entered upon their march. They reached the Gallisteo and encamped, without any hostile demonstrations on the part of the Indians. The citizens travelled on foot, protected by the soldiers on horse-back, who examined the country in their route down the valley of the Rio Grande. The pueblos were deserted and the country desolate. After reaching Sandia, they came in sight of the Indians, but the fugitive Spaniards were reinforced at Alamillo by thirty soldiers who were marching to their relief from the south.

Provisions were seldom to be found on the march, and the fugitives suffered greatly from hunger. The inhabitants who had been gathered at Isleta had fled to the south before them. They were obliged to halt and send forward to El Paso for food, and four carts loaded with corn were sent to them. At

Saliente, they held a council whether they should return to New Mexico, and decided to encamp at San Lorenzo, about three miles from El Paso, where wood and water could be obtained, and report to the Viceroy their defeat and expulsion from New Mexico.

The number of fugitives who escaped from New Mexico, including several hundred village Indians of the Piros and Teguas, was 1946. The official reports make the number of Spaniards who perished in the two or three days of massacre to be four hundred and one, including twenty-one priests and seventy-three able-bodied men.

The condition of the exiles became pitiable. The women, barefooted, mixed mortar to plaster the walls of the rude huts they erected. Their supplies of beef and corn received from El Paso were insufficient, and they often had to subsist on herbs and wild fruit. Hostile Indians surrounded them, by whom they were often attacked, and they were obliged to remain at El Paso in poverty and discouragement for several months.

When the Indians beheld the retreat of the Governor and the hated Spaniards from Santa Fé, they were filled with amazement at the speedy success of their revolt, and a scene of savage revelry began which was like the loosing from confinement of thousands of wild animals. All traces of their civilization seemed to have been obliterated at once. They gave themselves up to astonishing fury, casting off all marks of their Christian education. They plundered and destroyed everything in the Capital which had been the property of the Spaniards, saving only the few provisions that could be found. They set fire to the church and to the convent, but could not burn their adobe walls, which remain in the restored building of San Miguel Chapel. They made burning heaps of the furniture and relics of the church and the houses, and danced wildly around the fires, shouting that God the Father and Mary the Mother of the Spaniards were dead and the Indian God only was alive. Putting on the priests' robes, they rode furiously through the streets of Santa Fé, with yells of joy. Establishing the four cardinal points of the compass as their visible Church, they erected stone enclosures in the plaza, dancing the cachina, and offering flour, feathers, seeds and grain to appease the gods of their country, whose worship they now resumed. Then running to the mountain stream that flows near the plaza, they washed their bodies with amoli to remove all the effects of the Christian baptism. They dropped their Christian names and marriage relations, and insanely rushed back to the debasements of heathenism.

The priests were regarded as the cause of their sufferings. Their treatment of the Fathers in the massacre was most cruel and revolting. The old priest at Jemez, Friar Juan de Jesus, sleeping in his cell at night, was roused by a band of savages, who stripped him naked and having mounted him astride a hog, with torches and yells, beating and cursing him, drove him through the village. Then they compelled him on his hands and knees to carry them, till he fell dead, and his body was cast out a prey to the wolves. A priest at Acoma met a similar fate. He was stripped and tied with a rope and paraded in fiendish triumph, beaten to death with clubs and stones and his body thrown into a cave. A priest at Zuñi was dragged from his cell, stripped, stoned and shot on the plaza, and his body burned in the Church.

The grounds of complaint against the Spanish rule, as stated by the Natives in an official examination before and after the rebellion, were comprised in the statement, first, that they were angry that the priests and the Spaniards had taken away their idols and worship handed down to them from their ancestors; and secondly, that they wished to live as they pleased and not according to the laws of the Spaniards, which were not good. "They wished in a word to re-establish the old order of things—the old religion, the old customs, the old social and political order. We have seen what that signified; now the Pueblos were free, nothing hindered them from going back an age." *

Popé, like any other sorcerer, was not any where visible during the siege of Santa Fé, nor during any of the conflicts, but at once came forward to inspire the orgies of the Indians after the town was in his possession. His power and influence were greatly increased by the success of the rebellion. His influence and word was for a while supreme. He shared largely in the booty, and profane honors were bestowed upon him. But conflicts arose. Discussions increased every day. The northern pueblos fought

*A. de F. Bandelier.

DEATH TO THE SPANIARDS.

with the southern, then the Teguas and Pecos tribes went to war. The Apaches and Navajoes renewed their attacks upon all the Pueblo nations. Plunder and murder everywhere devastated the villages and the corn fields. Famine ensued. The northern tribes were starving, when the southern had plenty. Disease and death were everywhere destroying the populations, after their return to heathen customs, food and worship. Popé soon died of poison. Catiti, who had been the principal leader in the siege, had more power; but there was no more union among the tribes. The wretchedness and suffering of their lives were increased, because discarding every form of civilization, and their Christian faith, they understood better the degradations of heathenism.

All these changes and desolations were made apparent and freely acknowledged by some of the tribes, when in 1681, Governor Otermin attempted, under the orders of the Viceroy, to re-conquer New Mexico. The Franciscan friars at El Paso supplied his expedition with almost everything needed by the soldiers. Corn, beef, cattle, wagons and ammunition were freely provided by this peaceful brotherhood, in the hope of recovering their lost missions. New armor was manufactured of ox hides. The families of the colonists were left at San Lorenzo. The inhabitants of Santa Fé were especially zealous to recover their homes, and the priests, to Christianize the apostate Indians.

Infantry, cavalry and a body of friendly Indians composed the effective force of the army, which departed from El Paso November 5th, amid the acclaims of the citizens. They reached Isleta December 5th, and captured it. The village was in a sad condition. The church and convent were damaged by fire, the church turned into a cattle corral, and every cross thrown to the ground. The people were ordered to assemble in the plaza, and there they were severely chided by Otermin for their impiety. The father Ayeta was the next day received into Isleta with great ceremony, and addressed the people, commanding them to return from their apostacy into the fold of the church. They received absolution, communion and the baptism of their children. The royal flag of Spain was then unfurled, and saluted with three rounds of musketry, amid the shouts of the natives, and the reconsecrated bells rang out in loud peals, as the vesper service closed the exercises of the day. The next day Otermin addressed the people, and extolling the King and his care of his subjects, bestowed the King's pardon on them without their request, but they meekly received his clemency in place of their independence with some exhibitions of pleasure.

Thus the southern pueblos were visited one after the other and reconciled again to the Spanish regime, and Otermin undertook the subjugation of the northern tribes. He went as far as Cochite, where the tribe under Catiti were hostile. They grossly deceived the Governor and the priests under a pretense of submission and penitence, but only to gain time for the gathering of their forces, and securing of advantages against the Spaniards. The aspect of these tribes was so serious, that both the Governor and the priests were disheartened. The Indians would hold no conferences, and remained in the mountains, where they had built, during the period of their independence in anticipation of the return of the Spaniards, many strong refuges and pueblos for their defense.

The council held at Cochite decided, with the advice even of Father Ayeta, to return to El Paso. The expedition had lost 125 horses and only 136 were in a condition for service. The people of Isleta went with the Spaniards, destroying their pueblo and casting their fortunes in with them. They numbered 385 of all ages. Their return to their Christian religion was thus apparently sincere.

Otermin showed neither energy, courage or persistence worthy of such an effort to recover his province. He spent only a month in New Mexico, meeting but little resistance from a large portion of the people. His failure left New Mexico for several years in the undisputed possession of the savages.

The office of governor was taken by Domingo de Cruzate, a very able general who held the title until 1687. Santa Ana was taken by storm in an expedition made by Pedro Posada, a governor for a short time. Cruzate again made an attempt to bring the pueblos back to subjection. A few Franciscan friars accompanied the last expedition in 1688, but in vain did Cruzate carry to them the commands of the King, though he took possession of some towns as far north as Cia, and held them for a short time.

PERIOD V.

SPANISH RULE.

1692 TO 1821.

CHAPTER IX.

CAMPAIGNS OF VARGAS AND HIS SUCCESSORS.

IN 1691, Don Diego de Vargas Zapata Lujan succeeded Cruzate. He was a man of great force of character. He combined the endurance, courage, tact and persistence of a Spanish warrior with religious zeal and entire devotion to the powers and dogmas of the Roman Catholic Church. He was a conqueror first by the victorious faith whose banner he was ready to defend and carry forward at the point of the sword. When all its persuasions failed to subdue the recreant and apostate natives, he was unrelenting in his measures, prompt and energetic in the use of violence and the destructive forces of war.

With eighty mounted Spaniards and one hundred friendly Indians he made an armed reconnaissance from El Paso in the first year of his office. In twenty-three days he rode into Santa Fé amid the

Tanos, who had built a pueblo around the plaza, leaving the old town in ruins. They had anticipated his approach and collected by swift runners warriors from the northern pueblos to oppose him. Early in the morning of the 13th of September they attacked their ancient foes. De Vargas, a brave soldier and intrepid leader, inspired his troops in front of his men, choosing the most favorable points of counter attack to the Indians. Not till the middle of the afternoon did they surrender.

Santa Fé had fallen, without any bloodshed. The natives were convinced of their weakness before such determined foes. Twelve pueblos in the group around Santa Fé offered no further opposition to the authority of Spain. Then the priests came forward to reconquer them by the Christian religion. Their children born since the rebellion were baptized, and seven hundred and sixty-nine persons were received into the communion of the church.

De Vargas reported to the Viceroy his success and urged upon him to hold this country by colonizing it on a larger scale. He asked that garrisons be placed at different points, surrounded by at least five hundred colonists.

Meanwhile he subjugated the pueblos of Taos by peaceful measures, and there learned that the people of the Moquis towns, of Jemez, Queres and Pecos, and a tribe of Apaches were in council and preparing to attack the Spaniards in overwhelming numbers. De Vargas enlisted the Taos Indians in his new perils. They promised to join him in eight days at Santa Fé, where he arrived on the

12th of October, having subdued in one week, Taos, Picuries and San Ildefonzo, three of the largest northern pueblos, without the loss of a man.

The soldiers of De Vargas had little opportunity to test their valor in conflict with the warriors of New Mexico. The descendants of five great families occupied this extensive country, who were destitute of all national instincts to unite them in face of a common enemy. The pueblo peoples were not much inclined to wars. De Vargas was mightier among them by the religious symbols on his banner, than by the sword. A devotee of his religion, he seemed to exult more in the conquests of the Holy Faith. But he was worthy of better foes as a warrior to test his hardihood and vigor. The natural difficulties of the country—the hunger, thirst and cold and heat to which his soldiers were exposed—imposed greater tests of their endurance than these Indians with ineffectual weapons and superior numbers. Yet De Vargas was ready for the emergencies which their treachery and desperation would sometimes present.

From Santa Fé he marched first to Pecos. The people of that important pueblo awaited him with the cross reinstated in the plaza, arches at the entrance of the pueblo, and a chorus chanting a hymn of praise of the sacrament of the Host. The people submitted in a body in the plaza, receiving absolution from their sins, and two hundred and forty-eight were baptized. Then a Governor, magistrate and war-captain were appointed and installed.

Thus he went from village to village down the Rio Grande, to San Domingo, Cochiti and Cia, their people welcoming the Spanish General and bowing reverently to the priestly rites of the church.

At Jemez the people were prepared to resist him. Three hundred Indians surrounded the troops as they reached the top of the mesa on which the pueblo was situated. They mingled with them, brandishing their spears and arrows, but committing no violence. De Vargas, suspicious of these hostile movements, asked the cause of them. The Indians perceiving no signs of fear in the soldiers, said it was to express their pleasure at their presence, and leading the Spaniards to their chiefs and warriors held in reserve in the pueblo, they all knelt, chanting a Christian hymn. Then embracing the General they led him into the pueblo.

The plaza was crowded with Indians, and they now began their war-dance. Somewhat alarmed, De Vargas ordered them to lay down their arms and bring in their women and children. Then holding a council with them, he explained their allegiance to the King of Spain and their desert of punishment for rebellion and apostasy. Commanding them to renounce their heathen customs and to receive pardon and baptism, Vargas and the priests, still fearful of treachery, were invited into a room where good food was provided for them, but they would not remain on the mesa during the night.

The next day a delegation of Apaches came to him saying that they wished to make a treaty and live at peace with the Spaniards. De Vargas coldly

IN OLD SANTA FÉ, CHRISTMAS EVE.

received them, but promised in a year to return and treat with them.

Seventeen provinces had already yielded to De Vargas. It was a conquest worthy of a Christian soldier. None had fallen victims to his sword. It had been tempered with mercy. It offered peace with submission, nor had it thirsted for blood. One thousand, five hundred and seventy captives had bowed their knees to receive Christian baptism and do honor to the cross in this campaign.

The Zuñi and Moqui towns had not yet sent tokens of repentance and loyalty. De Vargas immediately prepared to conquer and reduce them with his force of only eighty-nine soldiers and thirty Indian scouts. His men and their horses were, however, in the highest degree of efficiency. On the 30th of October, he set out on the march of three hundred miles into a hostile country. Isleta was found deserted and in ruins. Acoma and the camp-fires of the hostile Queres came next into view, but they offered no violence, and after long parleying for fear that the Spaniards were, under cover of Christianity, seeking to get the natives into their power in order to hang and shoot them, they finally yielded themselves and their fortress, and were pardoned and restored to allegiance without the shedding of blood.

The Zuñians received the General with great cordiality, declaring themselves friends and brothers and entertaining the Spaniards with great hospitality. De Vargas' peaceful conduct of his compaign had been announced before him, and the Indians found that nothing was to be gained by resistance.

The Navajoes, whose country bordered on that of Zuñi, endeavored to arouse the Moquis and the Apache tribes against him. The Moquis at first fled to the mountains before his approach from Zuñi. But when they received messages of peace, they returned and received him to their towns, at first with war-dances and other threatening demonstrations. De Vargas, with only sixty-three soldiers and two priests, preserved a calm exterior, ordered the chiefs to dismount, and himself with his soldiers on foot, entered the first village bearing the royal standard and an image of the Virgin. He returned to camp and for that night and the next day these people, among whom had been a stormy war-party, demanding that De Vargas should, with his soldiers, be put to death, quietly submitted to the King's authority and to the rites of the church. The other villages in like manner returned to their allegiance and to the Christian faith.

De Vargas now determined to return to El Paso, without attempting to subdue the wandering and hostile Apaches, by whom he had lost many horses stolen from his troops, and several times had been attacked. He was guided by three Indians to the Rio Grande near Socorro, whence he arrived at El Paso on the 20th of December. He had in four months reconquered twenty provinces, and rescued seventy-four Spanish women and children who had been in captivity for twelve years since the rebellion. He had demonstrated the availability of kindness in treating the Indians according to the principles of the Christian religion. With but little bloodshed he restored these provinces to the royal domain, from which they had separated with the rage and ferocity of savage warfare. He also brought back to a superficial confession of Christian piety, 2214 Indians who had turned back to the idolatrous worship of their ancestors.

The subsequent conduct of many of these tribes showed their insincerity and deep-seated hatred of the Spaniards, to whose military force they submitted, since its stay in their country was for a few days. But when it departed they prepared anew to offer a stubborn resistance to the return of colonists who should take possession of their country and homes.

The success of De Vargas increased the desire of the Viceroy to hold the country by permanent settlements. Funds were provided by the royal Junta of Mexico for the necessary expenses to equip a colony and provide for the long journey. Vargas received $42,461.12, at different times, for the recruiting and support of colonists in the presidio of Santa Fé.

Fifteen hundred persons joined the expedition, and there were three thousand horses and mules. Each family received from ten to forty dollars for the purchase of supplies. The colony with its military guard left El Paso Oct. 11, 1693, ascending the valley of the Rio Grande. Their sufferings soon became great from the insufficiency of food. There had been a failure of crops in the country and the Indians were very destitute of food. They had gathered in a great council at Santa Fé, formed an alliance and determined to resist the settlement of the country. Their plan was to deceive De Vargas with fair promises at first, and the appearance of submission; then to steal or destroy their horses one by one, till they should be compelled to fight on foot, and be overwhelmed by superior numbers, in cañons and ambuscades on their marches.

This course was pursued in the lower pueblos, where with more or less sincerity the people received the Spaniards. De Vargas marched with great caution to Santa Fé. He received large gifts of provisions on the way from the Queres and even from the Tanos pueblos, and was received with apparent cordiality in Santa Fé, which he entered on the 16th of November, with an imposing array of banners, armor, horses and trumpets.

Santa Fé was at this time a fortified pueblo with only one entrance. There was "a round-house for the defense of the redoubt with trenches in the form of a half moon; on the south side there were two round-houses and also two on the north side, and three estufas in the enclosure. There were plazas, and their dwellings three stories high and many four stories." It furnished lodgings to fifteen hundred persons, with other and separate apartments for the priests. Six months after, Mexican families to the number of three hundred persons joined them, and were also provided with lodgings. "There were no doors or windows in the outer walls of the houses, and the only entrance was secured in a military form. The place was surrounded by trenches and our people were secure."*

* Certified Report of De Vargas.

The occupation of the buildings by the soldiers and emigrants was a grievous offense to the Tanos. The weather was very cold and the Spaniards were famishing. De Vargas called upon the Indians for one hundred bags of corn, which were supplied without complaint, but a second request for two hundred was refused. The conspiracy long cherished now broke forth. The Spaniards were encamped near the present Rosario chapel. Daylight one morning in December, revealed the Indians in large numbers shouting defiantly at the Spaniards, who were approaching to assault them. Vargas at first tried his powers of persuasion, with which he had so often overcome these pueblo Indians. They were requested to lay down their arms, but refused. They however consented to hold a council, hoping meanwhile for reinforcements from the Apaches and other pueblos. Vargas allowed them until afternoon to surrender, and withheld his troops, but sent for the aid of the Pecos Indians to recapture the town.

The attack was not made until the next morning, when the Indians, beholding the troops standing in line and receiving absolution, opened the fight from the intrenchments, hurling arrows and stones in desperate defense of their homes. The Spaniards advanced with the old war-cry, Santiago. They assaulted the single entrance to the pueblo, near the present military head-quarters, but unable to break it down, built a fire against it, and the troops thus forced their way into the principal estufa.

The plaza was still defended by the high solid walls of the pueblo, which it was necessary to scale and take at every hazard, since the reinforcements of the Indians were now in sight. Beams and hastily-constructed scaling ladders were now placed against the walls, but their defenders, encouraged by the approach of their countrymen, hurled stones, arrows, and hot water with such energy that the Spaniards were forced back and defeated in their effort to undermine and carry the walls.

Vargas now drew up his troops so as to prevent the reinforcements from reaching the garrison. They were mounted and sent in five squadrons to disperse them before they entered Santa Fé. At the first charge five warriors fell, but the Indians were only scattered for a time. As they approached the town again, they were dispersed with the loss of four warriors. Night was near and the fighting ceased on both sides, without any decisive result. But the Tanos chief was killed and they were much discouraged.

The next morning, therefore, they permitted Vargas to march in triumph into the plaza. Planting his standard in the midst of the plaza, and a cross over the entrance to the pueblo, which had been carried there the day before, he again took possession of Santa Fé in the name of the King. The town was now searched and the severities of war against rebels were inflicted upon the defenceless inhabitants. Many wounded Indians were found hidden in the estufas. Others were taken prisoners. Seventy of these were piously absolved by the priests and executed by orders of Roque Madrid, adjutant to Vargas. Ninety others had been killed in the capture

GOVERNORS OF ZUNI.

of the city. The women and children were reduced to slavery. Four hundred were assigned to the Mexican families among the colonists. About three thousand bushels of corn, besides beans, wheat and other provisions were seized, and divided among the soldiers and colonists. The Indian Governor of Santa Fé was found already hung before the Spaniards entered the town.

A wooden cross was no longer the conquering weapon of De Vargas. He had now changed his character as a warrior. Hostilities with all the Indians of New Mexico began again with the fall of Santa Fé. They were always ready to attack the Spaniards whenever they left the walls of the town. In a country populous with enemies the operations of the colonists could not be carried on in safety. Fields could not be cultivated nor towns established. The captured supplies were soon exhausted. The guns of the Spaniards were disabled in the conflict at Santa Fé. Their ammunition was nearly expended and the Indians became bolder in their attacks, though the Apaches, whenever captured were immediately executed after being absolved by the priests.

Vargas, alarmed at the situation, sent a detachment of troops to Durango in Mexico for ammunition. Meanwhile he met many attacks of the Indians, who captured the animals of the Spaniards and harassed them in their foraging expeditions.

In March, 1694, with only twenty soldiers, he set out to subdue the northern pueblos. He found the hostile Indians securely entrenched on the Mesacita of San Ildefonzo. This was a favorite resort of the northern tribes. It rises abruptly from the banks of the Rio Grande, a steep black rock with walls of lava and tufa, and with difficulty ascended by any one. On its top, which contains about one hundred acres, in a basin surrounded by rugged masses of rock, in which are natural reservoirs several thousand Indians could be comfortably and securely sheltered.

A snow storm raged for three days after Vargas started from Santa Fé. He therefore reconnoitered the enemy's position and retired to the pueblo of San Ildefonzo after capturing seventy horses. The next day he attempted to take by assault the stronghold, but could only carry the small hill at the base of the rock.

The Spaniards again attempted to climb the steep sides over the broken lava, but were repelled and derided by the confident Indians. De Vargas' troops, who had been reinforced from Santa Fé, were still greatly weakened and reduced, and he had but about fifty effective men. He devised a way to take the stronghold by cutting off the Indians from their water supply. This, too, was ineffectual. The Indians came to the brow of the precipice and in derision poured water from vessels upon their hands and faces. They had a secret pathway to the Rio Grande.

By the 19th of March the patience of the General was exhausted, and he left the Indians, five hundred in number, secure upon the rock, and returned to Sante Fé, after capturing one hundred and fourteen horses and mules and killing thirty or forty Indians. His defeat was humiliating and unfortunate, for it restored confidence to the tribes north and south which had banded together to overcome the Spanish arms. Swift runners carried the news to the western tribes. Cia and Santa Ana, friendly to Vargas, entreated his protection from threatened attack, but he could not give it without imperilling the safety of Santa Fé.

A third time he besieged and attacked the mesa of San Ildefonzo, distributing his troops into three divisions and assaulting the rock on three sides. The Indians attempted to take the fields below the mesa, but were driven back to their stronghold. They finally surrendered and returned to their villages.

The colonists receiving assignments of land around Santa Fé, were encouraged to sow the ground, and De Vargas with troops then went south to pacify the Queres pueblos.

The increase of the Spanish colony was surely forcing the natives to peace and submission. There were enough restless people in the northern provinces of Mexico to keep open the trails into New Mexico. Usually the colonists were of the poorer classes, and the soldiers of the Spanish families, whose purses were not equal to their pride, and whose vanity was not content with the poor returns of idle lives without adventure. Loyalty to the church and King, whose realms could thus be extended, was a motive to emigration in some few instances where priestly influence prevailed. They usually arrived in Santa Fé, the acknowledged capital, greatly impoverished, worn out and sick from the hardships and sufferings of a journey of one thousand miles overland, through hostile tribes and often barren regions.

The successes of De Vargas and assistance offered by the Viceroy stimulated emigration. Large tracts of land, long cultivated by the Indians and often under irrigating ditches, were distributed as the fruits of conquest. The interruptions of their simple occupations, the culture of corn and vegetables, and the tending of sheep, caused the pueblos to decrease in numbers. The contact of a stronger race with a weaker one was fatal; but the Spaniards were inferior as colonists to the industrious peoples of Northern Europe, settling on the Atlantic shores.

The summer of 1694 opened with Apache disturbances. The planting season was over and the Indians renewed their raids; De Vargas went against the Teguas and again reached the pueblos of Taos, which were deserted. There he followed the inhabitants to their mountain refuges, and ordered them to return. They refused, and their villages, in which were great quantities of provisions, were given up to plunder. De Vargas returned through the Ute country, where he had some slight conflicts with these Indians, who were generally on friendly terms with the Spaniards. They were soon pacified, and gave renewed pledges of friendship. Then following the Chama river to the site of San Gabriel, the soldiers directed their course down the Rio Grande to the pueblo of San Juan, where the General encamped. Thence, with part of his troops, he marched by way of San

Ildefonzo, where he was again challenged by the Teguas to fight on their old battle-ground. De Vargas declined, and pushed on to Santa Fé.

The refractory inhabitants of Jemez now demanded his attention; they had frequently attacked the pueblos of Cia and Santa Ana and San Felipe on account of their loyalty to the Spaniards. These towns sent a strong body of warriors to join De Vargas as he crossed the Rio Grande; but the people of Jemez had fled to the mountain and had partially erected there a new town. In two columns, De Vargas advanced upon this position at sunrise, having dismounted his men. From the top of the hill by which the mesa was approached, the Indians for a while, hurling arrows and heavy stones, made a spirited defense. The Spanish forces gained possession of the hill and assailed the Indians in their houses. These were soon set on fire and their defenders, attempting to escape, hurled themselves in desperation over the steep sides of the mesa. There was great loss of life. Eighty-two were killed, and three hundred and seventy women and children were taken prisoners. A great quantity of corn was captured and nearly two hundred sheep. Seven hundred and fifty bushels of shelled corn were supplied to the capital from these expeditions. The Jemez Indians sued for peace, and made a treaty which they kept till 1696.

The devout General remembered the tragic death in 1680, at Jemez, of Friar Juan de Jesus. An old Indian and his wife, who had also preserved the tradition, declared that they could find his body in the old pueblo, and led him to the vicinity of an old estufa where were the bones of the martyr with a portion of his clothing and of an arrow sticking in the spine. With much solemnity they were transferred to Santa Fé and buried in the parish church.

In 1696, a famine which desolated the colony of New Mexico, broke out, while De Vargas remained Governor at Santa Fé. The distressed people were in a starving condition. Every species of animals and herbs were used for food, and the people went out upon the mountains searching for them like wild beasts.

It was the last opportunity of the Indians. In June, 1696, they arose in another rebellion in which fourteen pueblos joined. Thirty-four Spaniards were massacred. Five priests were slain, their churches burnt, and their religious symbols desecrated. But this rebellion was quelled, aided as the Spaniards were by the general destitution in the country. Many Indians perished in the mountains, and many others permanently deserted their pueblos and united with the Apache tribes. De Vargas lost his office soon after, and was succeeded by Pedro Rodriguez Cubero in 1697, as Governor. De Vargas was put in prison on accusation of large robberies of public property, but he was acquitted from these charges in Mexico, and returned in 1703, re-established in office.

Meanwhile the colony had regained prosperity while the pueblo peoples had been reduced during their state of independence. There were scarcely ten thousand left.

CHAPTER X.

A CENTURY UNDER SPAIN—1700 TO 1800.

BUT a century of unprogressive life followed, such as is frequently discovered in the history of Spanish colonies. There was a monotonous succession of Governors. There were political jealousies and legal quarrels. The missions languished. They had failed to touch the individual life of the natives and raise them to civilization. A religion of forms scarcely stirred their sentiment. It did not excite ambition, intellectual powers, or energy in the races it should have brought in two centuries to a high condition of life. Idolatrous worship was not abandoned, but concealed. There were four centers of trade in 1780 with Chihuahua and Mexico. These were the towns of Santa Fé, Albuquerque, La Cañada and El Paso. Each had a population of about two thousand. The Apaches, Comanches and Navajoes were incessantly at war throughout the territory, and the Spanish colonists were often involved in conflicts with them.

We do not dwell upon the official periods of thirty Governors under the power of Spain and the short-lived empire of Iturbide till the beginning of the Mexican Confederation in 1821. There was but a succession of ordinary events in a frontier province during a century of slow development.

The northern provinces of Mexico in the seventeenth century are stated by Humboldt to have been very thinly inhabited. The natives withdrew as the conquering Spaniards advanced toward the north. The people of New Mexico were in continual warfare with the Indians in the eighteenth century, and were in a similar condition to the inhabitants of Europe in the middle ages. They did not lack energy of character. They dwelt in towns rather than in the country, on account of greater security, and by the superiority of their enterprize and warlike traits as well as by the power of the religious teaching of the devoted Franciscan priests and monks, maintained a supremacy.

Humboldt gives the population of New Mexico in 1803, at the beginning of the nineteenth century, as 40,200. The province of New Mexico contained at that time 5,709 square leagues, making an average of only seven inhabitants to a square league.

There were three villas or towns in this province — Santa Fé, Santa Cruz de la Cañada or Taos, and Albuquerque.

There were three parishes, nineteen missions of the Franciscans and twenty-six pueblos or Indian villages, with a population of 29,153.

Santa Fé had a population of 3600 at the time Humboldt wrote, in 1808, based on the enumeration made in 1793 of the entire extent of Mexico by the Spanish Government.

Albuquerque or Alemada was estimated at 6000, and Santa Cruz de la Cañada or Taos, was estimated at 8900, of which a large portion were Pueblo Indians, dwelling in the vicinity of these towns.

Paso del Norte was one of the most important and attractive settlements in this province. All travelers stopped at this point to lay in provisions on their journey to Santa Fé, the seat of government and chief destination of all incomers to the province. The route along the broad valley of the Rio Grande to the capital was an easy one, even for carriages, and the scenery was described as remarkable for its mountainous features and groves of cotton-wood, mesquite and fresh poplars along the fertile banks of this river, which assumed great size and volume when filled with the melting snows of the Rocky mountains.

With the experience of a world-wide traveler Humboldt thus describes El Paso at the beginning of the nineteenth century: "The environs of El Paso are delicious, and resemble the finest parts of Andalusia. The fields are cultivated with maize and wheat, and the vineyards produce such excellent sweet wines that they are even preferred to the wines of Parras in New Biscay.* The gardens contain in abundance all the fruits of Europe — figs, peaches, apples and pears. As the country is very dry, a canal of irrigation brings the water of the Rio del Norte to the Paso. It is with difficulty that the inhabitants of the presidio can keep up the dam, which forces the waters of the rivers when they are very low, to enter the canal."

* Grapes were introduced into New Mexico by the Franciscan friars as early as 1630. The first vineyard was planted in Senecu, eighteen miles below Socorro, founded and inhabited by the Piros Indians in 1626, who abandoned it in 1675.

PERIOD VI.

NEW MEXICO UNDER THE MEXICAN CONFEDERATION.

1821 TO 1846.

CHAPTER XI.

ANCIENT DWELLINGS OF NEW MEXICO.

THE ancient homes of the people of New Mexico are called by a name common to the buildings and the people who inhabited them. Pueblo is the Spanish word for village, and was properly applied to ruins and to the existing dwellings of the sedentary tribes of the south-western country. Their ruins are especially noticeable in the valleys of the Rio Grande, Chaco, San Juan, and other northern rivers. They are equally remarkable on the Los Animas and Gila rivers and in many parts of southern New Mexico and Arizona. The larger dwellings were erected on the lofty table-lands above the cañons and valleys, where the smaller villages, composed of detached houses, are found. These castle-like pueblos were probably of later construction, the type growing out of the necessities of defense. They were large communal houses of great extent and height. They are classified by Prof. A. de F. Bandelier, who has given them a very extensive personal exploration. He describes them as they are found in—" (*a*) groups of two or three constituting a village, (*b*) or in one polygonal pueblo of many stories, (*c*) or of large scattered houses disposed in an irregular manner—sometimes eighteen of these edifices making one village, (*d*) artificial caves, like the many-storied pueblo building, (*e*) or many storied dwellings with artificial walls erected in great natural caves."

There were many cells or small rooms in all these edifices. Their masonry varied greatly in material of lime or sand-stone, or lava rock, or adobe, and in the care in which the walls were built; and there was the greatest variety of material in houses erected in close proximity. Estufas were common to all these communities or villages, and watch-towers for guarding crops or military defense were frequent, and also large and small mounds within the court-yards or just outside the walls.

These ancient houses were sometimes built of cobble-stones, but usually of rectangular sand-stones, about two feet long, six or eight inches wide and three inches thick, laid in native cement, or in mud. The faces of the walls were often smooth and the stones carefully matched; but if built of tufa rock or cobble-stones, they were more roughly constructed. The walls of buildings from two to five or six stories high, were three to five feet thick. The great spaces enclosed were, in the lower stories, divided into small rooms, usually opening upon the courts and seldom communicating with each other. There were no underground chambers in these buildings, and but slight depth to their foundations. The rooms were low, and had no doors nor windows; the small doorways and holes admitted light and air. The walls were plastered with gypsum, and painted with red and yellow ochre. The successive stories of the buildings were approached by ladders. As they receded from within, outward, they made an unbroken wall on the outside for fortification, and portals on the inside, where the people were usually engaged in their various occupations. These great buildings, from their lofty sites, commanded magnificent views of the surrounding cañons and mountains, and the parks which stretched below them. They were reached by steps worn into the face of the perpendicular sides of the mesas, ascending on the side of the wall along the crevices in the rocks. On the grassy surfaces of the mesas, around them, embracing often hundreds of acres, reservoirs of stone are still visible, where they collected water from the melting snows or copious rains of summer. Innumerable fragments of pottery are scattered over the sides of the cliff, the relics of the utensils of the people washed by the floods over these steep ledges. And the industrial products of stone are in all these ruins, throughout New Mexico, found to be of the same materials, though they must have been brought from very distant localities. These are lava metates, crushers, mauls and hammers· basalt or diorite axes, hatchets and smoothing-stones; obsidian knives; flint, quart-site, agate and jasper arrow-heads; knives and crushers, and similar implements for their simple arts.

The capacity of these communal houses for habitation was sufficient, in some instances, for fifteen hundred people, but generally about one-third of this number could have found accommodation in them. Hungo Pavie, one of the smallest of the ancient pueblos of this class, whose ruins are seen in the Chaco cañon, was three hundred feet long, one hundred and forty-four feet wide, and three stories high, with walls built in terraced form of sandstone laid with adobe mortar. It had one hundred and forty-six apartments, and they would have sheltered, in their simple life, at least five hundred people. Pueblo Chapillo, about thirty miles from Santa Fé, above one of the cañons of the Upper Rio Grande, measures about three hundred and twenty feet long by three hundred feet wide. Its walls standing two or three feet high, show the division and size of the rooms, which were about ten feet by eight—but its height cannot be known. In the same vicinity are two pueblos much larger on the ground plan, Questa Cita Blanca and Pajarito, situated within a few miles from each other, so that, from each, friendly aid could be rendered in cases of attack. These were probably sufficiently large for a thousand persons, if they were of the usual height.

In 1874 an interesting pueblo and burial mound was discovered in the valley of the Rio Chama, near Abiquiu, on a mesa one hundred feet above the river.

The town was built in the form of a double L, with a continuous double wall of lava probably two stories high and divided up into rooms ten feet square. The estufa was formed by digging into the ground a circular pit from ten to twenty feet in depth. This was crowned by a wall two or three feet high built around the rim of the excavation, upon which are laid beams which are covered with brush and mud for a roof. The burial place was within thirty feet of the pueblo. The skeletons were found six or eight feet below the surface of the ground, buried face downward, the head pointing to the south. Two feet above one of these were two smooth, black "ollas," or vases, containing charcoal, parched corn, and the bones of small animals and fowls, the possible remains of a funeral feast. There were no signs of clothing, ornaments or weapons. This skeleton was entirely preserved and sent to the Army Medical Museum in Washington.

There is not a finer structure of this class of ancient buildings in New Mexico than the pueblo Pintado in the Chaco cañon, where, in the rainy season, is a stream tributary to the San Juan river. The southern and western walls are standing, indicating at least four stories. On the lower story one hundred and three rooms are plainly visible. Three towers are built on the other walls so as to defend the ground between the pueblo and the stream. The materials were wholly of stone and wood, with no part of metal. Then plates of sandstone with edges dressed by the hammer, were laid in coarse mortar filling every chink, with regular layers at intervals of fifteen or eighteen inches, of thicker stones, to strengthen the masonry, which was smooth and in perfect plumb. At each story the thickness of the wall decreased by the width of a slight beam for the girders of the floor, the larger beams of which were set into the wall. The rooms were lightened only by occasional port-holes in the upper stories, and by doors leading from the rooms.

Lieutenant Simpson, of the U. S. Army, in 1850 thus describes this remarkable edifice:

"We found the ruins of Pueblo Pintado to more than answer our expectations. Forming one structure and built of tabular pieces of hard, fine-grained, compact, gray sandstone (a material entirely unknown in the present architecture of New Mexico), to which the atmosphere has imparted a reddish tinge, the layers or beds being not thicker than three inches, and sometimes as thin as one-fourth of an inch, it discovers in the masonry a combination of science and art which can only be referred to a higher stage of civilization and refinement than is discoverable in the works of Mexicans or Pueblos of the present day. Indeed, so beautifully diminutive and true are the details of the structure as to cause it, at a little distance, to have all the appearance of a magnificent piece of Mosaic work.

"In the outer face of the buildings there are no signs of mortar, the intervals between the beds being chinked with stones of the minutest thinness. The filling and backing are done in rubble masonry, the mortar presenting no indications of the presence of lime. The thickness of the main wall at its base

is within an inch or two of three feet; higher up it is less, diminishing every story by retreating jogs on the inside, from the bottom to the top. Its elevation at its present highest point, is between twenty-five and thirty feet, the series of floor beams indicating that there must have been originally at least three stories. The ground plan, including the court, is about 403 feet. On the ground floor, exclusive of the outbuildings, are fifty-four apartments, some of them as small as five feet square, and the largest about twelve by six feet. These rooms communicate with each other by very small doors, some of them as contracted as two and a half by two and a half feet; and in the case of the inner suite, the doors communicating with the interior court are as small as three and a half by two feet. The principal rooms, or those most in use, were, on account of their having larger doors and windows, most probably those of the second story. The system of flooring seems to have been large unhewn beams, six inches in diameter, laid transversely from wall to wall, and then a number of smaller ones, about three inches in diameter, laid across them. What was placed on these does not appear, but most probably it was brush, bark or slabs, covered with a layer of mud mortar. The beams show no signs of the saw or ax; on the contrary, they appear to have been hacked off by means of some very imperfect instrument. On the west face of the structure, the windows, which are only in the second story, are three feet two inches, by two feet two inches. On the north side they are only in the second and third stories, and are as small as fourteen by fourteen inches. At different points about the premises were three circular apartments sunk in the ground, the walls being of masonry. These apartments the Pueblo Indians call estufas, or places where the people held their political and religious meetings.

"The site of the ruins is a knoll some twenty or thirty feet above the surrounding plain; the Rio Chaco coursing by it, 200 or 300 yards distant, and no wood visible within the circuit of a mile.

"The quarry from which the material was obtained to build the structure seems to have been just back of our camp.

"We came to another old ruin thirteen miles from our last camp, called Weje-gi, built like pueblo Pintado, of very thin, tabular pieces of compact sandstone. The circuit of the structure, including the court, was near 700 feet. The number of apartments on the ground floor was probably ninety-nine. The highest present elevation of the exterior wall is about twenty-four feet."

Lieutenant Simpson says of the pueblo Bonito:

"The circuit of its walls is about 1300 feet. Its present elevation shows that it had at least four stories of apartments. The number of rooms on the ground floor at present discernible is 139. The apartments in the east portion of the pueblo, not included in this enumeration, would probably swell the number to 200." He estimates that the four stories of rooms, with retreating terraces, had as many as 641 rooms. "The number of estufas is four; the largest being sixty feet in diameter, showing two stories in height and having a present depth of twelve feet. All these estufas are cylindrical in shape, and nicely walled up with thin, tabular stone. Among the ruins are several rooms in a very good state of preservation."

The following description, by the U. S. Assistant-Surgeon, J. F. Hammond, on the same expedition with Lieutenant Simpson, of a room in the ruins of the pueblo Bonito, in the Chaco cañon, remarkably indicates the advance in masonry and architecture of the unknown builders:

"It was in the second of three ranges of rooms, on the north side of the ruins. The door opened at the base of the wall, toward the interior of the building; it had never been more than two feet and a half high, and was filled two-thirds with rubbish. The lintels were of natural sticks of wood, one and a half to two inches in diameter, deprived of the bark, and placed at distances of two or three inches apart; yet their ends were attached to each other by withes of oak, with its bark well preserved. The room was in the form of a parallelogram, about twelve feet in length, eight feet wide, and the walls as they stood at the time of observation, seven feet high. The floor was of earth and the surface irregular. The walls were about two feet thick, and plastered within with a layer of red mud one-fourth of an inch thick. The latter having fallen off in places, showed the material of the wall to be sandstone. The stone was ground into pieces the size of our ordinary bricks, the angles not as perfectly formed, though nearly so, and put up in break-joints, having intervals between them, on every side, of about two inches. The intervals were filled with laminæ of a dense sandstone, about three lines in thickness, driven firmly in, and broken off even with the general plane of the wall, the whole resembling mosaic work. Niches, varying in size from two inches to two and a half feet square, and two inches to one and a half feet in horizontal depth, were scattered irregularly over the walls, at various heights above the floor. Near the place of the ceiling, the walls were penetrated, and the surfaces of them were perpendicular to the length of the beam. They had the appearance of having been sawed off originally, except that there were no marks of the saw left on them; time had slightly disintegrated the surfaces, rounding the edges somewhat here and there. Supporting the floor above were six cylindrical beams, about seven inches in diameter, passing transversely of the room, and at distances of less than two feet apart, the branches of the trees having been hewn off by means of a blunt-edged instrument. Above and resting on these, running longitudinally with the room, were poles of various lengths, about two inches in diameter, irregularly straight, placed in contact with each other, covering all the top of the room, bound together at irregular and various distances, generally at their ends, by slips apparently of palm leaf or marquey, and the same material converted into cords about one-fourth of an inch in diameter, formed of two strands hung from the poles at several points. Above and resting upon the poles, closing all above, passing transversely of the room, were planks about seven inches wide and three-fourths of an inch in thickness. The width of the plank was uniform, and so was the thickness. They were in contact, or nearly so, admitting but little more than the passage of a knife blade between them, by the edges, through the whole of their lengths. They were not jointed; all their surfaces were level and as smooth as if planed, excepting the ends; the angles as regular and perfect as could be retained by such vegetable matter; they are probably of pine or cedar, exposed to the atmosphere for as long a time as it is probable these have been. The ends of the plank, several of which were in view, terminated in line perpendicular to the length of the plank, and the plank seems to have been severed by a blunt instrument. The planks — I examined them minutely by the eye and touch, for the marks of the saw and other instruments — were smooth and colored brown by time or by smoke. Beyond the plank nothing was distinguishable from within. The room was redolent with the perfume of cedar. Externally upon the top, was a heap of stone and mud, ruins that have fallen from above, unmovable by the instruments we had along.

"The beams were probably severed by contusions from a dull instrument, and their surfaces ground plain and smooth by a slab of rock; and the plank split or hewn from the trees, were no doubt rendered smooth by the same means."

The pottery of the New Mexico pueblo ruins has been carefully examined and described by Prof. F. W. Putnam, of Harvard College. In the volume on the United States Explorations under Lieutenant Wheeler, already mentioned and quoted from, he makes these general remarks upon it:

"A comparison of this ancient pottery with that made by the present inhabitants of the pueblos shows that a great deterioration has taken place in native American art, a rule which I think can be applied to all the more advanced tribes of America. The remarkable hardness of all the fragments of colored pottery which have been obtained from the vicinity of the old ruins in New Mexico, Colorado, Arizona and Utah, and also of the pottery of the same character found in the ruins of the adobe houses and in caves in Utah, shows that the ancient people understood the art of baking earthen ware far better than their probable descendants now living in the pueblos of New Mexico and Arizona. The gray clay seems to contain a large amount of silicious material, which, on being subjected to a great heat, becomes slightly vitrified. The vessels made of the gray colored clay have apparently received a thin wash of the same, upon which the black ornamentation was put, before baking. The intense heat to which the vessels were afterward subjected has vitrified this thin layer of clay, which now appears like a thin glaze. The polish is probably due to smoothing the surface with a stone before the thin wash was applied, as is now done by several tribes in the United States and Mexico. The black substance, uniting with the clay-wash, was burnt in and became a fast color. The red color was produced by the addition of a large proportion of red ochre, or oxide of iron, with the gray clay, and thus, according to the greater or less amount of iron used, the clay is more or less red throughout. To some vessels a thin wash of clay, containing a large proportion of the ochre, was applied before baking, which resulted in a deep red color, and in these the black ornamental lines were burnt in with the ochre-clay wash. The same method is probably followed by the present pueblo tribes, but as their pottery is not so well baked the colors are not as permanent, and the vessels made are generally far inferior in construction, as they are thicker and more porous than the ancient specimens.

"Among the many fragments of ancient pottery that I have examined, from the region named above, I have not seen a piece in which more than a single color was employed in its ornamentation. With very few exceptions, in which the ornamental lines are of a brownish color with a metallic lustre, the pattern consists of black lines and figures on either the red or the gray ground-color. In the modern vessels, from the pueblos on the Rio Grande, the prevailing colors are white and black over a red clay. In some, however, the black figures are painted directly upon the red or primary color of the vessel.

"It is a little remarkable that, both among the ancient and present Pueblo tribes, the ornamentation on the vessels of clay should be so confined to figures expressed in color. I do not remember having seen a specimen of this class of smooth red or gray pottery, on which incised work appears, and I may further remark, that, so far as my examination has extended, I have seen, on pottery of this character, only expressions of geometrical figures. On the recent pueblo pottery, there is, now and then, an attempt to represent natural forms, such as leaves, birds and deer; but this realistic ornamentation is poorly executed, so far as I can judge from the limited material at my command. It is also worthy of remark, that while the present pueblo tribes, particularly the Zuñi, often model vessels and other objects in clay, to represent men, birds and other natural forms, so far as my knowledge extends, only a single fragment of such a form has been found under circumstances indicating antiquity."

"Among the ruins of the Gallinas the pottery was usually of a bluish ash color, but is occasionally black, brown and, more rarely, red. It is never glazed, but the more common kind is nicely smoothed so as to reflect a little light. This pottery is ornamented with figures in black paint, which are in lines at right angles, or enclosing triangular or square spaces; sometimes colored and uncolored angular areas form a checker-board pattern. The coarser kinds exhibit sculpture of the clay instead of painting. The surface is thrown into lines of alternating projections and pits by the use of an obtuse stick, or the finger nail; or it is thrown into intricate layers by cutting obliquely with a sharp flint knife. Thus the patterns of the ornamentations were varied to suit the tastes of the manufacturers, although the facilities at their disposal were few."

The indubitable evidences of the stone age in the

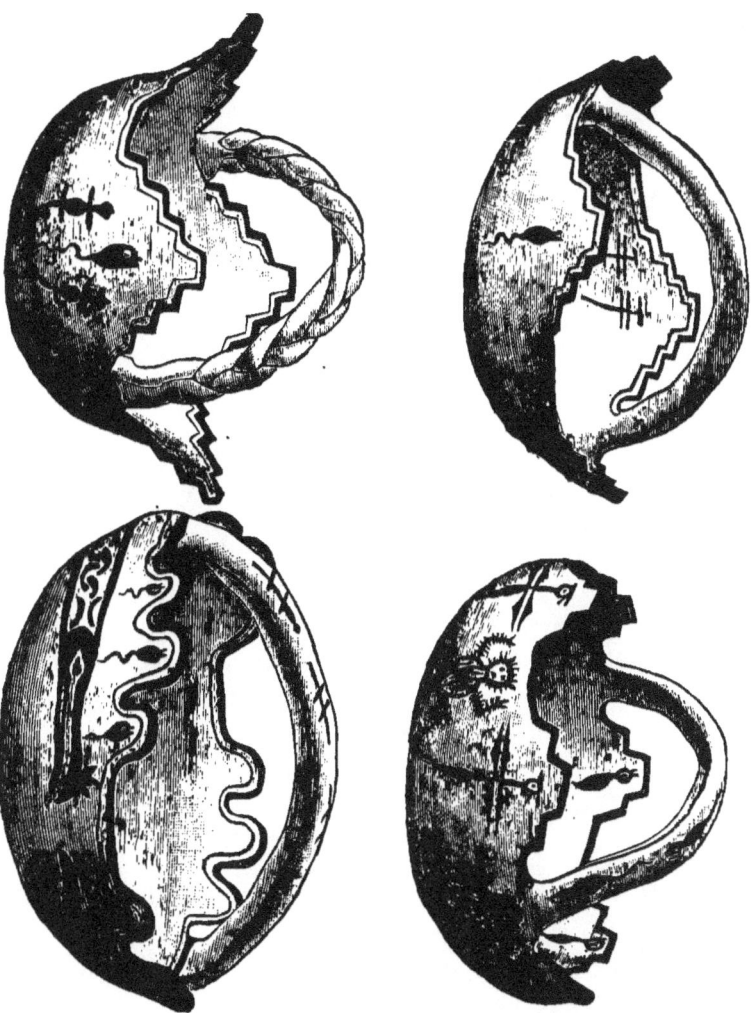

ZUÑI CLAY BASKETS.

original inhabitants of the ruined pueblos and cave dwellings already described, are confirmed by the great numbers of weapons and utensils that are found in and around these dwellings. They consist of knives and spear heads of jasper, flint, quartz, obsidian and chalcedony. Some of these are of the most beautiful minerals. The stone hatchets are made of the highly-polished stones of the same varieties, with perfect grooves for the withes with which they were bound to their handles, and of the most varied colors. There are hammers of jasper, actinolite and lava, polishing stones for the manufacture of pottery, mortars of sandstone, metatas of every variety of coarse or smooth surfaces for the preparation of flour, meal and paints; well-worn mano stones with which the grinding was done in these stone hand-mills, weighing from one to forty or fifty pounds. Many ornaments of stone, necklaces, pipes, arrow-head molders, and implements for sewing and weaving, and architecture of stone, beside the innumerable shapes and sizes of vessels of pottery, indicate the inventive and mechanical skill, the taste for the arts of peace as well as of war which characterized these people of such a remarkable culture and origin.

Prof. A. de F. Bandelier says of the cave dwellings on the Gila and Sapello rivers: "These cave dwellings are properly but one story high, but the compulsory adaptation to the configuration of the ground has caused an accidental approach to two stories. They are instructive for the study of the development of the terraced house of the Pueblo Indian,

Perfectly sheltered, and therefore quite well preserved, the cave villages are, perhaps, larger than the open-air ruins—compactness compensating for the limitation in space. But they illustrate the fact that the foundations remaining of villages built in the open air are frequently only those of courts or enclosures—the mounds alone indicating the site of buildings. . . . The fireplace was a rectangular hearth, as I found it at Pecos, and placed in the center of the room. The pottery and stone implements are identical with those of the neighboring open-air ruins. But the dryness of the air inside the caves has preserved the more perishable remains. These show that the yucca plant, common over the whole country, has played a commanding part in the textile industry of the people—that it has supplied the dress of the inhabitants in summer, as did furs in winter. Nowhere, from the highest Gila to Mangas Springs, west of Silver City—a stretch of sixty miles—have I found or heard of cotton fabrics, as on the Upper Salado. But kilts plaited of yucca leaves, analogous to the bark kilts worn to-day by the Yuma Indians of the Gulf of California, and strings of 'pita' (yucca fibre) wound around with strips of rabbit fur, such as are used by the Moquis to manufacture heavy mantles for winter use, have been found. Mats of yucca, decorated with painted figures, were met with at Mangas. All these plaitings, as well as the sandals and baskets, are identical with those discovered in Southern Colorado, in the Cañon de Chezi (Chelly), at the Tule, on the Salado, and along the whole course of the Gila. While the art of tanning, probably with Rumea Venosus, was evidently well known, it is strange that the buck-skin dress and moccasin of to-day are wanting among the aboriginal remains of the caves and cliffs.

"I have heard of a rude stone idol found in a cave on the Upper Gila. Wooden idols were exhumed at Mangas Springs; also, a fetich of obsidian, and prayer plumes similar to those of the present Pueblo Indians, all deeply embedded in bat manure. Turquoise beads are abundant on the Sapello."

To add interest to this story of these old dwellings and their strange people, the author invites the kind reader to follow him in some of his personal adventures among these ruins in the cañons of the Rio Grande, in 1881.

The pueblo of the mesa Chapillo was built above a wild volcanic fissure, whose sides are still blackened and scoriated from the heat of internal fires now extinct, which once broke these mountains into the dark billowy fragments that fill the basin. The mesa stands between two great cañons made by cliffs of glittering gray tufa-rock and sandstone of bright red and yellow hues pierced by dark-mouthed caves two or three hundred feet from their base.

As we approach the steeper part of the cliff, we follow in imagination these old cliff dwellers, as centuries ago they climbed to their lofty habitations. A winding zigzag path is before us along a trail worn into the solid rock. Step by step, it leads up the perpendicular face of the cliff; we gather with lively interest the sherds of pottery so variously colored and decorated, and chips of agate and flint. We fancy that we behold the cliff-dwellers' wives and maidens, clothed in deerskin and cotton garments, bearing on their heads the *ollas* filled with cool water from the springs and little stream in the cañon we have left far below, to the pueblo above us. It would be strange if their water jars were not often dashed in pieces on these dizzy heights. We put our feet into the well-worn tracks to mount the last seventy feet of that vertical face of the cliff, which we ascend along a slightly jutting ledge. As we reach up with our hands, our fingers clutch the places made for them long ago in this long-enduring tufa rock. The right hand finds a firm hold above us, then the fingers of the left sink into another hole just fitted to the stature of a man in the act of climbing, when his feet touch the foot-tracks below. Pulling ourselves up, our knees find a smooth resting place sunk in the rock. Our hands secure another firm hold, and so we slowly rise, seeming to ourselves to have leaped across the centuries, and to touch the feet of the ancient people who are leading us to their home near the clouds. This fancy makes us forgetful of all danger, and with an intense historic glow, we climb toward the summit, upon which at last we cast ourselves, panting and exhausted, while we look wonderingly around to see how the old cliff-dwellers will greet us. But we find no Rip Van Winkles here. Our Pueblo Indian guide is pointing us to the silent and deserted homes of his far-off ancestors. The sun is casting its last rays upon them. We look around, bewildered for a moment with the magnificent grouping of cliffs and mesas, cañons, dark pine-covered valleys, and snowy mountains beyond, and above them all against the deep-blue sky, and then we hasten forward toward the greyish white stones, lying in confused heaps and fragments of walls, on the level, grassy surface of the table-land. This is the pueblo Chapillo. We hurriedly examined its ruins ere the twilight deepened. Its walls, two or three feet thick, were strong enough to support three or four stories. Circular depressions indicated the estufas. Stone implements—grinders, hammers, chisels and axes—were scattered among the wall rocks on their surface. What might not be revealed by digging into the deposits of sand which the centuries have piled over them? This was evidently the home of several hundred people. We linger here in the shadows of the twilight, which warns us to leave this mysterious spot, and we regretfully begin to clamber down the cliff into the gloom of the cañon, where we walk by the light of the stars back to the camp two miles away, our arms burdened with treasures of the past and our thoughts busy with the strange histories of this land.

Near this castle-like dwelling are the cave houses, to which our guide led us the next morning. They are about fifty feet from the top, on the south-western face of the plateau. Descending by the same rocky trail, we reach an irregular terrace or shelf from three to ten feet wide, along the face of the cliff, on which at intervals of thirty or forty feet are these cave dwellings cut into the white, porous tufa stone which forms one of the upper strata of the table land. They are of various shapes, rudely constructed from natural caves. But some are in the form of half a sphere, with a door-way three feet high and two feet wide, having both lintel and threshold of stone. The rooms are generally rectangular and sometimes carefully hewn. Some of them are double, each twelve feet by fifteen, and over six feet high. The ceilings are smooth and often blackened with smoke, which escaped through one or two holes in the ceiling, slanting toward the face of the cliff. Sometimes one room is excavated above another, entered by holes only large enough for one to crawl through. The inner rooms were used for storing food or for comfortable sleeping places. Little cuddies are hewn into the sides of the caves. Some of the walls are neatly frescoed with yellow paint, upon which are figures in red ochre. The floors are level and hard, but usually covered with mold in which we may find blackened corn-cobs, and the heads of grain stalks, which are, however, as likely to have been carried thither by the crows and bats and other birds, as by human beings.

The pictographs cut into the ceilings and sides of these caves are representations of feathered and double-headed snakes, circles, men and women, eagles, chiefs with feathers on their heads, birds, bows, plummets, trees, lightning, rain, clouds and various animals.

As we sit in these caves, we ask ourselves of the people who once lived in such rude habitations.

We look out upon the same hills and majestic mountains and picturesque valleys, in sight of which their dreamy lives were spent. Sitting in these doorways, they could espy their friends or foes approaching; they could take refuge on the top of the cliff or repel them from these narrow ledges on its side. As we searched for their tools and weapons, we found no traces of metal, but such implements would long ago have disappeared — picked up by roving savage tribes. The silence and emptiness of these once populous dwellings, of the caves and the pueblo, seemed like the desolations described by the Jewish prophet, of Edom — as rude a people as were these: "O thou that dwellest in the clefts of the rock, that holdest the height of the hill: though thou shouldest make thy nest as high as the eagle, I will bring thee down from thence, saith the Lord, and Edom shall be a desolation: every one that goeth by it shall be astonished, and shall hiss at all the plagues thereof. . . . No man shall abide there, neither shall a son of man dwell in it."

CHAPTER XII.

THE PUEBLO INDIANS.

AT the time of the Spanish invasion, and during the succeeding century of exploration and occupation by Europeans, there were about 150,000 native inhabitants within the present limits of New Mexico and Arizona. Three-quarters of this population belonged to the roving tribes of the Athabaskan family; about 40,000, including the Pimas, were of the sedentary tribes called Pueblos by the Spaniards. These were of different language and descent, and belonged to the three great people-stocks — the Keresan, Zuñian and Tanonan — while far to the west were the Moquis of the Shoshonian stock. They occupied twenty-six provinces; eleven of these were in Southern New Mexico, and are easy to identify amid the numerous and extensive ruins of their towns, found chiefly in the river valleys of that region.

These southern provinces were named by the early conquerors and friars, or by the historians of their expeditions, from the characteristics of the people, or from their own designation in their native speech; but these names covered a very indefinite extent of country. They are frequently mentioned as the provinces of Marata, Acu (Acoma), Totonteac (of the Moquis), Acha, Tabaras, Sumas, Jumanas, Conchos and Passaguates (savages of Chihuahua), the Jerez of Sonora, Piros, and the Mansos, who are reduced to sixteen persons at the present time. Isleta is the only inhabited pueblo in New Mexico, among all these ancient provinces. The Piros are still extant in Sen-e-cu, six miles from El Paso del Norte. Of the Sumas, there is but one descendant still living at San Lorenzo.

The province of Hubates or Taños, held the region of the Placitas and Sandia mountains, and the province of Tiguas, part of the Rio Grande valley below Albuquerque. They embraced the towns which were visited by the Spanish soldiers under Coronado and by Espejo, and their ruins still bear the names of Ziguma, San Lazaro, Guika, San Marcos, Gallisteo, Los Tanques. The ruins of Ziguma, in the cañon of the Rio de Santa Fé, near Cieneguilla, belong to this group.

Queres was a province between the Rio Jemez and Rio Grande, where five pueblos still exist, and the ruins of extinct towns are frequent. Cicuyé was the important province on the Pecos. In the first century of the Spanish occupation, its people, diminished by disease and other causes, moved to the region of the Jemez mountains, where they were mingled with people of the same stock, whose language was similar to their own.

The provinces of Taos and Piccuries, in the vicinity of the upper Rio Grande, are still marked by important, pueblos, whose populations have maintained their numbers and been prominent in the various struggles of the Pueblos for independence of their Spanish rulers. The pueblo of Taos was frequently occupied by the Spanish soldiers.

The tribal connections of the natives of New Mexico are definitely traced by the kinship of their languages. Of the seven linguistic stocks represented in the Pacific States and Territories, four are found in New Mexico. The great Tinné family is represented in the Athabaskan tribes, called now the Navajoes and the Apaches; the Shoshones in New Mexico are now the Utes and Moquis.

The Rio Grande Pueblo languages are distinct from the speech of these more barbarous tribes, yet are divided into three linguistic classes: I. Zuñi. II. Kera. III. Tanonan. The Zuñi embraces a single group of villages. The Kera dialects are scattered from the Upper Rio Grande to the San Juan river and embrace the Queres pueblos of Santa Ana, Silla, Tsea (or Cia), San Felipe, Cochite. Santa Domingo and the South-western pueblos of Laguna and Acoma.

The Tanonan dialects included four subdivisions:

1. Tehua, embracing San Ildefonzo, San Juan,

Santa Clara, Pojoaque, Nambe, Tesuque and the Tehuan town on one of the Moqui mesas.

2. The Tiguas, including Sandia, Isleta, Taos and Piccuries.

3. Jemez, with the Pecos pueblo on the Jemez river.

4. Piros, in Chihuahua, near El Paso.

Ninety-seven inhabited pueblos have been carefully enumerated by A. de F. Bandelier as existing at the beginning of the seventeenth century (A. D. 1600) in New Mexico and Arizona. Of these, fifty were situated in the valley of the Rio Grande and its branches. From the plans of several hundred ruins which he has personally sketched, he estimates an average of not more than 400 souls to each village, so that not more than 30,000 or 40,000 constituted the entire Pueblo population in the provinces, when colonization by the Spaniards was begun under Oñate. There were about 30,000 just before the rebellion of 1680.

At the beginning of that century (1600) the government of the Pueblos recognized for each of these scattered tribes a supreme authority in the Council. Its decrees were communicated to the village by a public crier. An executive officer superintended the execution of the decisions of the Council, and there were captains who directed each the labor, the hunting, the fishing and the wars of the pueblo. Each pueblo was absolutely independent.

The Spanish dominion established for the Pueblos the communal system by granting, through an order of the King in 1682, community lands to each settled tribe. These were inalienable except through consent of the whole tribe. The King required them to elect without any interference from Spanish authorities whatever, every year, their governor, treasurer and alcaldes or justices of the peace, and report them to the Governor of New Mexico for his confirmation. The protectors or agents appointed by the royal decree to attend to the concerns of each tribe, had no jurisdiction over them. Yet the communistic ideas of the tribe were diverted from full sway over the Pueblos by these incentives of personal ambition, through rotation of office. And at the same time they became mindful of ownership of the land, and of the authority of an invisible power, to which they were subject with others, which also protected and cared for their improvement. They were made wards of the Spanish government, and under its supremacy their original form of government was maintained, while it was the purpose of the Spanish legislation that the Indian should be gradually led from his savage tendencies, superstitions and childish follies up to civilization and a higher manhood.

The new laws and ordinances for the government of the Indies made by the Spanish kingdom in 1543, were in force over this part of the American continent in the next century; for Spain, in the hundred years from Columbus, surpassed every European nation in extending her dominion over the new world from the latitude of northern New Mexico even to the extremity of South America. These laws were well devised. Distance and the lapse of time from the issue of the King's decree at Madrid to the reception of it by his officials, greatly impeded their administration. The laws were unfaithfully executed often, but retribution surely though tardily followed. The official was obliged to make his report in detail; the inspector was sure to visit him unawares; the priest and the missionary were required to inform the Council in Spain of the abuses of the native subject as well as of the colonists.' For punishment, long journeys were taken, and the prison waited for the oppressor, or defaulter, or disloyal officer, like Diego de Peñalosa and Louis de Rosas, military Governors of New Mexico, many months after the offense was committed. Thus decrees were delayed in execution, like that one granting four square leagues of land to each Indian pueblo. It was made in 1682—but the lands were not staked out till 1704, and for some of the principal pueblos till 1726, and as late as 1865.

Among the abuses of administration in New Mexico were the enforcement of tributes, personal service to the Governors and other officials, and the compulsory labor for the benefit of the colonists. The small salaries of the Governors, amounting to only two thousand ducats, were thus supplemented by tributes of cotton and maize from the Pueblo Indians.

In 1709 the Marquis de Peñuela, Governor of New Mexico, compelled the Indians to serve him personally, for which he was reprimanded and threatened with a heavy fine of 2000 pesos (dollars) by the

Viceroy of Mexico if he continued to disobey the royal edicts. But slavery was a punishment for crime in that age. Revolt against the authority of Spain, therefore, brought these Pueblos often to this condition of slavery as prisoners of war, if their lives were spared. But these revolts were partly the results of grievances committed against them contrary to Spanish law. It is evident from the records that as early as 1725 compulsory labor was allowed in the service of the missions as a means of education and civilization. But as the Indian was averse to labor, it became a hardship, often working prejudice against the influence of the missions.

There was much less compulsory labor in mines in New Mexico than has been generally believed, because there is no good evidence that mining was generally practised there by the Spanish colonists. The report of Pedro de Rivera, the military inspector of this presidio to the crown, in 1725, concerning New Mexico mines, states positively that up to that date they were not worked to any extent because of the low grade of ore.

The severities of war prevalent in those centuries among European nations were doubtless inflicted on these natives when rebellious. So that summary executions of prisoners and floggings and imprisonments occurred among these peoples, corresponding to their own savage customs. The ecclesiastics of the missions often interfered with the military powers on account of them, for they were sincerely attached to their proselytes. The more savage

AN INDIAN IDOL.

tribes, by their incursions upon the natives and the colonists, also hindered the peaceful government by Spanish officials of these subjects of the crown, but there was doubtless some reason for the complaint of the colonists that "the Pueblo Indians were treated better than themselves, for everything was done for them and nothing for the colonists." The prevailing sympathy of the missionaries and other religious authorities for the natives, as well as the records of these missions, contradict the assertions that the rigors of the Inquisition were ever visited on the pueblo peoples, though they were inflicted upon some of the Spanish officials in New Mexico.

The pueblo peoples often hunted by villages, surrounding the game in a district by a cordon of men and women, who gradually closed in upon the affrighted animals. They trafficked according to their locations, in skins, tanned leather, cotton and other vegetable products, mantles, utensils of stone and pottery, weapons, provisions of meat and maize, and ornaments of turquoise.

The Pueblos worshipped the sun and the waters, to which they made the most sacrifices; but they had many idols of stone and clay, for which they had shrines, where they prayed, in the same manner as the Spaniards had crosses along the roads where they offered adoration. The worship of the devil was most constant. In each of the villages there was a house or temple to which they carried food for the demon. Their fetishes were numerous and their worship complex, in which animals played a prominent part. They had no idea of a Supreme God.

There was a constant conflict between the warriors and sorcerers for control in a tribe.

The Franciscans, by right of discovery and the martyrdom of six of their missionary friars, have held these Pueblo tribes for evangelization for three centuries under the title of the "Custody of Saint Paul of the Conversion of New Mexico." These natives seemed to have received the Christian religion only to enlarge by it their own traditions and superstitious fancies. They accepted easily the Christian doctrine of a Divine Providence watching over their physical welfare, for it coincided with their own belief in the Shinana, Those above. They had many rites and ceremonies, and by these and their prayer plumes, were always honoring their numerous deities; yet they gave up none of their gods or devils, and easily relapsed from their newer faiths.

But the Franciscans taught them simple industries. They employed the Pueblo women to build churches. They taught the people the use of tools, and somewhat improved their cultivation of the soil with grains, fruits and vegetables. They also introduced to their country the domestic animals, like the horse, cow, burro, sheep, goats, dog and various fowls. The missionaries did not easily learn the Pueblo languages, and consequently their influence in the teaching of religious truths was limited, and the progress of the missions was slow, when to teach these natives, there was lacking every modern instrumentality of education.

Among the ancient Pueblos there was much less

association of men and women in the family. The adult males lived mostly in the estufas, while the women and their children occupied the houses. The boys also slept, ate and were taught in the estufas, where the women brought the simple meals, to be taken by the men apart from their wives, and these round houses served as places for lounging, as well as for councils and sacrifices.

There were marriage customs among the primitive Pueblo tribes which were of little avail to prevent sexual license. The children were brought up in utter disregard of modesty or chastity. The education of the boys was carried on in the estufas, and consisted of the repetition of prayers, chants and historic narrations, which the youth learned little by little to memorize, and so preserve traditions hidden in fanciful myths. The girls learned to grind corn and prepare food. The crushing and grinding of corn was done on three matates by three women, grinding to a regular measure, and chanting in which the men assisted.*

Pueblo farming has been gracefully described by a journalist: "The Pueblo Indian caught the mountain torrents and held them secure in rude reservoirs until he should require their waters to nourish his crops. He was practically independent of the elements. From a crooked stick he devised a plowshare; a cedar bough served as his harrow. With these crude implements he prepared the soil as best he could, and the round, plump, native species of wheat, oats, barley or rye were scattered broadcast.

* Bandelier.

Then three times during the summer the water was turned on through the ditches that lined his field; and these irrigating canals contributed both moisture and fertilization at one and the same time."*

The principal crop of the Pueblos was corn, which would grow on the lofty mesas with no other watering than the rains. As far north as Santo Domingo near Sante Fé, they raised cotton. Their communal stores were first cultivated and first gathered from the fields; but the individual crops were then harvested for the benefit of a family; for each male could cultivate a plot within the tribal limits and bequeath it to male children; but neither the land nor crop could be disposed of except within the tribe or clan. As the houses were built by and belonged to the women, when the crop was stored in them, it became the possession of the family.

MODERN PUEBLO INDIANS.

The modern Pueblo Indians occupy thirty-four towns and are classed by distinctions of language into eight tribes. So many dialects are in use that, with the exception of four tribes, they are obliged to communicate with one another in the Spanish language.

The Pueblo people are in comparison with other Indians very interesting to observers. They are generally finely formed and of noble appearance. In stature their height is medium, their bodies muscular and their chests large. They are erect and

* Daily New Mexican.

stand lightly on their feet in dignified attitudes, and move swiftly in the race with great ease. They are very hospitable and courteous to strangers, with a gracious speech to their guests. Though generally peaceful and industrious they have been repeatedly proved to be valiant warriors and efficient allies.

The present Pueblo communities are located on lands well supplied with water, pasture and a fertile soil. The Spanish emperor, Charles the Fifth, caused the smaller villages to be abandoned, and bestowed grants of land upon those which were occupied, which gave an irrevocable title to a section of land four miles square around the pueblo. This was confirmed by the United States by the provisions of the treaty of Guadaloupe. The Pueblo Indians have reservations embracing 700,000 square acres in New Mexico and Arizona. These are generally valuable lands, well irrigated and under good cultivation in the vicinity of the villages.

The Spaniards governed the Pueblo tribes easily by reason of their missions or churches in each community. They could use the authority of the priest in religious matters to secure order and obedience to the Spanish government of which he was made an agent. The present mode of government of the Pueblos is the same as that of three centuries ago. It is neither despotic nor republican. There are five chiefs or head men of the tribe. The first is the cacique or spiritual ruler. He performs marriage ceremonies, sanctions betrothals and has power to punish for irreligious acts. He is regarded with much reverence, and in some pueblos the young men decide by lot each year who shall be so fortunate as to take care of the cacique, whose office is during life. The Governor rules the temporal affairs of the community, assigning work to each member of the tribe, determines the hours of labor, and otherwise acts as a civil magistrate, but is elected annually. His cane is used as a judicial summons, or as an instrument of punishment.

The war chief is elected like the Governor. In time of war he defends the town and leads the fighting. In time of peace he controls the pasture lands and hunting grounds. There are some other subordinate officers who act as police.

Most of the decisions for the conduct of a community are made in a council. Anything of interest or importance to the village is announced from the housetop by a public crier. They cultivate their land to a high degree, so that they have an abundance of corn, wheat, oats, barley and fruit, to supply their simple wants. In some villages the people almost abandon their houses in the season of cultivation, and erect temporary booths near their fields, where they guard their grain and fruits from inroad and theft. Their thrashing floors are enclosures from thirty to fifty feet in diameter, made of posts hung with bags and old blankets. Into these a dozen horses are driven and kept in motion by an Indian boy, urging them to trample with their hoofs the grain thickly spread under them. The thrashing is watched in silence by a score of men standing outside, who winnow the husks and grain, and the women carry it in baskets on their heads to the pueblo.

"It is vain to deny that the South-western village Indian is not an idolater at heart, but it is equally preposterous to assume that he is not a sincere Catholic. Only he assigns to each belief a certain field of action and has minutely circumscribed each one. He literally gives to God what, in his judgment, belongs to God, and to the Devil what he thinks the Devil is entitled to, for the Indians' own benefit. Woe unto him who touches his ancient idols, but thrice woe to him who derides his church or desecrates its ornaments."*

Though the converts of Roman Catholic Christian missions and believing in the Mass and in Baptism, most of the Pueblos are still worshippers in secret of the sun and forces of nature combined with the ceremonies to which they have been faithfully trained by the Church Missionaries. At night and in the morning they chant in minor tones hymns to the sun, most of which are sad and mournful in character. They regard with veneration household gods, and preserve ancient mysteries in their native language and in estufa ceremonies which are little known. They use the Pueblo tongue for their deliberations in councils and to communicate their traditions to one another.

With the estufas of ancient and modern Pueblos are associated the secrets of their religion, their councils and their traditional orgies. An American, in 1875, was permitted to visit one of the five

* "Archeological Institutes of America." Bandelier.

belonging to the Pueblos of Taos, and described it thus:

"It was a large, circular chamber under ground, the entrance being through a small trap-door on top, surrounded by a circular stockade containing numerous antlers of deer and having a narrow opening. Descending to the chamber by a ladder, it was found to be probably twenty-five or thirty feet in diameter, arched above, and about twenty feet high; around the wall at a height of two feet from the ground was a hard, earthen bench. On the floor in the center was an oblong pit two feet deep and nearly three feet long. In this it is said the sacred fire is kept burning, and we were shown some live embers beneath the ashes.

"Behind the fire-pit is a sort of altar constructed of clay, the use of which it was impossible to ascertain. From a peculiarly sweet, aromatic odor, which seemed to fill the atmosphere of the room, we inferred that probably in these rites sweet-smelling grasses or wood are used as incense. The war-chief informed us that it should be considered a great favor to have been permitted to view the interior of this estufa, as such a favor was seldom shown to Americans and never to Mexicans."

The custom of marriage is established as an official act; but within the same tribe or clan there is a positive and general disregard of its moral obligations. There is no prevailing rule of chastity which preserves personal virtue between the sexes. The keeping of more than one wife, however, is not allowed by the community, and the separation of man and

PUEBLO BASKET-WORK.

wife is a cause for scandal. As the perpetuation of the clan and tribe is of the first consequence and the children are regarded as belonging to the clan of the mother, the social system of these communities is founded on the necessity of child-breeding, and recognizes no higher law in conflict with this idea, and some of the dances and religious rites are the unrestrained expression of this view of social privilege and duty.

Though their domestic life has been said to be protected by strict laws, as related to those out of the tribe, there is great carelessness in the training of children, and the promiscuous life of these communities, as well as some of their heathenish dances, tend to great licentiousness. The Pueblos are somewhat industrious, and preserve the skill of their ancestors in pottery-making, weaving and basket-work. Each community, village or district has its distinctive quality, shape and decoration in its pottery. The variety in color and grace of form in these manufactures is very remarkable, but their imitations of animal, bird and plant life are crude and grotesque, rather than artistic.

The Pueblo Indians have not claimed the privileges of citizenship in the United States, though always loyal and friendly to the government. They have refrained from voting and sought thus to avoid taxation. But by recent legislation in Congress, and by acts of the territorial legislation, they are as liable to taxes and subject to laws of the United States as other citizens. They have manifested much interest in the education of their children and in sending them to industrial schools, recently established by the government for them at Albuquerque and Santa Fé.

Much time is spent by the Pueblos in their amusements and religious festivals, but the traditional dances which are degrading have been as far as possible repressed by both the Spanish and American governments.

A number of their dances, which could be reproduced with propriety, were exhibited in the exposition in Santa Fé which celebrated the three hundred and thirtieth anniversary of the European settlement of New Mexico. The Pueblo Indians vied with the Apaches in attracting the attention of the thousands who came, from all parts of the country, to witness these strange performances.

A religious dance of the Zuñis, celebrated by the order of the cacique only in times of great drought, was specially indicative of Indian traits. The costumes in this dance, in which the women are personated by young men, are extremely high-colored, and varied in texture and artistic designs. Skirts of rich color hung from the hips to the knees. Blue tunics, with scarlet borders and flowing sleeves, completed the costume, with ornaments of eagle feathers in deep yellow dyes. A knot of these feathers fastened to the top of the head, with long, flowing black hair, was the distinctive badge of the leader. The male dancers, in white woolen blankets and a colored border in diamond pattern, girded by a green and red sash, with a bunch of white strings over the right leg and a fox-skin behind, had their heads crowned with yellow plumes and their faces hidden by a yellow mask. Their waists and ankles were encircled with garlands of hemlock and fir, woven with bright berries, and in their right hands were held gourds partly filled with pebbles. By rattling these, they marked time for the dancers. The costumes of those representing women was similar, their faces also concealed by a mask. The dancers stood in two rows, facing each other, four feet apart. The leader at one end, in full view of the other dancers, regulated their movements with the rhythm of a chant, marked in measures by the stamping of the right foot.

The leader, at intervals, taking a pinch of flour, scattered it to the four quarters of the heavens as a prayer to the deity to send them rain. The chants, performed by carefully trained voices, were accompanied by a small drum. There is but little grace in the motions of the dancers, and the continuance of the same figures for a long time becomes very monotonous to the spectator.

The Antelope dance of the Acomas and the Elk dance of the Piccuries, at the same Exposition, were novel sights. The performers in each were clothed in the skins of these animals. Bending down, and holding slender sticks in their hands for forelegs, they imitated the motions of antelopes or elks in alarm, fright, feeding, roaming over the plains, fighting and running away from their pursuers. Finally a party of Indian hunters drove them away captives. These dancers had studied every graceful motion of the animals they represented, keeping time in all these figures to the tom-toms and chants. The Piccuries, with wide branching elk-horns on their heads, and using stouter sticks in their hands for forelegs, decorated with boughs of trees, imitated the bold motions of elks, which they hunt in their native wilds, and attracted the most interested attention of the crowds gazing curiously on this drama of Indian life.

In the Zuñi war-dance, which succeeded these lighter plays, there were forty of this tribe, their bodies painted from head to feet with fiery red, green and blue pigments, and with various war-symbols, in white, on their chests and backs. Their hideous faces and howls, yells and wild gestures with spears and bows, recalled to mind the descriptions of atrocious scenes among the early colonists of America.

Among the Zuñi, as well as the Pueblo Indians, of the Rio Grande, the unit of society is the clan, with descent in the female line, and inheritance in the same direction of everything except lands. There is a complex grouping into four clusters within the thirteen clans, which takes the place of the phratry.

These clusters are secret societies, or guilds, based not upon descent, but upon individual fitness for perpetuating certain special kinds of knowledge. The Medicine order preserves the secrets of knowledge for healing the sick; the Hunters, the secrets for preserving game; the Keepers-of-the-faith have charge of the worship of the deities, both public and secret; while the order of the Bow is devoted to the military art. Starting with a few simple acquirements, a complicated ritual with a symbolical regalia has gradually been developed. The basis of religious belief is a system of dualism, resembling that of ancient Mexico, according to which a pair, with the attributes of sex, have created the world and mankind, and continue to uphold all life; while the host of supernatural agencies worshipped are all created beings, forming a series of deities organized after the fashion of the various groups of their own tribe.

Each order has its own history in the shape of myths and fables, folk lore and traditions; and thus have been preserved what recollections of the past are still in existence. These tales appear to establish the fact that at some remote time their home has been shifted from some point in the North-west about the boundary of Utah to their present location. These traditions resemble those of the Queres nation in claiming that after descending from the North-west, they turned northward and settled on the Rio Mancos, a tributary of the San Juan in the south-western corner of Colorado, where remarkable cliff-dwellings have been discovered, from which place they migrated to their present home. This spot on the Mancos is called by the Zuñis Shi-pap-u-luma, and the Queres point to the same region as their former home, and call it Shipap. In the mythology of both tribes it is a sacred spot, and has given the name of the final abode to which their spirits will return.*

* Archeological Institutes of America.

CHAPTER XIII.

RELIGIOUS CUSTOMS AND GENERAL CONDITION OF THE PEOPLE IN 1837–40.

THE Roman Catholic religion was established by law in New Mexico at this period, as it had always been recognized by peculiar privileges, since it was in competition with no other form of Christianity. There was toleration for no other religion. Foreigners could worship in other forms or creeds only in their own houses. The military and church powers were closely united; there was, in fact, a military hierarchy in control of the province. Industry yielded to its demands in the observance of successive feast-days and parades, till the life of the people was robbed of all progress and enterprize attendant upon diligent labor. Superstition was encouraged. Miracles were claimed to be wrought for trivial ends, and with a concurrent credulity on the part of the people truly astonishing. The tradition of the apparition of Nuestra Senora de Guadalupe—Our Lady of Guadalupe, the patron saint—is a notable illustration of the impositions practised upon the misled people. The apparition is still preserved in their religious observances, as sacredly as the nativity of Christ, and is one of the most cherished dogmas of their faith. In 1831, a medal commemorating this apparition was manufactured in Birmingham, England, for the Mexican market, to perpetuate this devotion. Nine-tenths of the population of Northern Mexico wore these medals, of which 216,000 were struck for distribution. On one side of these is the Virgin, in a blue-spangled robe, with the date A. D. 1805, and on the other, the motto—*Non fecit taliter omni nationi*—(She) hath not dealt so with any nation. The current version of this miraculous appearance is a household tradition in New Mexico.

The power to perform miracles was implicitly ascribed to all the canonized saints. Their images were carried to the bedside of the sick; the patron saint was paraded through the fields and meadows about the time of the beginning of the rainy season, to bring the needed rains; the Sacred Host was carried with great pomp to the dwellings of those dangerously ill, while the people knelt in the streets as the procession passed.

The arrival of the Bishop of Durango at Santa Fé, in 1833, was attended with characteristic scenes of enthusiasm and devotion. Brilliant and profuse decorations of the streets were made with rich cloths, shawls and carpets, for the processions to pass over. The people fell on their knees before the Bishop when he appeared upon the streets, kissed the pastoral ring upon his hand, and received the apostolic benediction. Priests were often likewise recognized in their official character in public places. The people performed the duties of public worship with great punctuality, and the hour of vespers daily caused a momentary hush of all conversation, and cessation of business in shops and stores and fields, when the bell sounded for prayers, till in two or three minutes, its livelier tones released the population from the duty of reverence, and the ceremony ceased with *Buenas tardes,* "Good evening," passed from one to another like the morning salutations of the present day.

The *fiestas*, feast-days, kept continually in mind the religious sentiment, and caused a disregard of industrious labor. The Holy Week observances absorbed all the thought and time of the people, and especially did Good Friday demand observance with great pomp. An image of Christ large as life nailed to a great wooden cross carried in procession, other images of the Virgin, Mary Magdalene and the apostles, made a solemn spectacle to the multitude; and the shameful rites of the penitents in some of the towns were the occasions of self-imposed torture and agony, degrading to the Christian faith. The sufferers were often the most wicked and abandoned criminals. Though these abuses of devotion were

prohibited by the Holy See, as early as Pope Clement the sixth, they had a singular attraction to the mixed Indian and Spanish race — in its lower elements — and while often prohibited by the highest church authorities, continue in some localities among the New Mexicans to the present time.

The religious solemnization of marriage among the New Mexicans during this period of degeneracy of the church and people, was difficult and expensive. Marriage lost much of its sacredness and was commonly disregarded. The marriage fees imposed by the priests varied from five to five hundred dollars, according to the pomp with which the rite was celebrated. Marriages were generally arranged by parents, and the wishes of the young people were seldom considered. There was but little preceding courtship, and very often marriage covered the disgraces of unmarried people.

Baptism was not a costly sacrament for the children, but burials were so much a source of revenue to the priests and impoverishment to the relatives, that corpses were often deserted, or secretly deposited in churches at night, when priests were obliged to perform the ceremony without pay, unless the relatives could be discovered.

The immoralities of the people were fostered by the examples of the priests, who were prominent at gaming tables, fandangoes, saloon drinking, and in violation with their people of their professedly celebate lives.

Death was but a release to the people from much extortion in the name of religion, and the beginning of compensation for faithful submission to the church. The baptized child was decked in its coffin in the gayest colors, and with the liveliest music the gayly-clothed bearers bore the uncoffined corpse to the burial. The scenes of interment among the scattered relics of others in the consecrated earth were of a character to deaden the sentiment of respect and tenderness for the remains of the deceased.

The progress of intelligence in the people of New Mexico, in 1837, reflected on the condition of the Mexican Confederation. There were no newspapers published in the province. The only attempt at such a publication had been made in 1834, when "The Crepuscule" (Dawn). was issued weekly for a month to about fifty subscribers. It then ceased, having accomplished the election of its editor as a representative to the Mexican Congress. There were no professional lawyers in New Mexico in this period. There was no native physician in practise, and foreign doctors had found it impossible to maintain themselves, on account of the unwillingness or inability of the people to pay for their services.

There was no opportunity for a carpenter or cabinet-maker to exercise any skill in his labor, as sawed lumber was unknown in New Mexico, and the boards used in building had to be hewn out with an axe.

The architecture of the people betokened their backward condition of intelligence and enterprize. The material used was mostly unburnt clay, and the pattern of buildings of the most primitive type,

AN ADOBE HOUSE.

which had come to them from the Indian pueblos and the old Spanish colonists. Their churches and the official residences, even to the Governor's *palacio*, were constructed of the same rough and unsightly blocks of dried clay. The dwellings did not lack comfort, on the inside. They were thus described in 1837:

"A tier of rooms on each side of a square, comprising as many as the convenience of the occupants may require, encompass an open *patio* or court, with but one door opening into the street—a huge gate, usually large enough to admit the family coach. The back tier is generally occupied with the kitchen, provision store and granary, and other offices of the same kind. Most of the apartments, except the winter rooms, open into the *patio*; but the latter are most frequently entered through the hall, which, added to the thickness of their walls and roofs, renders them delightfully warm during the cold season, while they are perfectly cool and agreeable in summer. In fact, hemmed in as these apartments are with nearly three feet of earth, they may be said to possess all the pleasant properties of cellars, with a freer circulation of air, and nothing of the dampness which is apt to pervade those subterranean regions.

"The roofs of the houses are all flat terraces, being formed of a layer of earth two or three feet in thickness, and supported by stout joists or horizontal rafters. These roofs, when well packed, turn the rain off with remarkable effect and render the houses nearly fire-proof. The terrace also forms a pleasant promenade, the surrounding walls rising usually so high as to serve for a balustrade, as also a breastwork, behind which, in times of trouble, the combatants take their station and defend the premises.

"The floors are constructed of beaten earth, 'slicked over' with soft mortar and covered generally with a coarse carpet of domestic manufacture. A plank floor would be quite a curiosity in New Mexico. The interior of each apartment is roughly plastered over with a clay mortar unmixed with lime, by females, who supply the place of trowels with their hands. It is then white-washed with calcined gypsum, a deleterious stuff that is always sure to engraft its affections upon the clothing of those who come in contact with it. To obviate this, the parlors and family rooms are usually lined with wall-paper or calico, to the height of five or six feet. The front of the house is commonly plastered in a similar manner, although not always whitewashed. In the suburbs of the towns, and particularly in the villages and ranchos, a fantastic custom prevails of painting only a portion of the fronts of houses, in the shape of stripes, which imparts to the landscape a very striking and picturesque appearance."

The population of New Mexico, in 1840, was about 45,000. Not more than 1,000 were white Creoles, or those born of European parents. The mestizos, of Spanish and Indian origin, numbered about 35,000, and there were 10,000 Pueblo Indians. This population was confined mainly to the valley of the Rio Grande, which was cultivated and inhabited with a few towns, or centers, for a distance of 100 miles above Santa Fé, and 140 miles below.

To support these people, agriculture was the chief reliance. It was carried on in a very primitive way; the soft, rich soil of the valleys was cultivated with the large hoe and the wooden plow—a section of a tree, two feet long, pointed at one end and running flat like a shovel-plow, and guided by a projecting branch for a handle. Not a particle of iron was used in the construction of these plows, or of the great lumbering carretas or Mexican ox-carts, whose wheels were made of sections of great trees, supported by rude axles which creaked hideously under their loads. The method of cultivation by irrigation gave a surety to crops, and the farmer was content with small fields of grain, to cultivate which the necessities of irrigation would have made too laborious, if greatly extended. The fertile valleys were sometimes the sites of haciendas, or large estates. They usually belonged to Spanish families and were cultivated by peons; and, with their ancient trees, far-reaching fields of grain, thousands of cattle and sheep on the pastures, and numerous small houses around some central quadrangular block of white walls, afforded a very attractive appearance.

CHAPTER XIV.

AMERICAN EXPEDITIONS — ARMIJO.

THREE Frenchmen had reached New Mexico as early as 1693, being deserters from the expedition of La Salle, and in 1739 nine French Canadians entered New Mexico, two of whom remained till Oct. 19th, 1743, when one of them was shot at Santa Fé, for fomenting a rebellion among the Pueblos against the Spanish power. The French traded with the Comanches north of Mora in 1748, but though New Mexico was nearly defenceless for fifty years after this date, no one sought to wrest this territory from the Spaniards.

The first approach of Americans to New Mexico, across the plains, was made as early as 1805. James Pursley, wandering near the Rocky mountains, was guided by some Indians from the Platte river to Santa Fé, where he remained several years. A French Creole had previously, in the same way, entered Santa Fé, on a trading expedition, which he made profitable to himself, but **never** reported to his employer—an American named Morrison, of Kaskaskia. The Louisiana purchase aroused the interest of the United States in these vast regions, and Lieutenant Zebulon Montgomery Pike was sent on an exploring expedition, in 1806, up the Arkansas and Red rivers. He was instructed to establish friendly relations with the Comanche and other Indians of the plains, and to avoid all offense or alarm to the settlements of New Mexico.

The head waters of the Canadien river were mistaken for those of the Red river, and Lieutenant Pike, with his party, were lost in the valley of the Arkansas river—to which the stream had led them again, in the middle of winter—after wandering for two months in search of the sources of the Red river. The party became separated in their search, having crossed the mountains on foot with incredible perils and sufferings. They finally encamped on the banks of a stream, supposed to be the Red river, and built a fort, as they believed, within the United States territory. Here the men of the expedition were gradually gathered, but in the midst of their operations in strengthening their fort, they were surprized by the presence of a body of Mexican troops, despatched by Governor Alencaster from Santa Fé, with one hundred horses and mules, to bring the company to Santa Fé. Astonished at finding themselves on Spanish soil, Lieutenant Pike struck his flag and yielded to the polite demands of the Mexican officer.

Lieutenant Pike had established his fort on the Conejos river, five miles from its junction with the

Rio Grande, and from a hill south of his camp, had a view of the magnificent San Luis Park — a luxuriant vale, surrounded with great and lofty mountains — which excited in his men intense enthusiasm.

Their march to Santa Fé took them first to Ojo Caliente, one hundred miles from the fort. Thence to the Chama river and the pueblo of San Juan, where the people most hospitably received them. Santa Cruz, and San Ildefonso and Tesuque were visited on the way to Santa Fé, where they arrived March 3, 1807, in the most astonishing plight for an expedition of United States soldiers.

The capital city presented an equally strange appearance to the eyes of the Americans. It was about a mile in length, situated on the banks of the creek and three streets in width. It resembled a fleet of flat-boats on the Ohio river, as seen by Pike from a distance. He discovered the north side to have a public square occupied by the government building, the soldiers' houses and guard's quarters on the north and the opposite side given up to the dwellings of the clergy, the churches and the public offices. The houses, with their portals, made very narrow streets not more than twenty-five feet wide. The population of the town was about 4500.

Governor Alencaster received Lieutenant Pike in the palace, the floors of which were covered with buffalo and bear skins. After an examination of his papers and commission, and a short colloquy in the French language, Lieutenant Pike was treated with the courtesy which his character as a gentleman and a man of honor demanded, and the next

THE PUEBLO OF SANTA DOMINGO.

day was hospitably entertained at a dinner in the palace.

He was, however, informed that he must go to Chihuahua with his men, not as prisoners of war, but with an escort of dragoons, and a certificate from Governor Alencaster that he was obliged to march thither. They set out with the Governor, who accompanied them for three miles and cordially parted with his recent guest. On the route Lieutenant Pike describes the pueblo of Santo Domingo as containing 1000 people. At San Felipe they crossed over a bridge made of eight arches. Near Albuquerque the men were put in charge of Don Facundo Melgazes, who treated them with great gallantry and honor, and delivered them on April 2, to the general commanding, Salcedo, of Chihuahua, who despatched them to Texas. They were very hospitably treated by the Spanish Governors of Coahuila and New Leon, and on the 1st of July, 1807, entered Nachitoches, grateful and happy to stand once more on the soil of their own country.

From the observations of Pike it appears that the industries of the people of New Mexico at this period were confined principally to stock-raising and agriculture. At El Paso, his party was entertained by a planter, Don Francisco Garcia, who possessed 20,000 sheep and 1,000 cows. There was but one mine in operation in latitude thirty-four degrees. probably in the vicinity of Socorro, which produced 20,000 mule loads of copper annually, furnishing all that was needed for the provinces. The annual exports from New Mexico consisted of 30,000 sheep, tobacco, wrought copper vessels and skins of deer and buffalo. Fine imported cloths were from twenty to twenty-five dollars per yard, flour two dollars per hundred and beéves five dollars each. The Pueblo Indians manufactured rough leather, pottery, cotton and coarse woolen cloths and blankets. Mechanical operations were confined to the Indians, and agriculture carried on by the Spaniards. The New Mexicans were continually subject to military service, their frontiers being exposed to the incursions of Apaches and Navajoes, so that dragoon escorts were required for the trading caravans between the province and states of Mexico. They had become thus inured to war, and, isolated from the civilization of the kingdom of Spain on the south, were a brave people, and kind and hospitable to all who came within their borders.

The end of the Spanish rule in Mexico and its provinces came with the proclamation of the Independence of Mexico by Iturbido, in February, 1821. Iturbido, at first declared regent, was soon proclaimed emperor of Mexico, with the title of Augustine I. His reign was short. In March, 1823, he was forced to abdicate, and banished from his country. Iturbido and his family sailed for the Mediterranean, but returning secretly to Mexico, in May, 1824, in a vessel chartered in England, he was declared an outlaw, seized and shot, July 19th, 1824, five days after his landing.

The Mexican republic was created, Nov. 19th, 1823. A constitution, resembling that of the United States, was adopted, and New Mexico became part of the federation of nineteen states and four territories. In the Mexican republic, each territory was allowed a representative, but a Governor was appointed over it by the President, and a territorial Legislature was elected by the people.

Bartolomè Baca was the first Governor of New Mexico appointed under the Republican rule. He held office from 1824 to September, 1825, and was succeeded by seven Governors, each holding his position for a brief term, till 1837, when New Mexico was created a department of the Republic under Albino Perez, who was assassinated by the Pueblo Indians in their insurrection at Santa Fé, Aug. 9th. Josè Gonzalez, proclaimed Governor of New Mexico by the insurgents, was deposed by Manuel Armijo, who had stirred up a counter revolution in favor of the Mexican Republic; and Gonzalez was executed with some of his followers, Jan. 27th, 1838, by Armijo, who was recognized by the National Government in the City of Mexico, and managed to continue in office from 1838 to 1846, with a short intermission of a few months, when he was at that time suspended, but again elected as Governor, the last time under Mexican rule. He yielded only to the United States troops, when they took formal possession of New Mexico, by proclamation of General S. W. Kearney, Aug. 16th, 1846.

On the 14th of September, 1841, after incredible privations and sufferings from famine and every kind of disaster from their wanderings on the plains, that portion of the Texan-Santa Fé expedition which had reached the Mexican settlements, set forth toward Santa Fé. with instructions and letters showing the peaceful intentions of the large trading expedition from Texas to which this party belonged, and from whose calamities they had barely escaped with their lives. Passing one night at Anton Chico, as they were the next day nearing San Miguel, they were suddenly surrounded by more than a hundred soldiers well mounted, but armed indiscriminately with old carbines, lances, bows and arrows, and swords, under the command of Domasio Salezar, who placed the Texans under arrest, examined their papers, and then proceeded to rob them of arms, equipments and everything on their persons, and led them out to be shot.

By the interposition of an interested Mexican, Don Gregorio Vigil, this murderous purpose of Armijo's trusty officer was prevented, and the five prisoners were driven on foot toward San Miguel. The next day they were hurriedly marched through the town in charge of a villainous lieutenant, Don Jesus, and after great hardships, toward sunset, came upon a numerous cavalcade surrounding General Manuel Armijo. Governor of New Mexico, mounted on a gayly-decked mule of great size. The first salutation of the Governor was friendly, but his hostility to the Texans was soon manifested when he ordered them to be marched back under guard to San Miguel that night. To a remonstrance of the officers in charge that they were hardly able to walk all the way back that night, Armijo replied, "They are able to walk ten leagues more. These Texans are active and untiring people. I know them; if one of them pretends to be sick or tired on the road, shoot him down and bring me his ears! Go!"

Under this penalty of failure, the company reached San Miguel in a few hours, and were placed in a temporary prison. The same evening, they saw a comrade who had been taken prisoner previously to themselves, shot in the back by the guard, in the prison yard. They were then taken by a strong guard from the prison, and brought before the house where Armijo was quartered, and examined. The Governor meanwhile questioned a concealed witness behind him as to each member of the party. This proved to be one of their bravest companions, Howland, from whom they had parted on the plains, in their desperate effort to save themselves from the horrors of starvation.

No sooner had his testimony been taken than Armijo came forward and told the captives that their lives were safe, as he had found their report of themselves confirmed by this other prisoner. He had previously been captured, and taken to Santa Fé, but attempting to escape from his confinement, had been re-captured. He was now led forth to his execution before their eyes, but Armijo remanded him to prison till the following day, when he was shot. The next day Captain Cooke, with the rest of the expedition, was captured, through the treachery of an officer named Lewis. This traitor had also delivered another detachment, under General McLeod, into Armijo's power. After twenty days in prison, Armijo sent all the prisoners on a cruel march on foot to the city of Mexico, 2,000 miles away. The indignities heaped upon these men, by the orders of Armijo, were indescribable. Starving, bruised, sore, ragged, shoeless, overcome by heat on the rough and dusty roads, shot at and mutilated if they fainted on the way, confined in horrible enclosures filled with vermin and filth beyond description, where disease, leprosy and death overtook many of them, this march was like the progress of a slave-gang under Arab overseers in Africa, and the terrible journeys of Russian convicts and exiles to Siberia.

In the insurrection of 1837, this man had risen to power through craft and impudence which fortune and the weakness of his countrymen made successful. The people of the province of New Mexico, under the Confederation, were moderately content with the change of government so long as the authority of the general government was represented by native officials. When the republic of Mexico was modified in 1835, and the federal power centralized in the capital, the change was displeasing to some of the provinces. Colonel Albino Perez was appointed under the new government at Mexico, to be Governor of New Mexico. At first the people of this distant province experienced no change in their financial interests, and no opposition was raised to the new regime till, for the support of the administration in New Mexico, it became necessary to levy a direct tax upon the people. Then discontent began to be secretly cherished, breaking out in the rescue by a mob of an alcalde or justice of the peace, who had been imprisoned in the north-

A HOSTILE PUEBLO.

ern district by the Prefect, Don Ramon Abreu. This was the beginning of a general insurrection.

A disorderly assembly of people, irrespective of nationality or condition, was gathered at La Cañada, twenty-five miles north of Santa Fé. The northern Pueblos were largely represented by their warriors in this mob. Governor Perez collected about 150 militia of the province, with the warriors of the pueblo of San Domingo, and marched from Santa Fé against the insurgents. This entirely insufficient force was ambushed near La Cañada, and the Governor, left with only twenty-five followers, the rest having deserted him, retreated hastily to Santa Fé, and thence fled southward for their lives. Governor Perez was overtaken, pursued back to the capital, and cruelly slain in the suburbs; his body was stripped and mutilated, and his head, carried into the city in triumph, was tossed about among the insurgents as a foot-ball. Prefect Abreu, with the Secretary of State, Francisco Alarid, and some other officials who had taken refuge in the farm-houses outside of the city, were also hunted out of their places of concealment, and their stripped bodies, pierced with lances, were subjected to the same indignities by the infuriated mob—mostly composed of the Pueblo Indians—whose savage natures were now thoroughly aroused.

Don Santiago Abreu, a former Governor of great note in the province, was most horribly tortured by them. His hands were cut off, his eyes and tongue pulled from their sockets while he was yet alive, and his body mangled, while his merciless foes taunted him with crimes. There were twelve of the more distinguished citizens who thus perished in this insurrection in the capital, whose bodies lay exposed in the fields to wolves and ravens.

Two thousand insurrectionists, including the Pueblo Indians, on the 9th of August, 1837, now surrounded the capital, which awaited with great fear the pillage and destruction that would follow its capture.

Better counsels, however, finally prevailed. One of the boldest leaders, José Gonzales, of Taos, was made Governor by the mob. The rebels now went through the form of confiscating the property of their murdered victims, by the decree of a council summoned by Gonzales, and their families were reduced to destitution. The property of the American and other foreign traders was not seized, but they lost all their claims upon the deceased officials, to whom they had largely given credit. These claims, presented to the American minister at Mexico, were never enforced by the government of the United States. But the merchants who had furnished means to Governor Perez to quell this insurrection, were accused of being instigators of it, and in some instances their property confiscated.

Among those most eager to profit by this insurrection, who had been also concerned in fostering it, was a character subsequently notorious and prominent in the history of the province, Don Manuel Armijo, of Albuquerque.

Probably no man more cruel or unscrupulous ever became prominent in affairs in New Mexico. He was Governor of the province most of the time from 1837 till its conquest by the Americans in 1846.

Having with his usual cowardice kept aloof from the fighting and carnage at the capital, he hurried to it from Albuquerque to be elected Governor. Finding his intrigues unsuccessful, he plotted a counter revolution in favor of the federal government. With the aid of the disbanded federal troops he returned to the capital in triumph, Gonzales having at his approach fled to the north.

Armijo proclaimed himself Governor and General and sent by couriers a boastful account of his valor in subduing the rebellion, to the general government at Mexico, by which he was at once recognized and confirmed as Governor for eight years. Four hundred dragoons and regulars were sent by the Governors of Zacatecas and Chihuahua to Santa Fé, who joined Armijo's force and marched in January, 1838, against the rebels again gathered at La Cañada.

The valiant Armijo in the presence of the enemy was about to retreat, when a captain of one of the companies of dragoons asked permission alone with his company to oust the rabble. Armijo gave consent, and the disorganized rebels fled precipitately. Gonzales was captured among the prisoners taken, and immediately shot without any form of trial.

Thus the government of the province was secured to Armijo, whose career as the last of the Spanish and native rulers, before the province became a territory of the United States, is worthy of some special notice.

Governor Armijo, directly after gaining power, assumed to himself all the functions of the chief executive, the legislature elected by the people but prorogued by him, and of the judicial department, which was appointed by him as a matter of form, and made subservient to his demands. Justice became a matter of sale, and the money and influence of a litigant before an alcalde or higher judge, neutralized all the justice, evidence and character opposed to him. Americans were especially obnoxious to Armijo, who lost no opportunity of humiliating and robbing them by an imposition of taxes and adverse decisions of his alcaldes.

In 1839, by exempting all the natives from the impost taxes on store-houses, shops, etc., but retaining them on all the property of foreigners, he threw the whole burden of the expense of government on foreign and naturalized citizens. He apportioned the taxes issued to meet the war levy made by the Governor of Chihuahua to carry on the wars with the Indians so that natives should pay but one-fifth that which was assessed upon foreigners, thus disregarding all treaty obligations between the United States and Mexico. The Americans paid twenty-five dollars per month, while native merchants with large stores and great stock ranches, paid but five to ten dollars each. Under Armijo imprisonment without trial was as common for debt as for larceny, highway robbery and murder. The prisoners were detained at will till release was purchased, the murderer escaping as easily as the debtor from punishment of his crimes. The debtor unable to buy his freedom became the servant or peon of his creditor at such small wages that he was kept continually in debt to him, and the service became life-long, or was transferred for consideration, with the accumulated obligations, to another master.

In 1839, by appointing his brother as collector of customs, he took the exclusive control of all the revenue, and, without law, arbitrarily imposed a tax of $500 upon each wagon-load of merchandize entering the province from the United States, without regard to its value or quality.

Armijo was not only Governor, commander-in-chief, legislator, custom-house officer, auditor, treasurer and judge, but in order to sustain himself, since his treasury was always bankrupt, he was also a merchant, and insisted on paying his officials, military service and other dues in his own merchandize, at exorbitant prices.

Armijo was accustomed to cane his native subjects in the streets, and to require his appearance on the streets to be heralded by a guard with the pomp of royalty, and abject obeisance made to him. Being a man of large and commanding frame and stern demeanor, he appeared to be brave, but, in fact, fulfilled his frequent manifestation and defense of bluster by his frequent expression, "It is better to be thought brave than really to *be* so."

With such a representative of the power of the Mexican Confederation over them, the people of New Mexico might welcome the American regime which, by the war of the United States with Mexico, was soon forced upon them.

PERIOD VII.

AMERICAN OCCUPATION.

1846 TO 1862.

CHAPTER XV.

THE COUNTRY AND PEOPLE.

BY the treaty of the United States with Spain in 1819, the boundary line separating the territory of the United States from New Mexico was thus defined. It extended from the Red river 100 degrees longitude west of Greenwich northwardly to the Arkansas river, then following the Arkansas to its sources, it stretched in a straight line north to forty-two degrees North latitude and followed the forty-second degree parallel to the Pacific. The south-eastern boundary of New Mexico was indefinite at the beginning of the war of the United States with Mexico, by reason of the claims of Texas made in 1836 against Mexico, to the disputed territory west of the river Nueces as far as the Rio Grande, and northward along the Rio Grande to its source, and thence to the forty-second degree north latitude. The state of Chihuahua formed the southern boundary of New Mexico along the parallel of thirty-two degrees thirty seconds east to the Rio Pecos or Puerco, and westward to the head waters of the

Gila, descending the river to its junction with the San Francisco. Here it met the undefined boundary of Sonora, which was usually considered to be the river Gila. The wide country between the Rio Colorado and the Gila, inhabited only by wild Indian tribes, was generally conceded to belong to New Mexico, and the desert tract northwest of the Colorado to California.

Though the widest limits of New Mexico would thus embrace the country from thirty-two degrees thirty seconds to forty-two degrees North latitude, and from one hundred degrees to one hundred and fourteen degrees longitude west of Greenwich, it was not all under Mexican jurisdiction and control. That territory, which was but partially settled, included within thirty-two degrees and thirty-eight degrees north and longitude one hundred and four degrees to one hundred and eight degrees west of Greenwich, was the province of New Mexico, properly considered, at the time of its occupation by the American army. This object of conquest by the United States government, enlarged by two degrees of longitude, became the present territory of New Mexico. Its surface presented in 1846, as at the present time, a succession of *mesas* or table lands from a height of 10,000 feet in the northern portion to 3800 feet in the southern borders. Over these extend five mountain systems from north to south and from east to west, varying in height from 6,000 to 13,000 feet above the sea. These mountains are composed of igneous rocks of granite, syenite, diorite and basalt. Many regions indicate volcanic action, and large tracts of malpie and streams of congealed lava are often met with on the plains or among the cañons. The finest pine timber covers the loftiest mountain levels, and dwarfed cedars, oaks and pines everywhere diversify the lower levels and sides of the hills and mountains. The *mesas* are covered with rich grass in the rainy seasons, amid great tracts of barren country, ridged and gullied by mountain torrents, which have gorged with deep arroyos the desolate sandy surface. Distant views of these sterile plains give them the appearance of billows of sand-hills, from which rise crags and cliffs and isolated buttes and peaks, carved by the elements into fanciful shapes of ruined castles, and temples, monumental pillars, and giant images of men and beasts, or lofty pinnacles, of various colors, in forming which the seas and winds, and frosts and floods seem to have indulged for centuries in a revel of power over the helpless earth.

Corresponding to these mountain systems are five large rivers with their tributaries, which are supplied by the abundant snows that cover the mountain tops for the greater part of the year, and melt in the rains usual in July and August. The Rio Grande is the main artery of this system, extending in New Mexico alone five hundred miles, having its sources in the Rocky Mountains near those of the Colorado river of the West, and the head waters of the Arkansas.

It is the longest river of New Mexico, running for over 1300 miles from its sources to the Gulf of Mexico. Steamboats can ascend from its mouth to

Laredo 700 miles, but within New Mexico its waters are not navigable, except in the rainy season, by any craft larger than canoes. Its valley averages a width of about five miles. Its waters, starting at the high elevation of the Rocky Mountains, have a fall within New Mexico of 2200 feet and at El Paso are 3800 feet above the Sea.

The tract of land thus subject to irrigation from this river within this territory embraces 2,000 square miles, and is as large as the State of Delaware.

The rivers Pecos and Canadien on the east, the Puerco and Gila on the west, and the San Juan and Chama on the north, bounded by great mountain chains, are also the sources of the fertility of the great valleys and plains through which they flow.

The soil of all these valleys, wherever irrigated, produces large crops of Indian corn, wheat, vegetables and fruits. Below the latitude of Santa Fé, often two crops can be raised in the lower part of the Rio Grande valley. The cultivated lands at the time of the American Conquest, around the towns and villages were located with a system of ditches, which formed instead of fences the boundaries of the plots cultivated; while the plains and *mesas* were held by herdsmen in common. Numerous large estates or haciendas occupied the best parts of the valleys and the vicinity of springs. There the old feudal system still prevailed in the relations of peons or serfs to the masters, who provided food, clothing and shelter for their dependents and kept

"THE MOST TREMENDOUS CHASMS AND GORGES ON THE CONTINENT."

them continually in debt and bondage; so that successive generations of slaves were attached to those large estates and were practically the property of the landlords under the Constitution of the Mexican Republic, which, though distinctly excluding slavery, permitted the enforcement of laws against debtors. The rivers of New Mexico constitute one of its boldest and most interesting features. Not one of them is navigable within the territory. Yet they flow through mountain ranges and lofty table-lands so as to form the most tremendous chasms and gorges on the continent.

The Rio Grande is over 2,000 miles long, with shoals and cataracts a thousand miles below Santa Fé. It flows through a deep and impassable cañon opposite Taos for an extent of fifteen miles on a rapid torrent. The bold explorer shrinks from looking down its precipitous, craggy sides to the foaming current in this dark chasm. Then it flows out into the fertile valley of San Juan, winds a serpentine course like a rivulet through a wide plain, till it receives the muddy waters of the Puerco and the clear mountain stream of the Rio Santa Fé, and stretches across the broad valley of the lower Rio Grande through the meadows of Albuquerque, Socorro and Messilla, till it skirts the plain of the Muerto and enters the defile at El Paso, to flow out upon the vineyards, orchards and cornfields, before it enters the barren district of Chihuahua.

The remarkable advantages for grazing in New Mexico made the raising of cattle, sheep, horses and mules, the chief industry of the people, which, however, suffered from the depredations of the Indian tribes to such an extent that these savage Indians were practically partners with the Mexicans in this business. The mineral resources of the province of New Mexico had also been developed under the Republican government of Mexico as little as under the Spanish crown. Some deposits of gold had been profitably worked in placer diggings. A few silver mines, in the mountains near Santa Fé, had been abandoned, while the far more extensive resources in the mountains and plains east and west of the Rio Grande had contributed scarcely anything to the industry or wealth of the inhabitants, though copper, lead, zinc, iron and coal were abundant. The lime and gypsum beds, which are distributed so richly over New Mexico, served only the immediate wants of the people for their simple dwellings. There were numerous salt lakes in the territory, from the shores of which vast quantities of salt could be gathered, but it was not an article of commerce with neighboring states.

New Mexico, at the opening of this war, was known to have a very attractive climate. Diseases were rare, and the people, though subject to some typhoidal fevers, lived with impunity in the prevailing dry and moderate temperature, under the privations of poverty.

The population, in 1846, was about 45,000, a few of whom were Spaniards. The rest were mestizos, partly Spanish and Indian by birth. In character they were generally indolent, and the men, sunk in ignorance and vice, were utterly unfitted for self-

THE COUNTRY AND PEOPLE. 263

government, while the women were affectionate, sympathetic with suffering, and rather attractive in personal appearance. There were about 8,000 Pueblo Indians and an unknown number of wandering savage tribes of Apache Indians in the province, who added nothing to the effective military strength of the province in resisting invasion.

New Mexico was ruled under the Republic, as a province, by a Governor and a legislature, called the Junta departmental. The Governors were very independent of the legislature in their exercise of power, and were often removed by revolutionary proceedings, so that they, without much form of law, held office at the pleasure of the people. The judiciary power depended on the Governor's will, and the clergy and military power each had their courts of justice. Only an indolent spirit in the inhabitants, and a prevailing ignorance, could tolerate such a condition. New Mexico exercised great independence of this general government, and resisted taxes and other tributes levied upon the province, unless concessions of equal value were made by the authorities in Mexico.

Don Manuel Armijo was the Governor in office at the time of the American conquest, and, therefore, the last one to be recognized as such by the national government in the city of Mexico. Armijo had held office from 1838 to January, 1845, and was again elected in December of the same year.

Santa Fé, the capital city of New Mexico, was at this time the town of most importance in the province. It contained about 3,000 inhabitants of

Spanish and Indian blood, and, with surrounding settlements under its jurisdiction, numbered about 6,000. Surrounded on all sides by mountains of commanding height and beauty, the appearance of its low, flat-roofed adobe houses and irregular streets was exceedingly disappointing to travellers who had made the toilsome journey over the plains. There was scarcely an attractive, clean-looking building on its narrow streets. The plaza was a desolate-looking square, on one side of which the long palacio, or Governor's palace, was standing. Its portico extended the entire length of one side of the square. It presented almost the only glass windows in the town—for ordinary houses had shutters instead of windows, or narrow openings glazed with crystalized gypsum. A singular ornament of this portico were festoons of Indian ears, for which the government had paid a bounty. In the long conflicts with hostile Indians this people had sunk to methods of warfare scarcely better than those of their savage foes.

The citizens of Santa Fé were naturally indolent, and consequently obliged to be extremely frugal in their mode of subsistence. They were extremely fond of smoking, dancing and gambling, and from frequent meeting of strangers, inclined to be sociable. The arrival of trading companies from the United States furnished the government with its means of support, and the people obtained most of their conveniences for living from these caravans. There were consequently a number of foreign residents in Santa Fé. They were mostly French or German, and generally the merchants were French,

A TRADING COMPANY

but a few Americans had become established in the town. The annual importation of merchandize over the plains, which was here distributed, was estimated at half a million dollars. In 1843, this commerce required transportation in two hundred wagons. The duties paid to the Governors on these wagons were from $600 to $1000, according to the impudence of the officials and the necessities of the administration. There was but little help against extortion, and the people were obliged in the prices paid for these articles, to remunerate those who had crossed the Santa Fé trail in the slow journeys with ox teams, and the merchants who dwelt in this outlandish place under such a government only for the sake of gain.

The other towns in New Mexico had the characteristics of all Mexican towns—adobe houses, filthy streets, idle population, and industries stimulated only by the actual necessities for existence. Albuquerque had about the same population as Santa Fé. It was the home of Governor Armijo, when out of office, and the place where he plotted to be reinstated as often as he was deposed. It extended along the bank of the Rio Grande on a sandy plain, with water so near the surface, that corn, wheat, fruits, and beans and red peppers, the principal food of the Mexicans, were easily produced, and its warmer climate and better soil were an offset to its lack of political importance in comparison with the Capital. It was said to be, if not handsomer, not a worse looking place than Santa Fé.

Las Vegas was a village of a hundred miserable

houses, with a Mexican population, who obtained a scanty living from the cultivation of the fields around the settlement, that were irrigated from the Gallinas creek flowing out of a beautiful cañon six miles above.

The smaller Mexican villages were absolutely without other characteristics than mud-houses, ill-featured and thinly-clothed inhabitants lazily working in surrounding fields, burros, dogs and poultry wandering about the narrow lanes, or with occasional sights of elevated racks of corn-stalks above threshing floors, or of wooden ploughs, and the creaking Mexican cart made without nails or iron, on two solid wheels cut off from the trunk of a big tree, and their bony, undersized oxen straggling in long lines before it.

And yet this country of New Mexico, in the summer months was very beautiful to behold, its grassy parks, diversified by endless groupings of low pines and cedars, its brilliant colors of cactus-bloom and a score of garden plants, growing wild in rich profusion; its mountain sides dark with pine forests, and crowned with brilliantly-colored faces of rocks, cliffs and gorges, under the clear blue sky, and its ever prominent table lands, measuring great levels against the horizon, and jutting into plains and headlands of a hundred different shapes, with an air exhilarating and pure, and a boundless extent of country rich with mineral wealth undeveloped, made this province a coveted possession to the government of the United States, and to that Administration which here hoped to enlarge the dominion of American slavery, and turn this unused country, by slave labor, into plantations and ranches that should add untold wealth and comfort to the people. For here, it was thought, could flourish that American aristocracy which degraded labor to classes of people who were only fit to serve their natural masters.

CHAPTER XVI.

NEW MEXICO IN THE WAR OF 1846-47.

THE Army of the West, one of the three divisions of the 50,000 troops authorized by Act of Congress in April, 1846, for the prosecution of the war with Mexico, was placed in command of Colonel Stephen W. Kearney, who was soon made Brigadier-General. The administration sought as the most desirable spoils of war the Mexican provinces of New Mexico and California. Kearney was ordered to push his division across the plains to Santa Fé, take possession of New Mexico and thence to extend his conquest westward to California. The ability, skill and intrepidity of Colonel Alexander W. Doniphan, who was second in command, gave the name of Doniphan's Expedition to the first part of this bold march of two thousand miles across the continent through the great American desert, over the Rocky mountains and two other continental ranges, to the shores of the Pacific. His command of 1658 men and sixteen pieces of artillery was composed, with the exception of one battalion of infantry, of volunteer companies of Missouri, mounted troops enlisted under the excitement which the Mexican war had aroused in the south-western frontier States. This little army departed from Fort Leavenworth, Kansas, June 26, 1846, and began their march over a thousand miles of green praries, through ravines of timber, across high table-lands and treeless deserts to Santa Fé. By July 2d, the column had fairly entered the Santa Fé trail and pursued a monotonous road 600 miles, till Fort Bent on the Arkansas river was reached, July 30th. The latter part of their march had been hindered by drenching rains, deep mud and then by exceedingly hot weather and the dust of the wind-swept plains.

Fort Bent was a trading post, thronged at this time, with men drawn by business or curiosity, diverse in nationality and color. It was in the land of the Comanches and Cheyennes, and there were many corrals and camps of caravan merchants in the vicinity of the military camp, waiting for an opportunity to make their accustomed trips to Santa Fé in safety.

While here recruiting his troops General Kearney had sent out an expedition of twelve picked cavalry men under Colonel Cooke, to enter the Mexican territory and proceed to Santa Fé under a flag of truce, to persuade the authorities of New Mexico to yield peaceably to the claim of annexation of all the territory east of the Rio Grande, made by Texas and reaffirmed by proclamation of General Kearney as having been annexed with Texas to the United States. The people of New Mexico were thus offered an escape from the humiliation of being conquered, which from their supposed indifference to the Mexican confederation, it was believed would be accepted. This embassy of peace crossed the Raton mountains and descending their western slope traversed the Mora valley to Las Vegas, where they were kindly received by the alcalde of this thoroughly Mexican town. From Las Vegas their route took them by the old Pecos church and pueblo ruins through a mountain park and rocky cañon, and on the 12th of August they entered Santa Fé and presented the communication of General Kearney to Governor Armijo in his palace.

The peaceful negotiations were without avail. The Governor sent a rather ambiguous message to General Kearney that he would meet him with an army of six thousand men. News previously received of the hostile preparations of the Mexicans under Governor Armijo, was confirmed by the report of these messengers from Santa Fé.

The main column of the army reached Fort Bent on the 30th of July, and leaving the sick and disabled at this point, resumed march on the 2d of August through an inhospitable desert southwardly toward the Raton mountains. There were neither grasses nor shrubs for the famishing animals, the water was scarce and of bitter taste, the wheels sank into the pulverized earth, and men and beasts were suffocated by the wind driving the fine sand

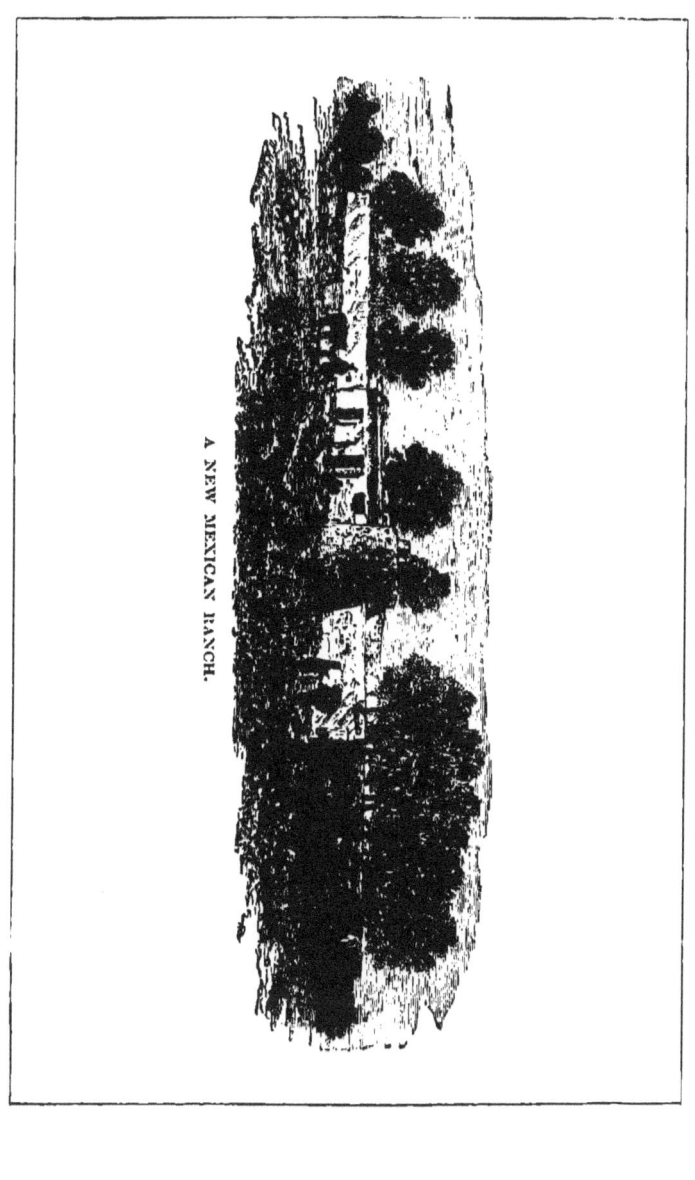
A NEW MEXICAN RANCH.

into their faces. For three days the column toiled through heat and dust till it reached the banks of the Purgatoire, a cool mountain stream in sight of the lofty Cimmeron and Spanish peaks, rising 13,000 feet above the sea level in snowy grandeur. The boundaries of the desolate plains were soon passed, and with new energy the men ascended over the rough roads and abrupt hills which led to the Raton Pass, where, entering upon a grand basin surrounded by steep hills, they enjoyed the first Sabbath rest allowed them since they left Missouri.

The little army now made rapid progress. General Kearney was in advance with five hundred men. The Mexican settlements were found to be in a country covered with groves of cedars and pines, or in valleys surrounded with corn-fields and gardens. The spirit of these volunteer soldiers was cheered by the news that two thousand Mexicans were encamped in a cañon six miles from Las Vegas to oppose this invasion of their country. The fatigues and hardships of the march of nearly a thousand miles were forgotten in the anticipation of a battle. The line was formed and the trumpet was sounded for the advance. The prominent citizens of Las Vegas took the oath of allegiance to the United States as the troops passed on to the expected engagement. But hurrying on to the cañon, they discovered that the Mexicans had fled, and the troops halted at the villages of San Miguel and Pecos to receive the people into allegiance as citizens of the United States.

New Mexico was declared by General Kearney

to have been annexed to the United States with Texas. He was instructed by the Secretary of War to establish a temporary civil government over New Mexico and California, should he conquer them, and release the people from their allegiance to Mexico. Much was left to his discretion in relation to the civil government of the conquered peoples, and their conciliation with the United States. But he exceeded his rightful authority, in his desire to give to the inhabitants the privileges and immunities cherished by the people of his own country. By proclamation from Santa Fé, soon after he reached the capital, he made New Mexico a part of the United States, and established a territorial government, denouncing, with the penalties of treason, any citizens found in hostility to the United States in the territory.

Governor Armijo had gathered 7,000 men to oppose the invaders; 2,000 were well armed and held Gallisteo cañon, where the Governor intended to give battle. Armijo had sent a message to Kearney that he would meet him at that cañon, and the latter hurried forward in expectation of a peaceful interview. But dissension had broken out among Armijo's troops, who had, by their fears, exaggerated the reports concerning the Americans and had fled in a panic. Only a breastwork of fallen trees and nine pieces of abandoned artillery opposed Kearney's progress to the capital. In this gorge, so narrow that but three or four men could walk abreast through it, 7,000 Mexicans with these batteries could have opposed a large army. But Governor Armijo had retreated toward Albuquerque with a few regular troops, and the road was clear to the capital, only fifteen miles distant. General Kearney peaceably entered Santa Fé, the same day, and planted the American flag in the plaza, in front of the palace. As the flag was raised, it was saluted by the artillery planted in the Loma (a hill behind the town), and the American cavalry rode with waving banners through the streets.

The New Mexicans were soon won to good will and submitted cheerfully to the new regime. Their property was unmolested, their homes secured from violence, and they were fully compensated for all supplies needed by the United States troops. General Kearney assured them that they were subject only to the laws of the United States, and counselled them to resort to no violence and take the oath of allegiance, announcing that all their officers would remain unchanged except the Governor, who had fled. On the 22d of August he formally declared by proclamation that New Mexico had become a part of the United States and its inhabitants endued with all the duties, privileges and penalties pertaining to citizenship of the great republic. Thus this vast territory, embracing 200,000 miles, with its inexhaustible resources of mineral wealth and soil and climate, without firing a gun or shedding a drop of blood, passed from the dominion of a race that had held it in dependence for 300 years, to the freedom of the most enlightened government and nation in the world.

General Kearney assumed the office of military Governor and was at once occupied by the delegations who came from all parts of the country to offer allegiance. The change of government was welcomed by the poorer people, who had long been subject to extortion and peonage. During the disturbances and changes in the central government, New Mexico had suffered greatly from the Indian depredations and civil feuds. There was but a weak sentiment of loyalty to the Mexican republic, and the native Indians were quite indifferent to the fate of the province. The Pueblos hailed the Americans as deliverers from Spanish and Mexican oppression, believing their traditions now fulfilled, which declared that help would come to them from the East. Even the chiefs of the Apache tribes came to hold a friendly council with the Governor-General and declare their friendship and peaceable intentions to the Americans.

The troops were comfortably encamped in the reservation on the north bank of the river now known as Fort Marcy, and greatly enjoyed the inviting and restful location of Santa Fé, surrounded by mountains and looking out upon the fertile plain which extended southward and was irrigated by the river whose cool waters flowed through the town. The indescribable strangeness of its low, fort-like houses, ancient churches, narrow streets and adobe walls gave a romantic interest to the surroundings of these soldiers. Exhausted by the long marches across the plains, and the presence of an army, and the crowds of strangers flocking to the capital to supply its needs, and become citizens with the Americans, gave unwonted life to the town

ALONG THE LINE OF MARCH.

which suddenly became populous with twelve thousand inhabitants.

One of the soldiers thus describes Santa Fé at the time of its occupation by the Americans: "The great square or plaza, level, unpaved and rather sandy, has on each side an accequia or canal, with rows of small cottonwood trees. This has a very pleasing effect in a hot, dry and barren country. It is further adorned with very comfortable porticoes, portales on three sides, including the palace. These are extensions of the flat roofs to the edge of the sidewalk, where they are supported by round pillars, which are white-washed. They serve as the only shelter for the market, and are lined with shops, nearly all kept by Americans. One or two streets are similarly improved, but in a general way are narrow and present to the passenger only a plain and nearly continuous wall; each extensive house having only a large, strong, folding door, and one or two windows; these have invariably a projecting frame and turned wooden bars, a sash seldom glazed, and strong shutters opening inward.

"On our first Sunday the bells invited us to worship. I went to the parochial church; although built of adobes, it is sufficiently lofty, and has two steeples, or towers, in which hang three or four bells. With the usual wax images, it is adorned with numerous paintings, one or two of some merit. There was some music of violin and triangle and no spoken service. The streets and shops were thronged, and nothing indicated that it was the Lord's day."

September 2d, General Kearney, with a force of

775 mounted troops, made an expedition southward into the valley of the Rio Grande to quell an insurrection which was reported to have been instigated by the deposed Armijo. For sixty miles they marched through vineyards laden with the finest grapes, and along farms well stocked with fruits, while game fowls of many kinds were swarming in the Rio Grande. The inhabitants of the Indian Pueblos received them with their traditional festivities, dances, races and religious celebrations, and the Mexican towns with deputations and military salutes. No opposition was encountered for one hundred miles, and the expedition having proceeded south to St. Tomé, returned after twelve days to Santa Fé.

In the meantime Fort Marcy, on the heights above Santa Fé, was constructed of adobes by the soldiers under Colonel Doniphan, with a capacity of one thousand men. Its guns completely commanded the town. Civil government was established. A constitution and laws for the territory prepared by Colonel Doniphan was translated into Spanish by one of the American officers, Captain David Waldo. The civil law, as adopted by Spain, was the basis of these laws, and the departmental decrees were revised and substituted for those which the legislation had made. An old governmental printing press found in the capital was utilized for the publication of these new statutes. General Kearney appointed Charles Bent of Taos as the Governor of the territory and Francis P. Blair, Jr., as district attorney; most of the other officials were Mexicans.

CHAPTER XVII.

CONSPIRACY AND REVOLT.

HEN the American forces in Santa Fé were placed under the command of Colonel Sterling Price, of Missouri (who arrived with 1200 men and several pieces of artillery, on the 28th of September, 1846), General Kearney received instructions to proceed westward to the Pacific and occupy California. He accordingly set out on this expedition, with an inadequate force, on the 25th of September. He was met, 150 miles west of Santa Fé, with the news that Commodore Stockton and General Fremont had taken possession of California and established a territorial government over it. General Kearney, however, continued his march to the coast, and subsequently engaged in conflicts with Mexican troops, who endeavored to recover that territory from the Americans.

The troops in Santa Fé suffered much from sickness and insufficient accommodations. Santa Fé was filled with visitors, traders, mountaineers, Mexicans and Indians, and 3500 soldiers. Its population was now estimated at 14,000 people. Detachments of troops and horses were accordingly sent to points suitable for grazing, eastward and southward, and Colonel Doniphan, Oct. 26th, before marching south to subjugate Chihuahua, was ordered to make an expedition to the Navajo country to bring that powerful tribe of Indians to submission. This expedition was full of hardships and perils, but resulted in a treaty with the Navajoes, by which they promised to refrain from future wars against the people of New Mexico.

Colonel Doniphan, after his return from the Navajo country, gathered his forces to march into old Mexico, and on the 14th of December, this expedition set out upon its remarkable adventures and brilliant victories.

Colonel Price had in his command 2,000 troops in different parts of New Mexico. Unaccustomed to the restraints of a severe military discipline, they gave themselves up to gayety and dissipation. Many Mexican citizens cherished great hatred against the Americans and the new order of things, and in nightly gatherings within the thick adobe walls of their houses, they plotted the overthrow of the American government. They determined to murder all who had accepted office under the Americans and nominated among themselves Don Thomas Ortiz for Governor, and Don Diego Archuleta as commander of their forces. The American troops were scattered and demoralized by these excesses, in which they were encouraged by the watchful Mexicans. The ringing of the church bells at Santa Fé, on Christ-

RINGING THE CHURCH BELLS AT SANTA FÉ.

mas eve, was the appointed signal for the uprising all over the territory. Communication with distant places was arranged by signal fires and swift runners.

The plot was revealed by a Mexican woman to Colonel Price, those principally concerned in it were arrested, and the conspiracy apparently defeated. Governor Bent issued a pacific proclamation to the people, but their crafty leaders and the priests who were in sympathy with them, continued to plot against the government. Another outbreak was arranged for January 22d, 1847. Secret orders were issued by Jesus Tafolla, Antonio Maria Trujillo, Juan Antonio Garcia and Don Pedro Vigil, the chief conspirators and officers, to leaders at different points in New Mexico, to concentrate their forces at Santa Fé, which was to be attacked, and to exterminate the Americans and those friendly to them in distant parts of the territory. On the 14th of January the insurrection began by the murder of Governor Bent and six other territorial officials, by Mexicans and Pueblo Indians, while on their way to Taos. On the same day seven Americans were cruelly slain at Arroyo Hondo, four others at Mora and two at Rio Colorado. By the 23d of January the insurgents had increased to a thousand, and occupied heights near Cañada, a small town about fifteen miles north of Santa Fé, near the Rio Grande. Colonel Price marched against them with four mountain howitzers and three hundred and fifty dismounted troops. He attacked the rebels stationed on the heights and in some adobe houses at the foot of the hills. This engagement continued from two o'clock till after sunset, and the insurgents were routed, fleeing in the direction of Taos, with a loss of thirty-six of their number killed.

On the 29th they were encountered again at Embudo, holding the mountain slopes overhanging the road, where a narrow gorge covered by brushwood, strongly defended them from attack. Price's men again boldly assaulted their position, rapidly firing as they climbed the sides of the mountain, and put the enemy to flight with a loss of twenty killed and sixty wounded. The town of Embudo surrendered to the Americans, and they pushed on in pursuit of the rebels through snow two feet deep, which they trampled down for the passage of their artillery and supply wagons.

The insurgents took refuge in the Pueblo de Taos, which was enclosed in formidable walls. Here were two large buildings six or seven stories high, each capable of sheltering five or six hundred men. A large church situated in the north-west angle rose near the outer wall. All the buildings and the outer walls were pierced for rifles, and the walls at various points were flanked by projecting buildings.

In this castle-like town the insurgents were sheltered by the Pueblos, who joined with them in resisting the attacks of the Americans for two days. They had taken their strongest position in the church, and Colonel Price selected for attack its western wing, upon which from a battery 250 yards distant, he opened fire on the afternoon of Feb. 3d. The cold and fatigue caused the troops to withdraw

A YOUNG PUEBLO HUNTER.

till the next morning to San Fernando. But on the 4th they returned to the capture of the town. The artillery was posted again on the west flank of the church. The mounted men took position on the opposite side of the town to cut off the retreat of the insurgents toward the mountain. The rest of the command was posted three hundred yards from the northern wall with a six-pounder and two howitzers. The front and eastern flank of the church were thus exposed to a double fire from two directions, yet for two hours it seemed ineffectual on the walls of the church. The troops then charged with axes upon the western and northern walls, and also set fire to the roof. Captain Burgeoin, commanding the attack on the west, in attempting to force the front door of the building was mortally wounded while thus exposed. The effort was fruitless. The western wall was, however, pierced sufficiently by this time to hurl shells by hand within the building. The six-pounder gun, which had been pouring grape shot into the town, was now posted within sixty yards of the church and effected a large breach in the walls. This was widened by axes, and a storming party entered and took possession of the church, which was so filled with dense smoke that they were protected from the destructive fire that would otherwise have been directed against them. The insurgents now retired from the western part of the town, seeking protection in the houses and escaping also to the mountains, but pursued by mounted volunteers. Fifty-one of them were shot down.

The next morning the vanquished rebels sued for

peace, which was granted on the condition that they should deliver up Thomas, one of the murderers of Governor Bent, and chief instigators of the rebellion. One hundred and fifty insurgents were killed of the seven hundred engaged in the battle of Pueblo de Taos. Their wounded were not known by the Americans, who lost seven in killed, and forty-five wounded.

The insurrection extended over the northern and eastern parts of New Mexico. The American garrison at Las Vegas, by their presence saved that town from scenes of bloodshed. A number of grazing camps in the vicinity were attacked and the animals stolen, and several sutler and army trains were robbed. At Mora eight Americans were murdered. One hundred and fifty insurgents held this town, and Captain Hendley, of the Missouri Volunteers, marched from Las Vegas with eighty men to avenge their death. There was a slight engagement outside of the town. Then Hendley entered it and fought from house to house. He had succeeded in taking one end of the fort with several men, when he was, with his followers, shot down by its defenders. As rebel reinforcements were approaching the town, the American troops were withdrawn to Las Vegas, leaving twenty of the enemy slain, at Mora. Hendley's death was avenged by the destruction of the town on February 1st, by Captain Merwin.

The New Mexicans and Indians now turned to the attacking and robbing of grazing camps, and captured on the Mora River two hundred horses. An expedition to recover these under the command of

Major Edmundson led to a severe engagement in a deep cañon of the Canadien River. Four hundred insurgents covered the hills on each side, but the Americans fought their way through the cañon, slaying forty-one of the insurgents and re-capturing the horses. The same officer also surprised the town of Las Vallas, where several Americans had been murdered. Forty prisoners were taken and sent to Santa Fé for trial, a number of whom, attempting to escape, were killed.

Colonel Price, during the summer, received a large reinforcement of Missouri troops. His force numbered three thousand men. The progress of the war in Mexico was wholly in favor of the Americans, and the inhabitants of New Mexico finally yielded to their destiny.

Of the leaders of the revolt who met with the due reward of their treachery and crime, Montoya and Chavez were killed at Cañada and Taos, Trujillo was hung as a traitor, and Thomas Ortiz shot in a private quarrel with his guard, while imprisoned at Taos. So effectually was this rebellion crushed, that no other attempt by the New Mexicans was ever made to return to independence.

PERIOD VIII.

NEW MEXICO IN THE CIVIL WAR.

1862 TO 1868.

CHAPTER XVIII.

THE CONFEDERATE INVASION.

THE invasion of New Mexico by the troops of the Southern Confederacy occurred during the months of February, March and April, 1862. It was part of a grand campaign which had been early planned by the leaders of secession, to take possession of the immense mineral resources of the south-west and the Pacific coast, and thus supply the Southern Confederacy with wealth which should not only be the basis of their credit and give value to paper currency and bonds, but furnish the material with which to build up immense manufacturing interests to rival the mechanical industries of the Northern States.

Bordering upon the vast country of Texas was the equal area of New Mexico and Arizona, with a native population of foreign language and customs, who were not supposed since their conquest to have become Americanized enough to confirm their loyalty to the United States. The presence of Confederate forces within their borders was to be the signal of a movement for the voluntary annexation of these great territories, which would thenceforth hardly need to be held as conquered provinces, and the same army augmented by New Mexican allies, was to be led to the capture of Colorado. Utah, with the open hostility of the Mormon hierarchy to the United States, would add new strength to the movement, which in a great campaign would take in Nevada and the glittering prizes of northern and southern California. The unequalled ports of San Francisco and San Diego would make of the Southern Confederacy the proudest maritime power of the world, with an immense stretch of sea coast on the Atlantic and Pacific Oceans, and the Gulf of Mexico, to which would flow the commerce of the Orient and of every other country and shore.

It was the boldest, and most comprehensive scheme ever plotted by the leaders of the rebellion, and one of the first to be put into execution.

The meagre resources of the Confederacy allowed only an unpretentious outlay for the beginning of this grand enterprize. It was started within the borders of Texas, from which New Mexico was to be drawn first into the Confederacy. To conquer the military posts of the United States in the territory, an expedition was ordered to be fitted out, as early as September, 1861, but as late as January, 1862, it consisted only of two and a half regiments, poorly armed, thinly clad, and almost destitute of blankets. Brigadier-General H. H. Sibley was in command of this poorly-equipped brigade. Small-pox and pneumonia had reduced the ranks, the ravages of which had been greatly increased by the failure of the quartermaster's funds to obtain necessary supplies.

However, it was determined to enter New Mexico as quickly as possible, trusting largely to the capture of United States government stores, and the friendly aid of the inhabitants for the needed subsistence of the troops.

A hospital for the sick was established at Doña Aña, in Texas, and during the first week in February the troops were marched toward old Fort Thorne.

On the 7th of February, a movement was continued to a point seven miles below Fort Craig, and on February 16th, a reconnoissance in force advanced to within a mile of the fort, and offered a battle on the open plain. General Sibley's effective force did not exceed 1750 men in the field, though 2600 were on service. There were three regiments of Texas cavalry, two batteries of Texas light artillery and one battalion of another cavalry regiment, who thus confronted at Fort Craig the Federal army, aggregating 3,810 troops. These consisted of eleven companies of United States infantry, seven companies of United States cavalry, a company of Colorado volunteers, the first regiment of New Mexico volunteers under Colonel Carson, fifteen companies of Graydon's spy company, and 1,000 hastily collected and unorganized militia.

General E. R. S. Canby was in command of the

United States forces, and strenuously sought to prevent an engagement with the Texans in open field, through distrust of the ability of the militia and New Mexico volunteers to sustain any movement under the enemy's fire.

Fort Craig was situated on the west bank of the Rio Grande. Opposite to it was the termination of a rocky *mesa*, from forty to sixty feet high, extending from seven miles below the fortress. This could be ascended by a bridle path, but at only one point over a road suitable for artillery. This *mesa*, covered with malpie projecting into the valley at one point only 1,000 feet from the post, if occupied by batteries could easily command the fortification.

Another *mesa*, three miles long and two miles wide, stood above Fort Craig, rising 300 feet above the level of the valley. The river can be approached at the southern and also at the northern end of this *mesa*, affording good location for camps beyond the reach of the artillery of the Fort.

The malpie was covered with sand ridges, from which protruded beds of lava. These ridges ran parallel to the course of the river, and the ravines between them were excellent covers for the movements of troops, and secure from attack by reason of the rough intervening ground, afforded great advantages to an enemy.

General Sibley discovered by his advance on the 16th of February, that it was impossible to attack Fort Craig from the front with his light batteries, and that the Federals were unwilling to engage in open battle. He therefore determined to cross the

ON THE LINE OF BATTLE.

Rio Grande to the east bank, flank the fort and force a battle at the recrossing above it. This required the crossing of the river in full view of the Federals, camping a mile and a half from the fort and directly opposite to it, till the next day, without water, and the following day to fight a battle.

The first crossing was accomplished on the 20th of February without any interruption. A camp was made in one of the ravines in the midst of a grove of pines. During the day General Canby ordered about 2500 men to cross the river and draw the fire of the Confederates so as to ascertain their position in the ravine. The Texans deployed as skirmishers and directed a few shots against the Federals, which threw the New Mexico volunteers into confusion,* but as the night was approaching the fighting was not long continued at this point. The volunteers were withdrawn under a demonstration made by the Federal cavalry, which was repelled by the Texans on the Confederate right. The Federal artillery and cavalry crossed the river and re-entered the fort, but their infantry was stationed so as to prevent the Texans from occupying the point opposite to the fort.

A serious loss overtook the Texans in the night. Their animals being imperfectly guarded, broke loose

* Gen. Canby (U. S. A.) says in his report of the first day's operations: "Preparations for the attack were made, and skirmishers thrown forward for the purpose of drawing the fire of his (the Confederate) batteries and developing his position. This was accomplished, but one of the volunteer regiments (Pino's) was thrown into such utter confusion by a few harmless cannon shots that it was impossible to restore them to any kind of order. This and the near approach of night rendered it inexpedient to continue the attack."

and ran wildly to the river for water. More than two hundred horses and mules were captured the next morning and brought into the fort. This interfered seriously with the movements of the Confederate supply train, part of which was abandoned, while the rest was moved over the sand hills. But the wagons thus lost contained all the blankets, books, papers and camp utensils of the Fourth Texan cavalry regiment, commanded by Colonel William R. Scurry, one of the most effective portions of their little invading army.

On the morning of the 21st the Texans held the position assigned to them the night before, and General Sibley, who had been too ill to direct the preliminary movements, now assumed command in person, taking the saddle at daybreak in order to bring on a battle at the crossing without delay. The Fifth and part of the Seventh regiment of cavalry and Teel's battery were ordered to make a strong movement on the fort, while an equal force under Colonel Scurry was directed to make a careful but steady approach toward the upper ford of the Rio Grande. At eight o'clock the movement of the Texans toward the river was discovered by General Canby, who ordered Colonel Roberts, with the United States regular and the volunteer cavalry to occupy the ford.

He was followed by four pieces of McRae's battery, two twenty-four-pounder howitzers, two companies of infantry and two selected companies of volunteers, while Graydon's spy company and five hundred mounted militia were dispatched to the eastern bank of the river to threaten the Confederate flank and watch their movements.

No Federals were seen in the vicinity of the river when Pyron's battalion of 250 Texan cavalry reached its banks, and they proceeded to water their horses, which for twenty-four hours had been without water. The groves of pine and cottonwood in the Valverde bottomlands near the river concealed the movements of the opposing forces from each other.*

* It has recently been stated by Lieutenant-Colonel J. F. Chavoz, one of the officers of Colonel Carson's regiment, of the New Mexico volunteers, that there were no groves for shelter of the troops, or trees for the concealment of their movements; and he attempts to justify his assertions by the present treeless condition of the land around Valverde. The official reports of both the Federal and Confederate officers in command at the battle of Valverde are directly contradictory to this criticism. Colonel Benj. S. Roberts, commanding the Fifth New Mexico infantry, says: "On reaching the crossing at the foot of the *mesa* of the Contadero, I discovered that the Confederate forces had already reached the river and occupied the large *bosques* in the Valverde bottom, with quite heavy forces of cavalry and several guns. Major Duncan, commanding the regular cavalry in advance, promptly crossed the ford, and dismounting his force, commenced the action by skirmishing on foot, and in a spirited and sharp skirmish with the Confederates, cleared the *bosque* of their forces, enabling me to establish the batteries, to cover the crossing and to shell the enemy *from the heavy timbers* he had already seized. A careful examination of the field of battle, made by me some months ago, impressed me with the importance of seizing and holding *the thick bosque at the lower ford*, the moment I discovered the Confederate forces had reached the river. . . . . Having received information that 500 Confederate cavalry had crossed the river *above* and threatened my rear, I placed Colonel Carson's regiment in a *bosque* higher up, near the main road to Valverde," &c. — Report of Colonel Benj. S. Roberts.

Major Thos. Duncan, Third U. S. cavalry, says in his report: "I was directed by Colonel B. S. Roberts, commanding column to cross the river and to hold the *bosque* on the opposite side, so as to prevent the enemy from reaching the water. On arriving at the ford I found two companies of Colonel Valder's mounted volunteers. These, as well as my own command, were crossed over as promptly as possible; but we had no sooner arrived on the river bank than a large force of the enemy's cavalry *could*

A portion of Colonel Robert's cavalry having reached the crossing at the ford of the upper *mesa*, forded the river, and dismounting, posted their horses behind a sand ridge about eighty yards from the river and parallel to it. These troops were commanded by Major Duncan, who soon had his men under cover of the low sand hills, logs and scattering trees, where they began a lively skirmish with the Texans, whom they quickly drove out of the woods at the crossing, and Duncan planted his guns in the heavy timber where they could shell the Texans and command the ford by their fire.

The Texans endeavored to ascertain the number of troops thus holding the ground, but were repelled by the sharpshooters, and left in doubt as to the

be seen in the woods, a few hundred yards to our front. . . . . As the enemy were greatly superior in numbers, had the advantage of a *thick cover of timber*, and by this time had brought up a piece of artillery and put it into position at close range to my front and right, I saw that it would be folly to move forward and attack him; I therefore dismounted my command."

Colonel Kit Carson, in a very brief report, Feb. 26th, 1862, says "his column, supported by the gun on the right, was moving forward to *sweep the wood near the hills*, when I received the order to retreat and recross the river."

The frequent allusions to "bosque," "groves," "woods," "timber" and "trees," both pine and cottonwood, in their reports by both Colonel Canby, commanding U. S. forces, Colonel B. S. Roberts, Major Duncan and Colonel Carson, are conclusive evidence in support of the statements made by the author in these pages. They are confirmed also by General H. H. Sibley, C. S. A., commanding, who says: "The forces of the enemy were kept well concealed in the *bosque (or grove) above the fort*, and within the walls." The other Confederate officers, in reports also made at the time, speak of "woods" and "cottonwood trees" on the plain — Major C. L. Pyron, C. S. A., Feb. 27th, 1862; and Colonel Thomas Green, C. S. A., Feb. 22d, 1862: "At the command to charge, our men leaped over the sand bank, which had served as a good covering to them, and dashed over the open plain, thinly interspersed with cottonwood trees, upon the battery and infantry in front."

strength of the Federals. The Texans, however, soon began to concentrate on this point the reinforcements which were coming down from the *mesa*. Finding that it was an exceedingly important position, a vigorous fight began to secure and hold it. On this position turned the final issue of the battle. Three attempts to dislodge Roberts and Duncan were made during the forenoon. Pyron's battalion and Scurry's Fourth Regiment dismounted, for two hours fought the Federals, who effectively used their guns and howitzers, to resist their assault and silence a light gun of the Texans.

At one o'clock in the afternoon the Confederates brought up two heavier guns, under the command of Captain Teel, and severely pounded the Federal left. The artillery firing grew more fierce since the Federals soon had eight pieces in action, disabling all but five gunners at the Texan guns. The Texans brought up some howitzers which did effective service during the day, and Scurry held his right with two pieces till he was supported by another regiment of Texan cavalry.

General Sibley was obliged early in the afternoon to give the command to Colonel Green, through exhaustion from recent sickness and the constant strain of the forenoon's battle. His troops were in a strong position behind a sand ridge, which covered his guns and men from the Federal shots, and shielded them from observation.

General Canby attempted to force the Confederate left flank by a strong force of artillery, dismounted cavalry and regular infantry, with a mounted squadron of volunteers in reserve. Pivoting on the left of his line Canby's right and center were moving up to enfilade the position of the Confederates, when Lang's Fifth Texan cavalry made a charge on Duncan's Federal battalion. This attack of the lancers was bravely resisted and caused them great loss; but the Federals being brought under the fire of the Confederate guns, suffered greatly while pursuing the Texans to the second range of hills, and were forced to retreat. Carson's New Mexican troops also repelled a column of Texans, charging upon a twenty-four-pounder gun, and severely beat them. Shortly before sunset an order came to the Confederates to charge all along the line. Suddenly darting from behind the ridge, the Texans dashed with ringing shouts upon McRae's battery of six guns, which was supported by columns of infantry and cavalry, from which grape, canister and musket balls were pouring upon their foes impetuously advancing upon them.

The Texans were approaching in a circular segment half a mile long, enveloping the left, front and part of the right of the battery. Armed only with double-barrelled fowling pieces and revolvers, with daring unsurpassed, they faced the deadly hail of missiles.

General Canby ordered Plympton, with four companies of regulars and one company of Colorado volunteers, to hasten to the support of McRae's guns. The volunteers supporting this battery on the other side gave way in a panic, and rushing through Plympton's line, carried his ranks away with them

LEAVING THE LINES.

in their flight. Some of the regulars, however, rushed in upon the battery and drove the storming party back for a little distance, protecting the fugitives who were crossing the river.

Lord's squadron of cavalry now charged upon the Texans, who had regained the battery, and the cavalry flinched under the fire of the guns, which were now used most effectively upon the Federals. There was desperate fighting around the guns. The artillery men contended with revolvers, and the infantry with muskets, at close quarters, till half the Federals supporting the batteries had fallen, and they were driven from the ground by fresh troops of the Confederacy.

But Wingate's battalion now came forward on the double-quick, making the Texans recoil before their unexpected attack and sharp firing. Reinforcements, however, opportunely arrived to steady their confused ranks.

Colonel Roberts had led the Federal right too far toward the sand-hills, in pursuit of the Texans. His lines were broken, and General Canby ordered a retreat, protecting the troops from other parts of the field as they crossed the river. Roberts skillfully directed this withdrawal from the face of the enemy. The wounded were borne back from the hills; the ammunition wagons and even the arms of the fallen men were saved.

On the west bank of the river the regular troops, who had retreated from the fighting on the other side, were collected and ordered into the fort. Pino's New Mexican volunteers were in terrible disorder, and could not be rallied into line.* Only one regiment had entered into the fight across the river. A hundred men had deserted from his command and fled to the hills. The regular cavalry gathered in the stragglers and, under a flag of truce, removed the dead and wounded, and the whole command were returned to the protection of the fort.

But the Federal losses were serious. Sixty-eight had been killed, one hundred and sixty wounded and thirty-five were missing. Three prominent officers, among whom was Captain McRae, one of the most

---

* "Orders were accordingly sent to Captain Selden to fall back slowly and cover the retreat, and to the other commanders to recross the river. The movement of Selden's column, four companies of the Fifth infantry, in the immediate presence and under the fire of the enemy, was admirably executed, the command moving with deliberation, halting occasionally to allow the wounded to keep up with it, and many of the men picking up and carrying with them the arms of their dead comrades. The other columns, under the personal superintendence of Colonel Roberts, crossed over without disorder, confusion or loss.

"On the west bank of the river, the troops that had escaped from the battle were found to be much scattered, but the regular troops were easily collected and sent forward in the direction of the fort. Pino's regiment — of which only one company (Sena's) and part of another, could be induced to cross the river — was in the wildest confusion, and no efforts of their own officers, or of my staff, could restore any kind of order. More than 100 men from this regiment deserted from the field." — Report of Colonel Ed. R. S. Canby, U. S. A., commanding.

"The battle was fought almost entirely by the regular troops (trebled in number by the Confederates), with no assistance from the militia, and but little from the volunteers, who would not obey orders, or obeyed them too late to be of any service. The immediate cause of the disaster at Valverde was the refusal of one of the volunteer regiments to cross the river and support the left wing of the army. The contemporary operations of the right wing were eminently successful, but the confusion produced by the loss of the battery could not be remedied in season to retrieve the fortunes of the day. The retreat was effected in good order, and without further loss." — Reports of Colonel Ed. R. S. Canby, U. S. A. Feb. 22d, 1862 — March 1st, 1862.

brilliant and valiant in the service, had fallen while defending their guns. The Texans lost thirty-six killed and one hundred and fifty wounded.

Valverde was a complete victory for the invaders. They were strongly posted and their forces easily concentrated, but their valor was beyond question. These troops were handled with great skill, supporting with timely reinforcements those holding the hardest positions. When charging all along the line, they showed the determination and reckless disregard of death and wounds, for which Texan troops have always been famous. Some of their principal officers, like the heroic Colonel Sutton and Major Lockridge, fell within twenty paces of the batteries, to capture which they were leading their equally valiant troops. The Seventh Texas cavalry, in the front of the charging line, captured seven pieces of artillery and numerous small arms.

Two days were occupied by the Texans in burying the dead and caring for the wounded. The Federals made no efforts to renew the battle. General Sibley's men were left by the loss of their transportation with only five days' rations. It was perilous to attack the fort when thus destitute of provisions, and a council of war decided to push forward up the river as fast as possible to a point where supplies could be procured.

A march of thirty miles brought the Confederates to Socorro, where the sick and wounded found comfortable quarters, and reaching Albuquerque, they met no opposition from the United States troops, who had evacuated the town, leaving in their haste ample subsistence for the Texans in the hands of some of the inhabitants who were not unfriendly.

At Cubero, sixty miles west of Albuquerque, there was a depot of commissary and ordnance stores, including sixty muskets and 3,000 rounds of ammunition, under guard of twenty or thirty New Mexican soldiers, with a captain and surgeon in charge. Three or four sympathizers with the rebellion secured the surrender of this post, and turned over the stores to the Confederate troops.

The stores at Albuquerque were in charge of Assistant-Quartermaster Captain Herbert M. Enos. On the 1st of March, he learned that the Texan force, numbering 400 cavalry, had reached the town of Belen, thirty-five miles south of Albuquerque. All the ammunition wagons were at once started toward Santa Fé, and in the evening the rest of the stores were set on fire and the soldiers ordered to overtake the wagons. The burning provisions were rescued by the inhabitants, and some of the wagons were captured near the Sandia mountains.

The most valuable supplies were, however, at Santa Fé, and Major Pyron was dispatched thither with a sufficient force to capture the capital city. But the Federal officers had, on the 4th of March, sent forward to Fort Union a train of 120 wagons, under a strong escort, and finding Santa Fé untenable, had evacuated the city before the arrival of the Confederates.

General Sibley now determined to concentrate all his troops at Santa Fé, and make a similar movement upon Fort Union to that which had been so successful on Fort Craig. In a few days the sick and wounded were placed in comfortable quarters, at Fort Marcy, and his troops were supplied with clothing and food, his supply trains replenished, and restocked with fresh animals. A regiment of cavalry were ordered to take the Gallisteo pass, and hold it, while the rest of the troops were coming up from the south.

CHAPTER XIX.

ENGAGEMENTS AT APACHE CAÑON AND PIGEON'S RANCH—RETREAT OF THE CONFEDERATES.

THE exciting reports of the occupation of New Mexico by a Confederate army, and the defeat of so large a force of United States regular troops and volunteers at Valverde, had aroused the loyal people of Colorado to a determined resistance to the further progress of the rebel arms in the south-west and to the recapture of Santa Fé. A regiment of cavalry and one of infantry had been organized in Colorado, and placed under the command of Colonel J. M. Chivington, who set out with a force of 418 men to aid the loyal people of New Mexico to resist this invasion. These volunteer troops marched from Bernal Springs on the 26th of March, to recapture Santa Fé from the small Confederate force which was reported to hold it. They unexpectedly met Major Pyron with his Texan troops at Apache cañon, and a sharp engagement ensued.

The Colorado troops had made a march of thirty-five miles from the old Pecos Church, when at midnight they discovered the presence of Confederate pickets. The next morning, these were surprised and captured, and also two Confederate lieutenants. As the Federals moved forward into the cañon, a battery of two pieces, holding a good position in the road, opened upon them with grape and shell. Apache cañon is a gorge ten miles long, with hills from one to two thousand feet high on either side, and within close cannon-shot of each other. In some places one could not be out of the range of gun-shot in any position. The sides of the cañon were covered with low cedar and pine trees, affording good shelter to attacking parties.

The Colorado troops, finding themselves under a destructive fire from the Texan guns, deployed two companies of sixty men each as skirmishers on the mountain side to the left, and one company likewise advanced on the higher ground on the right.

The cavalry was unable to charge till the guns were silenced, and the Federal skirmishers from the steep sides of the cañon plyed them so vigorously with their musketry firing, that the Texan gunners were compelled to withdraw their pieces to a point one and a half miles within the gorge, where they took a better position, and by occupying both sides of the cañon with their own riflemen, effectively supported the guns which commanded the cañon before them.

The Federal troops advanced in the same order as before, deploying to the right and left and holding a company of cavalry under Captain Cook ready to charge as soon as the Confederates should give way.

For an hour the opposing infantry kept up a stubborn firing, when Captain Downing, commanding the Federals on the right, succeeded in partly flanking the enemy's position. As they showed signs of retreat Captain Cook made a quick charge with his cavalry, running the Texans down under the horses' feet. At the same time from the right they were sharply pressed by Downing's men, and the Texans were driven up another gorge on the left side of the main cañon, where Captains Wyncoop and Anthony received them with such vigorous volleys as to compel about seventy of the Texans to surrender. The sun had now set and the shadows were deepening in the cañon. Fearing reinforcements would overtake them in the darkness, the Federals gathered up their fallen comrades and fell back to Pigeon's ranch, where they encamped. Five were killed and fourteen wounded of the Colorado troops in this engagement. The Texans suffered much more, losing seventy-one prisoners, thirty-five killed and forty-three wounded.

On March 28th the Colorado troops marched to the old Pecos Church, where they were joined by Colonel Tappan with the rest of Colonel Slough's command, which had made a forced march of forty-five miles from Bernal Springs. These reinforcements consisted of three companies of the Fourth New Mexico volunteers, Lewis' battalion of Fifth Infantry, Ritter's battery of four guns, Claflin's battery of four small howitzers and Ford's company of the Second Colorado volunteers. The entire force, thus increased to 1312 men, was commanded by Colonel John P. Slough, of Colorado.

On the 28th these troops moved toward Apache cañon, and Major Chivington, with about 400 men, was ordered to ascend its heights and reconnoiter the Confederate force stationed at Johnson's ranch.

A march of sixteen miles over a broken country and without a road for half the distance brought them to an elevated point in sight of the ranch.

A wagon train was corralled in the vicinity of the ranch, guarded by one field-piece and two hundred men. It contained the supplies of the Confederates and consisted of eighty wagons. Perceiving the importance of its capture, Major Chivington ordered Major Wyncoop's company to pick off the gunners, while the rest of his men advanced upon the train at double quick. The gun was captured and spiked. The wagons and buildings were quickly surrounded, and seventeen prisoners captured, with thirty horses and mules.

The wagons were heavily loaded with ammunition, clothing, food and forage, and were immediately burned and their contents destroyed. The Texans offered a spirited resistance to this attack and did not yield this invaluable train to their assailants till they had lost twenty-seven men killed and sixty-three wounded. Among the latter was the Confederate chaplain, who was seriously wounded while holding a white flag in his hand.

By the loss of this train Lieutenant Scurry's Texan regiment was so crippled that they were for two days after the battle of Glorietta, which was fought a few miles distant, without food and blankets, and were obliged to fall back to Santa Fé, to obtain subsistence.

Colonel Scurry was encamped with about 1,000 men at Gallisteo on the 26th, when he was informed of the sharp engagement in Apache cañon. Called upon for reinforcements, in the afternoon, his column was formed with great promptness, and in ten minutes was on the march, and crossed the mountains in the night. The men dragged the artillery where it was too steep for the horses.

Scurry's effective force, after detaching the guard for his wagon train, which had moved in the direction of Johnson's ranch, did not exceed six hundred men, and three pieces of artillery. They formed a junction with Major Pyron's command at three o'clock in the morning.

The main column of the Federal troops was formed one mile west of Pigeon's ranch in Glorietta cañon, which was narrow and heavily wooded.

Colonel Scurry led his men into position, his infantry extending across the cañon from a fence on their left, to pine woods on their right. The cavalry was dismounted, and the artillery pushed forward toward a slightly elevated ground, and immediately opened fire upon the Federals. Pyron was on the right, Ragnet in the center and Scurry on the left of the Confederate line.

Colonel Tappan's batteries of eight guns and five howitzers were ordered up on the double-quick to within four hundred yards of the Texans, his infan-

AFTER THE SURRENDER.

try deploying to right and left on the hillsides as skirmishers. One company was retained to support the guns. For half an hour the artillery alone fought on both sides, the Texans being concealed in the woods, but exposed to the vollies of the Colorado skirmishers. The roar of battle within the comparatively narrow cañon was terrific.

On the Confederate left was a gulch running up the center of an enclosed field. The Federal infantry, under cover of this gulch, attempted to extend their line and get into the rear of Scurry's position. Perceiving this movement, Scurry led his men over the fence and across the open field for two hundred yards under fire, then dashed into the gulch with pistol in hand. There was a deadly struggle for a few minutes; then the Federals fell back, taking a new position in the rear of the gulch. Ragnet also charged his Texans down the center, followed by Major Pyron on the left. Thus their whole line was pushed forward, while their guns, one of which had been disabled by the Federals, were withdrawn from the fight.

The Colorado troops were now in line in front of Pigeon's ranch, and the Texans held the Federal position at the beginning of the engagement. Colonel Slough, with Tappan and Chapin, ascended the hill to reconnoitre for new and more favorable positions for their troops, while the fighting was being renewed below them. To prevent the capture of the Federal train of 120 wagons in their rear, which was now threatened, they decided to extend the line of skirmishers for nearly three-quarters of a mile, in a half-circle across the road on which the train was stationed. By this movement they repelled for four hours the attempts of small detachments of the enemy to ascend the hill, while the center was hotly engaged with artillery.

The Confederates now attempted to turn the Federal right. Three hundred men gathered in front of Tappan's position, which he was ordered by Colonel Slough to hold at all hazards. Scurry ordered a vigorous charge, when his column was within a few paces of Tappan's skirmish line. But it was thwarted by the gallantry of private Pierce, of the Colorado volunteers, who stepped forward and shot Major Schropshire, and captured Captain Shannon, who were leading the Texans on, just as an effective volley from the Federals checked the main body of the advancing line. Scurry now in person led his men against the Federals at the ranch, and Pyron and Ragnet opened a galling fire from their guns on the troops on the mountain side, driving them back. The Texans charged furiously on their center, and the Federals were again driven back to a ledge of rocks behind the ranch, protected by eight guns of Tappan's batteries, which hurled canister and grape shot with sad effect on the impetuous Texans, fearlessly advancing upon them.

The Confederates, elated by their success, now determined to capture this battery, but the troops supporting the guns contested, inch by inch, the ground they held. The Texan right and center doubled upon their left, to concentrate their utmost strength. Their intrepid and dauntless leaders,

Pyron and Ragnet, were everywhere inspiring their men, who pushed forward till the muzzles of their guns crossed those of the Federals among the rocks. Nothing could withstand such valor, and the Federals withdrew their guns one after another, with their wagons, under cover of the night, and yielded their last position, returning to Kolowski's ranch. The exhausted Confederates pursued their retreating foes but a short distance. They captured fifteen prisoners on the battle-field, where they remained during the night and all of the 29th to care for the wounded and bury their dead, during a temporary cessation of hostilities arranged for this purpose with the Federals.

The condition of the victorious Texans, after six hours of desperate fighting, was painful. Their wagon-train was destroyed, and they were without food or clothing, so that in a famishing condition they fell back to Santa Fé. Their losses in this gallantly-fought engagement exceeded that of the Federals. Thirty-six were killed and sixty wounded. Among their most lamented officers was Major Ragnet, who fell in the last fierce charge. The Federals lost twenty-eight killed and forty wounded.

The official reports for both armies were far short of the numbers buried in huge trenches on the battle-field—the Texans having been forced to leave many of their dead to be buried by the Federals.

This victory was disastrous to the invaders. It greatly weakened them in numbers, but it also crippled their subsequent movements, by the disabling of three of their guns, the loss of their ammunition and supplies, and the sense of the insecurity of their position, forced upon them by the presence of the Colorado troops and the loyalty to the Union cause exhibited by the New Mexicans.

Colonel Slough led his troops after their defeat back to Fort Union, unaware of the withdrawal of the Texans from Glorietta cañon to Santa Fé.

The strength and valor of the Texan troops, and the serious failure of the Colorado and New Mexico volunteers, aided by the regulars of the United States army, to crush this ragged and fruitless army of invasion, led General Canby to plan a combined movement of the forces at Fort Craig and Fort Union upon the enemy between them.

There was but little open sympathy for the Confederate cause among the people of the territory. A few were enthusiastic friends, like the Armijos at Albuquerque, native merchants of much influence, who gave their stores to subsist the Confederate soldiers, amounting to $200.000. The majority of the people were loyal to the United States. Many had enlisted in the Union service; a few had joined the Texan troops.

On consultation with his officers at Santa Fé, where they had remained in possession of the town for nearly a month, General Sibley decided to evacuate New Mexico.

To follow the Rio Grande down to Texas, a part of his force was transferred by ferry and ford to its west bank, on the 12th of April. These troops belonged to the commands of Pyron, Steel and Scurry. Colonel Greene descended the river to

Peralta to find a better ford. This was a place opposite to Los Lunas, which was on the west bank, where the remainder of the Confederates were halted awaiting their comrades.

General Canby having united the troops of Fort Union with his own, by a shorter route through a cañon after nightfall, overtook Greene's troops and in the morning turned his guns upon his camp.

The Texans, notified of their peril, at once crossed the Rio Grande to their relief. Scurry had safely made the passage with his artillery and General Sibley with his staff, when they were cut off from the rest of the force by the Federal cavalry and obliged to recross the river under a shower of rifle-balls. The whole day was spent at Peralta in artillery firing, no important movements having been made on either side. In the evening the Confederates retreated to the west bank and put the river between themselves and their pursuers.

To escape the Federals and save their artillery,* the Confederate officers proposed to take advantage of a great bend of the river to the west, and having abandoned part of the wagon train, to cross the mountainous country through cañons, which would cut off many miles of marching, and successfully elude the Federals, who would be unable to discover the direction in which they had disappeared.

This course was adopted. The movement was begun in the night. Seven days' rations were packed

* The Confederates on evacuating Santa Fé and also Albuquerque, buried at night several valuable field pieces near these towns. In 1889, those which had been thus concealed at Albuquerque were discovered, and when dug up were found to be uninjured.

on mules, the wagons abandoned, and all cumbrous baggage dispensed with. The route before them was difficult, without water or suitable roads, but no obstacle seemed to stagger the confidence of these Texans. They carried their guns up steep ascents, and dragged them into cañons with untiring patience and admirable spirit. In ten days, on seven days' rations, they reached a point on the river where supplies had been ordered to meet them.

The Rio Grande was rising rapidly, but its passage was safely accomplished to the east bank and the troops quartered in villages extending from Doña Aña to Fort Bliss in Texas.

The expedition to capture New Mexico was fruitless to the Confederacy. The territory remained loyal to the Union, and the Texans were greatly disappointed in the country and its resources. They, however, returned to Texas better clothed and equipped for service, acquired from the capture of United States stores and army supplies, and their prestige in fighting inspired confidence on other battle-fields.

PERIOD IX.

AMERICAN RULE.

1865 TO 1878.

CHAPTER XX.

NAVAJO AND APACHE WARS.

THE conquest of New Mexico by the United States, with the subsequent cession of this territory, gave rise to a long series of Indian wars. From 1849 to 1865, the government expended about $30,000.000 in the subjugation of the Indians in the territories of New Mexico and Arizona. The most fierce and hostile of these tribes belonged to the Apache nation. This people had for 300 years dwelt in this country, covering vast regions by their wanderings. They had thus occupied the most widely separated Mexican provinces. Their power had been felt in Southern Sonora, in the country north of the Gila, in New Mexico, as well as west and east of that province. They had occupied Chihuahua, held the basin of the Mapimi and Southern California, west of the Colorado river. They had roamed over Coahuila, through Texas and the south-western district of the United States, and swept over the whole of Durango, stretching their murderous raids into Zacatecas and New Leon. They originated in the northern regions, and belonged to the great Athabaskan family. Some of the tribes coming from this stock were large and powerful, and they were implacable enemies to the Pueblo peoples and also to their Spanish conquerors. The Spanish authorities had never been able to control them, nor the priests to convert them to the practice of their religious rites. Nearly all the tribes of the Athabaskan family remained Pagan, and preserved their lawless and savage instincts. Their rejection of Christianity increased the hostility of the Mexican-Spanish population against them, and led the Pueblos, through their adherence to the religion of the ruling classes in the territory, into frequent wars with their neighbors. The spirit of the Mexicans toward their hereditary enemies of the Apache tribes, was not much better than that of the savages. They invaded each other's countries, devastating corn and wheat fields, bringing back plunder of sheep and horses and cattle, and made captive women and children, who were alike by the Mexicans, the Navajoes and the other Apaches, treated and sold as slaves.

The authority of the United States was not sufficient to restrain these outbreaks. During the period from the American conquest in 1846 to 1865, for only four years were the Indians in New Mexico at peace, and then at but short intervals. In 1865 all the Indians in New Mexico and Arizona were hostile, except a few tribes on the Colorado river. From 1849 to 1851, there were two expeditions into the Navajo country; the first under the command of Colonel Washington, and the second under General Sumner. There was but little fighting in either of these invasions of the Navajo country, and the treaties or agreements between these United States officers and the chiefs were as ineffectual to secure a lasting peace as had been the compact made with Colonel Doniphan, who, in 1847, was the first American officer with command of troops to enforce upon them the authority of the United States.

In the fall of 1851 Colonel Sumner went into the Cañon de Chelly with several hundred troops, but after marching eight or ten miles, he was glad to retreat from it by night. The only good impression made on these Navajoes by these expeditions, beyond the capture of a few prisoners, was through the destruction of their corn-fields in the narrow valleys, and the pillage of their cattle and sheep and goats, which were turned over to the commissary department for the subsistence of the expedition, at a dollar each, paid to the soldiers of the command.

From 1851 to 1859, there were fewer raids made by the Navajoes, and comparative quiet in the territory, so that in many sections, considerable progress was made in opening up the mining resources of the territory. These miners were, in their scattered locations, subsequently, easy victims to savage forays.

In 1859 war broke out again with the Navajoes, and early in 1860 they attacked Fort Defiance, a post established in the previous campaign. Colonel

Miles led the forces sent to punish them. In a few months he was succeeded by Colonel Bonneville, who continued hostilities against them until Dec. 25, when a treaty was made, requiring the Indians not to pass a certain boundary, nor resist the passage of troops who should explore their country. But in the summer of 1860 General Canby was obliged to take the field against them in a long campaign with 2,000 troops, who were thus engaged through the winter, and hostilities again ceased in March, 1861. The Navajoes lost 200 warriors, and many cattle and horses and sheep, and quite disheartened they came into the post to beg for provisions, and peace. The troops were not withdrawn from the Navajo country till the following July, 1861.

The Confederate invasion under General Sibley required all the troops in the Indian country to be withdrawn, and the New Mexican ranches and settlements were exposed to the unrestrained depredations of the Apaches and Navajoes. Near Fort Stanton the farms were entirely abandoned. Many New Mexican families were murdered, and robbed of their stock. The miners were likewise forced to flee, and many were overtaken by the merciless Indian warriors.

Brigadier-General James H. Carleton relieved General Canby of the command September 18, 1862, and successfully conducted military operations in New Mexico and Arizona for the next four years.

The Apaches required his immediate attention. Kit Carson was sent to Fort Stanton with five companies of New Mexican volunteers, to punish the

NAVAJO INDIAN WITH SILVER ORNAMENTS.

Mescalleroes and Navajoes south-west of that post. By the unrelenting pursuit of these warriors, they were ordered to punish these tribes for their murderous outrages on the settlers and for breaking their treaties of peace. They were to slay the men without parleying, and capture the women and children and hold them as prisoners.

Carson's first conflict was with a band of Mescalleroes. They killed José Largo and Manueleto, two of their principal chiefs, and nine men, besides wounding several and capturing seventeen horses. The Mescalleroes soon discovered that a vigorous war was to be made on them and their chiefs, and went to Santa Fé with their agent to sue for peace. They consented to the terms required of them. They were to be removed with their families and with all who desired peace, out of the Mescallero country to Fort Sumner and the Bosque Redondo on the Pecos river, while the hostile Indians were being pursued and slain. They were promised protection and subsistence at Fort Sumner, till the whole tribe, after full submission, could be returned to their country, under strict conditions of peace.

This establishment of the Indian reservation on the Pecos, which was thus begun, caused a prolonged controversy between the interior and war departments at Washington, and finally received an investigation by a committee appointed by Congress.

There were now two parties among the Mescalleroes. The warring chiefs with their bands continued their outrages, and Colonel West, commanding the district of Arizona, closed in upon them from the west and south, co-operating with General Carleton on the east. Seven chiefs with their families and followers, numbering one hundred Mescalleroes, were transported to Bosque Redondo. They constituted a portion of the peace party, which was rapidly increasing.

Fort Craig in the Messilla valley was strengthened at the beginning of the year 1863. An expedition was sent against the Gila Apaches, who were fiercely raiding the ranches and ruining settlements at the head of the Mimbres river and the Pinos Altos. Magnus Colorado, a notoriously bad chief, was captured and brought into Fort McLeon. The next day, on pretence of escape, he was killed by the guard. Two engagements at the Pinos Altos mines resulted in the loss of forty-seven Indians, sixteen of whom, including the wife of Magnus, was wounded. The first cavalry California volunteers, who were the troops chiefly engaged in the Gila country, soon after following a trail of Apache warriors for seventy-five miles, discovered their camp. About sixty men dismounted and surrounded the camp, while the rest of the men made a charge upon it. They completely routed the Apaches, recaptured a herd of horses which they had run off from Fort West, and killed twenty-five warriors. On their return from this engagement, they were attacked by the Indians in a cañon, and again the soldiers turned the fight against them, even climbing one over the other the perpendicular walls of the cañon to dislodge their assailants, who hurled on them showers of arrows, but were again defeated with a loss of twenty-eight killed, while only one of the United States troops was slain.

By the end of February the Mescalleroes were completely subjugated in New Mexico. A hundred fled to Mexico or to join the hostile Gila Apaches; but these were vigorous fighters and afterward returned to commit depredations in the neighborhood of Fort Stanton. Four hundred Mescalleroes, including women and children, were under guard at Fort Sumner, and these were located on a reservation near at hand, while every Mescallero warrior at large was ordered to be shot.

New Mexico was believed to be like California, another El Dorado. The mines around Fort Stanton and in the region of the Mimbres river were attracting miners. Many of the California troops were men of this class and were allowed to spend a part of their time in mining, while guarding against the forays of the Apaches. Small bands of these Indians still roaming through the country, kept these mining settlements in alarm. Remarkable gold discoveries in Arizona were creating excitement, and many teamsters and other employees of the army were consequently leaving the service. The Navajoes and Apaches, however, under the excessively severe orders of General Carleton to kill without mercy these warriors, were forced to band together, and their barbarities became atrocious wherever they could dart out from their mountain fastnesses upon the settlements. The Mescallero Apaches gradually disappeared, and the attention of the department was directed specially to the Navajoes. Fort Wingate had been established and garrisoned by four companies of New Mexico volunteers in December, 1862. United States troops were stationed at Fort Defiance. The Navajoes, fearing a vigorous campaign, by a delegation of eighteen chiefs, who went to Santa Fé, sought for peace, but those who had no flocks and herds were unwilling to give any guaranties of peace, and an affair at Fort Defiance led to renewed hostilities which resulted in the entire subjugation of those of the tribe remaining in their country.

A negro, belonging to the officer in command, was shot by a Navajo, who had been exasperated by the treatment of the soldiers in shooting cattle belonging to the Navajoes. These had in a season of drought trespassed on meadow land reserved by agreement with the Indians, for the cutting of grass and the subsistence of stock belonging to the post. Satisfaction was demanded for the death of the negro. The Navajoes offered compensation in money, but refused to deliver the Indian who had killed the man, alleging that he had fled from the tribe. The military became hostile and irritated the Navajoes, who, as was their wont, when enraged, began to plunder indiscriminately, until the whole tribe became involved in these depredations.

The Navajo country is an **extensive** tract, one quarter as large as the State of Ohio. Its mountains are almost impenetrable. Its cañons are often twenty or thirty miles in length, with lofty walls, and are extremely dangerous for the passage of troops in a time of war. In their sides and crevices the ancient houses and fortifications afforded shelter for those who could attack with stones and other missiles, while they themselves were secure from injury or capture.

All the treaties hitherto made with the Navajoes had failed to keep them in peace; a change of policy, therefore, was decided upon by the United States authorities, in their treatment, which involved cruel measures of war. It was to slay all who refused to surrender at once, and be removed from their country to the distant reservation on the Pecos. The women and children when captured were to be transported thither, and their lives spared under any circumstances.

The Navajoes were allowed until the 20th of July to come in with their families to Fort Wingate. Notice was sent to the different chiefs and their followers, by scouts and friendly Navajoes, that all who remained in their country after that date would be treated as hostiles. Meanwhile Colonel Kit Carson was put in command of troops to conquer this tribe. They were mostly New Mexican volunteers with friendly Ute and Mescallero Indians employed as scouts.

The reservation at Bosque Redondo, to which the Navajoes were to be transported, was four hundred miles distant. It was nearly as large as the State of Delaware and contained from 20,000 to 30,000 acres of land, subject to irrigation from the Pecos. Though mostly a level country, it was considered a healthful location. The Mescalleroes were already cultivating the lower part of it successfully. There was abundant grass for pasturage, and the land was fertile for those who would learn farming. Other industries were to be encouraged, and the young men fitted to become carpenters, blacksmiths, tailors and shoemakers. Less than 1,000 troops could here guard the 10,000 disarmed Navajoes, who, removed from their hereditary enemies, and free from the incursions of Mexicans retaliating for depredations, would more quickly become content with the peaceful occupations which should be taught them here. Peace might thus be established in New Mexico and its great mineral resources be developed. The Navajo country was reported to be very rich in these, and the lands opened to mining and stock-raising would abundantly repay the cost of a war, by which the heritage of the Indian would become the possession of the white man.

In the summer of 1863, there was an effective force of three thousand men employed in the Indian campaign, both against the Apaches and Navajoes. The latter were pursued wherever their forays were known, but they were in small bands and not easily captured. Scouting parties were sent out in various directions; Carson's troops captured a few women and children, but the warriors usually escaped. The Utes, being more successful trailers, in eleven days during August killed thirty-three Navajoes, captured sixty-six children, thirty horses and two thousand sheep. The Navajoes, as opportunity offered, attacked stages, wagon trains, and stampeded horses and other stock. They were shot down wherever found. The Pueblo Indians having suffered from these robberies, joined in pursuit of the Navajoes.

APACHE INDIAN BOY.

Their country became a vast hunting ground. The game was free to all who could shoot and capture it. It often turned fiercely upon its pursuers. But the odds were against the Navajoes, and the captives having increased in numbers, were transported to Fort Sumner.

This still more exasperated the Navajoes. In November a band numbering sixty or seventy crossed the country and extended their ravages as far east of the Rio Grande as San Miguel county, where they captured one or two herds of sheep and drove them back to their own country. As the winter season drew nigh, many Navajo women and children were captured in a very destitute condition. Without blankets or provisions they were perishing from cold. Still the warriors were at large. A herd of 7,000 sheep belonging to one ranchman was driven by them from San Miguel county into the remote portions of their country. By an engagement with 130 Navajoes, thirty-five miles north of Fort Sumner, the troops recovered nearly 10,000 sheep. Thirty Mescalleroes, who the year before had been hostile, aided the troops. Three chiefs distinguished themselves, and one was mortally wounded in this fight. The Navajoes were partly armed with rifles. Twelve were killed.

During the year 1863 the number of Indians killed by the vigorous military operations under General Carleton was 301; 87 were wounded and 703 captured. Their depredations in only five counties of New Mexico caused the loss, as stated in official records, of sixteen citizens killed, 224 horses. 4,178 cattle. 55,040 sheep and 5,901 goats; other counties suffered equally, and the estimate for several previous years was not less. In January, 1864, the citizens of Colorado and the Ute Indians were pressing the Navajoes from the north on account of their robberies of stock in that direction. The troops were pushing hard upon the scattered bands, taking advantage of the snows and severe cold of the season to increase their distress and thus move rapidly to accomplish their subjugation. The purpose of the Navajoes to resist so powerful an enemy was broken. On the last day of February, General Carleton reported that 3,000 Navajoes had either been captured, or surrendered for removal to Bosque Redondo. For the first time in 180 years these brutal and fierce savages were acknowledging their defeat. As quickly as possible they were transferred to the reservation, but their sufferings on the journey were very great. Many died from their exposures to the cold, while those who were driving their flocks across the mountain ranges, were greatly hindered by the deep snows.

Extensive preparations were made to cultivate the land for their subsistence. Irrigating ditches were made for great distances and land ploughed for the crops. Meanwhile the commissariat department of the Government troops was severely taxed to provide for so many extra rations as were required. Those Indians who brought their stock with them were permitted to retain it, and were paid for whatever was needed to supply the captives with meat. On the 6th of March, 3,656 Navajoes and 450 Mescalleroes, were upon this reservation, forty miles square. Every man, woman and child who could handle a tool was set to ploughing, spading and hoeing the ground, to keep them from starvation during the next winter. General Carleton aroused every energy in his officers to get at least 3,000 acres under cultivation. This reservation had been warmly commended by the New Mexico legislation, but was violently opposed by Dr. Steck, the superintendent of Indian affairs representing the Interior Department at Washington. The War Department was influenced by his representations, and General Carleton contended with innumerable difficulties in the care of so many prisoners.

The indomitable spirit of the Navajoes was, however, thoroughly humbled. They came in great numbers to Fort Canby and Los Pinos, and wherever they could surrender to United States troops. Over 3,000 gathered at Canby. At one time 2,000 were transported to Bosque Redondo. They were in a pitiful plight. Their hardships brought sickness and death. One hundred and twenty-six died in two weeks, at Fort Canby. The trail of 400 miles between this place and Fort Sumner was marked by the dead bodies, or graves of hundreds of exhausted warriors and famished or frozen women and children. Ignorant of the cause of their removal, their distress cannot be even imagined. These Navajoes had been compelled to yield their country of over 2,000,000 of acres, in exchange for a narrow reservation within whose limits sickness, suffering and the pangs of starvation and death awaited them.

General Carleton urged upon the authorities at Washington and on Congress, that the Navajoes in their change from a nomadic to an agricultural life, might be guarded from imposition and their reasonable wants supplied, while they should be encouraged in their labor. In his official report he thus pleaded for them:

"The exodus of this whole people from the land of their fathers is not only an interesting but touching sight. They have fought us gallantly for years on years; they have defended their mountains and stupendous cañons with a heroism, which any people might be proud to emulate; but when at length they found it was their destiny, too, as it had been that of their brethren, tribe after tribe, away back toward the rising of the sun, to give way to the insatiable progress of our race, they threw down their arms, and as brave men, entitled to our admiration and respect, have come to us, with confidence in our magnanimity, and feeling that we are too powerful and too just a people to repay that confidence with meanness or neglect, feeling that for having sacrificed to us their beautiful country, their homes, the associations of their lives, the scenes rendered classic in their traditions, we will not dole out to them a miser's pittance in return for what they know to be a princely realm."

Private as well as public opposition had been encountered in the establishing of the reservation at Bosque. The New Mexican people had profited by the expenses of transportation of supplies for the Indians and for the troops, in the Navajo country.

There was a great amount of business incident to the Indian wars. These unscrupulous traders and contractors saw in the colonization of such a tribe as the Navajoes an end to their enormous profits out of the miseries of others. The same motives seem to have influenced agents of the Government in the settlement of the military troubles through the reservation at Pecos.

The Navajoes were disturbed at the prospect of losing their new homes. The rivalry long existing between the Interior and War Departments, as to the control of Indians in other sections of the country, was now manifesting itself here.

But the submission of the Navajoes to their hard fate still went on. In April, 2400 Navajo prisoners were removed to the Bosque reservation. In the march nearly 200 perished amid the heavy snows and inclement winds, which chilled them in their almost naked condition. In May, 800 more prisoners were sent to the reservation, where 7,000 were now under guard and generally at work for their own support.

Neither the Government nor missionary associations, though importuned by General Carleton. would send teachers to instruct these poor people. though there were more than 3,000 youth of school age gathered there. But one lay teacher ever ventured upon this needed labor, and that for but a few weeks. No provision was made for a school-house by the Government. Two store-houses for grain, a hospital and a blacksmith's shop were erected. Congress appropriated $100,000 for the support of 8,793

Apaches and Navajoes here, in 1864. The supplies received from the beginning of the reservation, amounted to $414,852.66. The Indians were industrious and generally eager to accomplish their entire support by labors in the fields. Elevated sites had been chosen for the villages, well supplied with water by irrigating ditches, along which 2,000 shade trees were planted in avenues. The location of the reservation was considered to be healthy. But both the Navajo and Apaches were much discouraged by the mortality which prevailed. There were 216 deaths in sixteen months, ending June 27th, 1865.

The idea and conduct of the reservation was again vigorously assailed by Dr. Steck, in his report to the Interior Department, and Congress ordered an investigation, which was made by an able committee during the next two years, the results of which were fatal to the continuance of the reservation.

CHAPTER XXI.

SUBJUGATION OF THE NAVAJOES AND CHIEF VICTORIA.

COLONEL KIT CARSON determined to pursue the subjugation of the Navajoes yet remaining in their country, and strike them in their deepest cañons, to which they had retreated. On the 6th of January, he had organized and ready for new operations, an expedition at Fort Canby, New Mexico, with fourteen commissioned officers, and seventy-five enlisted men, to penetrate the Cañon de Chelly, and drive the Navajoes from its ancient fortifications and cliff dwellings, where they considered themselves in an absolutely secure retreat.

The Cañon de Chelly is one of the most famous in the south-west. It was entered in 1849, by Lieutenant Simpson, on a similar expedition, who described it then as having a width of 150 to 400 feet, at the mouth, with low walls of red amorphous sandstone. These walls, three miles from the entrance, reached a stupendous altitude, with perfectly vertical faces, as smooth as if they had been chiseled by the hand of art.

He followed from the point a branch of the cañon to the left, from 150 to 200 yards wide, for half a mile, till a second branch turned to the right, of narrower width, with sides 300 feet in height, still vertical and smooth from top to bottom, except at one point, where a cave sheltered a cool spring, near which the gorge terminated with a steep impassable wall.

Returning to the primary branch, this was then followed to its head, 300 yards above the fork. Its majestic sides contained some commodious caves and small habitations, made up of over-hanging rock and artificial walls, laid in stone and mortar, the latter forming the front portion of the dwellings.

Again returning to the main cañon, it was traversed for a mile, till upon the left hand wall there was observed, fifty feet from the bottom, unapproachable except by ladders, a small pueblo ruin, in which was the circular wall of an estufa. Occasionally, where the bed of the cañon widened, would be found a peach orchard, or a field of maize, belonging to the Navajoes. The walls became more imposing in their grandeur, presenting at intervals façades, hundreds of feet in length and three or four hundred in height, and which are beautifully smooth and vertical.

"These walls looked," says Lieutenant Simpson. "as if they had been erected by the hand of art, the blocks of stone composing them not unfrequently discovering a length in the wall of hundreds of feet and a thickness of as much as ten feet, and laid with as much precision, and showing as handsome and well-pointed and regular horizontal joints as can be seen in the custom-house of the city of New York."

The cañon was explored for a distance of nine and a half miles, but no Navajo fortress was discovered in it. The sides were 500 feet high at this distance from the mouth, and the groups of Navajoes sometimes seen on their tops, appeared as specks upon the sky. The Indians at that time had no permanent habitation in the cañon. In winter they sought the mountains, where wood abounds, and in summer they lived near their cornfields and pasture grounds, feeling secure against their enemies, since their country was so unapproachable.

Colonel Carson, during the first four days of his expedition, overtook scattered bands of Navajoes, of whom he killed twelve, and captured a few women and children, and a small flock of sheep and goats. A detachment entered the cañon at the east opening and passed through it without loss, taking nineteen prisoners and killing three Indians. About 200 Navajoes also voluntarily surrendered during this expedition, the moral effect of which upon the Navajoes was far greater than the immediate results indicated.

The third year of the Navajo war opened with the

prospect of the complete removal of this tribe from their country to the restraint of the reservation, before the year should close.

Early in February, several chiefs of the Navajoes came to Santa Fé to confer with General Carleton. They were notified again that all who should refuse to deliver themselves to the military forces, and go upon the reservation with the rest of their people, would henceforth be treated as hostiles, and annihilated. It was believed that about 1,000 remained in their country, though those Navajoes who were rich in herds and flocks had been transferred to Bosque, being permitted to retain their property.

With a dignity and spirit worthy of the highest praise in the heroes of other nations, some of the chiefs still resisted the entire expatriation of their people. Faithful to the traditions of their tribe, they preferred to be hunted as fugitives in their native wilds, rather than tamely herded and fed as prisoners surrounded by the narrow limits of a reservation. None were more worthy of the respect of those waging relentless war against them than Manuelito. Having held out for three years against the troops, he with his brother was sent for in February, 1865, to come to Zuñi and confer with the five chiefs who were acting as delegates from the commanding General to warn their people. With about fifty men, women and children, who constituted half his band, Manuelito met these messengers, among whom was Herrera Grande, sent to offer to the Navajoes the last terms of peace from their conquerors.

KIT CARSON.
(From a photograph in possession of Mrs. Fremont.)

Manuelito brought in his stock. There were but fifty horses and forty sheep. Pointing to them he said, "Here is all I have in the world. See what a trifling amount. You see how poor they are. My children are eating roots. My stock is so poor it cannot travel to the Bosque now."

Herrera said to him, that if he and his band remained, they would not only lose their stock, but their lives. The women and children began to cry, foreseeing the consequences of their chief's refusal.

Manuelito was, however, sustained by his brother, who said that his stock was also too poor to travel 300 miles; and he wanted to remain for three months, till he could get them in condition for this journey. The chiefs said they were not allowed to offer any delay to the fulfillment of the terms made by the Government officers, and urged in view of the desperate condition of the people, that Manuelito should yield at once.

After moody silence, which wrought no change in his stubborn spirit, Manuelito said that he had concluded not to go. "His God and his mother lived in the west, and he would not leave them. There was a tradition that his people should never cross the Rio Grande, the Rio San Juan, or the Rio Colorado. He could not pass over three mountains, and he could not leave the Chusca mountains, his native hills. He would remain and suffer all the consequences of war and famine. He had now nothing to lose but his life, and they might come and take that whenever they pleased, but he would not move. He had never done wrong to the Americans or the Mexicans. He had never robbed, but had lived on his own resources. If he were killed, innocent blood would be shed."

Herrera the chief, then said to him, "I have done all I could for your benefit. I have given you the best advice. I now leave you, as if your grave were already made."

Herrera reported to General Carleton that all the Navajoes who remained in their country now consisted of six small bands in different parts of their widely-extended land. They numbered 480 in all, most of whom were subsisting on nuts and roots. He thought that seventy or eighty of these would probably soon surrender to the troops, and among them part of Manuelito's band.

General Carleton at once issued orders that Manuelito should be captured on some of his trading visits to Zuñi and shot down if he attempted to escape. He hoped thus to compel his band to come in and be transferred to the reservation.

Manuelito was never reported as captured, and is to-day the principal chief of the Navajoes.

In 1867, under the administration of General Grant, and the authority of Congress, an Indian Peace Commission was organized to consider the causes of war, and to present some plan for the civilization of the Indians. The ability and experience of this commission could not be questioned. It was composed of Generals W. T. Sherman, Harney, Terry and Augur; Colonels W. F. Tappan and John B. Sanborn; Senators J. B. Henderson and N. G. Taylor. In 1868, this commission reported that during fifty years, to the beginning of 1867. the United States Government spent $500,000,000 and 20,000 lives in Indian warfare. Our wars, they said, with Indians had been almost constant, and they unhesitatingly affirmed that the Government had been uniformly unjust toward the Indian.

According to the records of the Indian Department, Vincent Collyer, another United States Commissioner, declares, "That the Apache Indians were the friends of the Americans when they first knew them, and they have always desired peace with them. When placed upon reservations, in 1858–9, they were industrious, intelligent, and made rapid progress in the arts of civilization. The peaceable relations of the Apaches with the Americans continued, until the latter adopted the Mexican theory of extermination, and by acts of inhuman treachery and cruelty made them our implacable foes; and this policy resulted in a war that in ten years, from 1861 to 1870, cost $40,000,000 and 1,000 lives." In one year the Apaches killed 363 citizens and soldiers of the United States, wounded 140, and devastated a country five times as large as New England.

On the 1st of June, General Sherman and Colonel Tappan, of the Peace Commissioners appointed by President Grant, signed the treaty with the Navajoes, by which they should be returned to their country, schools should be established and schoolhouses built for every thirty children between the ages of six and sixteen years among them, their education made compulsory, the heads of families given 160 acres of land for individual ownership, seeds and agricultural implements, flocks and cattle, and $100 the first year, $25 the second and third years, with clothing and other articles needed to encourage and aid them in beginning and living a civilized and industrious life.

But few of the provisions of this treaty by the Government were ever carried out, especially those that pertained to education and civilization. The Navajoes returned with joy to the country of their ancestors and resumed their pastoral and nomadic life. Their ability and industry, especially of the women, who chiefly kept the flocks and manufactured the famous Navajo blankets, and did much of the agricultural labor, is proved by the following enumeration of their progress from year to year, as producers of the necessaries of life.

Beginning in 1868, with 15,000 sheep and 500 head of cattle, this tribe in 1873, had 10,000 horses and 200,000 sheep and goats. In 1876, they were self-supporting. In 1878, they had become a prosperous, industrious, shrewd and intelligent people, having 500,000 sheep, 20,000 horses and 1500 cattle, while they tilled 9,102 acres of land. In 1884, they cultivated 15,000 acres; they raised 220,000 bushels of corn and 21,000 bushels of wheat. They had 35,000 horses, 1,000,000 sheep, and had increased in numbers from 10,000 to 17,000 in sixteen years. In 1888, they built fifty houses and cultivated still larger areas of ground.

The Chiricahua Apaches, when the reservation at Bosque Redondo was broken up, in 1868, by the peace commissioners, were placed upon the Ojo Caliente reservation in Grant County, New Mexico. Here they lived peaceably for ten years, till 1877, under the restraints of their chief Victoria, one of the most remarkable Indian characters that ever lived in the south-west. Victoria and his people had learned agriculture on the Pecos and were content with the quiet life that was opened to them in this occupation. Excellent buildings had been erected for him and his people at Ojo Caliente, irrigating ditches had been constructed and some progress made in cultivating the soil. "Let the Government leave me here alone," said Victoria, when it was again proposed to remove his people. But his lands were coveted by the white men. The Interior Department ordered the Chiricahuas to be removed to San Carlos reservation in Arizona. The military officers in New Mexico remonstrated at this unjust and needless offence against this tribe. Victoria declared that he would never go there with his people to stay; but the orders from Washington were imperative, and the removal was accomplished under the military guard ordered to enforce it. Twice Victoria broke away from San Carlos and returned to Ojo Caliente, only to be ordered or driven back. In April, 1879, Victoria in despair and rage since all his protests to the Government were in vain, took the war-path in desperate resolve never to leave it. With thirty warriors he stole away from the Mescallero reservation near Fort Stanton, where he had for some months found refuge. He surprised and killed the guard of six or eight soldiers on the Ojo

Caliente reservation, and captured forty-five horses of the Ninth cavalry. Then he was joined by about 150 of his people on the reservation, and began the most disastrous Indian war that ever desolated southern New Mexico, Arizona and Chihuahua. It continued with short intervals long after Victoria's death, and only ended with the capture of Geronimo in 1887. Its ravages in southern New Mexico were so fatal that 140 white people were killed from the beginning of Victoria's raid to Jan. 1, 1886, in Grant, Sierra and Socorro counties alone.

Victoria was a man of nearly fifty years when he made this last stroke for vengeance on the oppressors of his people. His long, gray hair hung over a wrinkled face, and from his short, stout body his left arm hung paralyzed. Nevertheless, with two head chiefs, Loco and Nanè, his son-in-law, and 200 warriors, this intrepid and desperate old chieftain defied the power of the United States and Mexico with their highly disciplined troops and experienced generals. For eighteen months he led in scorn of all their skill and resources, a career of bloodshed and rapine, the terror of which will not soon be forgotten in that vast region. Pursued by the United States cavalry over one hundred miles of territory in New Mexico, usually attacked by superior numbers, he successfully fought with them on mountain sides, in cañons and at the fords of rivers, then dashing away into the settlements, he avenged his warriors slain, by falling upon defenseless ranchmen or wayfarers, like hawks upon their prey. When too hardly pressed, he repeatedly crossed into Chi-

huahua and the mountains of old Mexico, where he roused against himself a foe that finally vanquished him. In these engagements his warriors never numbered more than 250, or 300. Usually he was attended by about 100 braves, and the women and children, who had cast their own unhappy lot with him.

But Victoria won renown in savage warfare that few Indian warriors have attained. He attacked, while still pursued by disciplined cavalry, ranches, mining camps, wagon trains, cattle guards, Mexican soldiers and United States army veterans. Reckless of dangers thus incurred, after terrorizing mining towns and larger settlements and inflicting all possible injury, he eluded his pursuers and appeared in some new quarter. He foiled in their campaigns against him two generals of the United States army and one of the Mexican forces. Victoria captured from the military Governor of Chihuahua in one campaign, 500 horses. He killed over 200 New Mexican citizens and one hundred soldiers of the United States, and 200 citizens of the Mexican republic. At one time the American and Mexican armies combined to overwhelm him, but he escaped them. At another time Colonel Buel, with 1,000 cavalry and 300 Indian scouts, pressing him on the north, Colonel Carr with 600 cavalry on the west, and General Grierson with the Tenth United States cavalry on the east, were only able by hard fighting to drive him back into Mexico, when attempting to cross again the New Mexican boundary.

At last Victoria's band was divided. The American and Mexican forces had separated in October, 1883. The Mexicans were returning through Chihuahua. They numbered about 300 men, under Colonel Terrazas. Late in the afternoon they discovered the Apaches encamped on the shore of a small lake at the foot of three basaltic hills, named the Tres Castillos, rising several hundred feet high in the midst of a prairie. There were with him about a hundred warriors, 400 women and children and nearly 800 horses and other booty. The Mexicans dismounted and began to surround the hills. The Indians ascended toward the crests, seeking shelter in the rocks. Then at dusk firing commenced and continued during the night in the bright moonlight. The flashes of musketry, lighting up the dark rocks and shadowy forms of the warriors, the reports of guns, the whoops of the savages, the wail of wounded women and children, made a scene of desperate and deadly conflict, that nerved the old chieftain to the energy of despairing rage, as he beheld his last opportunity of revenge with the last hour of his life. At dawn Victoria was seen on the summit of the crag. For an hour a sharp firing from his warriors continued, then suddenly ceased. Their ammunition was exhausted. The sun was shining brightly on the hills where these Apaches now fell beneath the pitiless fire of the Mexicans. Darting from rock to rock, they were shot down like wild beasts. Victoria, already several times wounded, was shot through the heart at eight o'clock, and the remnant of his disheartened band immediately surrendered. Eighteen women and children shared his fate, and seventy, including the squaws and little ones, were captured. In wrath and despair this old chief defended his children and wives to the death. With a price set upon his head, a hopeless Indian, a brave and successful warrior, he fell with as much desert of renown among all the Indian heroes of the south-west, as King Phillip for centuries has received on Atlantic shores.

This wasteful and bloody war was the result of the greed of the white settler, and the corrupt policy of the United States Government.

CHAPTER XXII.

CONQUEST OF THE CHIRICAHUAS BY GEN. CROOK.

THE southern portions of New Mexico and Arizona were again filled with dread of the murderous Apache early in the year 1883. General George Crook had been recalled to the command of the United States troops in Arizona, where ten years before, he had reduced the Apaches to quiet pursuit of agriculture and self-support on their reservation. They were now greatly disturbed by the encroachments of white men in mining operations and stock raising. The Chiricahuas were in open war against Americans and Mexicans. They had broken away from the San Carlos reservation *en masse*, after killing the chief of Indian police, who had accidentally shot one of their old squaws. Seven hundred and ten members of this tribe, old and young, had thus escaped from the reservation. They were fiercely pursued to the Mexican boundary 150 miles distant, but they left devastation and death behind them, murdering every one they met on their route. In Sonora they were attacked by Mexican troops, and lost eighty-five killed and thirty captured. Only fifteen of these were men. About 650 Chiricahuas, 150 of whom were warriors, reached the Sierra Madre mountains. From a secure stronghold in this impassable range they raided on the Mexican ranches and small villages, supplying themselves with an abundance of food, and driving back to their impregnable retreats, cattle, horses, mules and captives, loaded with plunder of goods, stores, money and jewelry.

The terror of the presence of these Apaches in Chihuahua and Sonora, spread beyond the American line. The only defense for this part of New Mexico was a patrol of a few United States troops under Captain Emmet Crawford, with a body of 150 Apache scouts, extending for 200 miles along the Mexican boundary.

In March, 1883, twenty-six Chiricahuas, led by the brave young Chato (Flat Nose) eluded this patrol, and, pushing their rapid course on freshly stolen horses seventy miles a day, swept through the country to the vicinity of Silver City. With the terror of a cloud-burst of human fury they startled the settlements. Judge McComas and wife, riding with their son Charlie, six years old, a few miles from Silver City, were suddenly attacked by this band. The parents were horribly murdered and mutilated and their boy carried away captive. Their fate aroused the settlers of the southern counties to their peril. This furious band of warriors, with amazing daring, had dashed from their retreat in the Sierra Madras, ridden 800 miles into the country of their foes, passed in the vicinity of 4500 Mexican soldiers and 500 American troops, and were hovering like winged demons around one of the principal towns and most populous regions of Grant County. Reports of their presence and atrocities spread through the country by telegrams and messengers, and in every way the people were put upon their guard. But in a few days these Apaches killed twenty-five Americans and Mexicans, and were safely returned to the mountains of Mexico, glutted by horrid bloodshed and rapine.

General Crook determined to unite the American forces with the Mexican troops for the thorough subjugation of this tribe. His only course was to trail this band back to their stronghold. The questions of international law involved in this course were referred to the governments at Washington and the City of Mexico. General Crook conferred personally with the Governors of Chihuahua and Sonora, and Generals Tapele and Carbo, of the National Mexican army. Formal agreements were made that the troops of either government should be allowed to pursue these hostile Indians over the national boundaries, while they were strictly enjoined to make no permanent encampment on foreign soil and to maintain treaty stipulations.

General Crook made rigid inspection of the arms, supplies and stock prepared for this arduous campaign, which was opened May 1st by an advance toward the retreat of the Chiricahuas. The American forces consisted of 150 officers and men, with about 100 Apache scouts from the San Carlos reservation. With these General Crook started April 23, from Willcox on the Southern Pacific Railroad, followed by a pack train supplied with stores for sixty days. Five days after Captain Crawford joined the command with one hundred additional scouts from the various Apache tribes. At San Bernardino Springs the final preparations were made, and the Mexican Generals were notified that the American troops would cross the border on May 1st. The Apache scouts began their war dances, which continued from sunset to sunrise, and their medicine men, in trances, made prophecies of great success on the war path. The officers and men were lightly equipped, carrying only their arms, one blanket and forty rounds of ammunition. Rations of hard-bread, coffee and bacon, with 160 rounds of extra ammunition each were carried on pack mules. The troops belonged with their officers to the Third and Sixth United States cavalry, and the scouts were from the Chiricahua, White Mountains, Yuma Mohave and Tonto bands.

Captain John G. Bourke, of the Third cavalry, acting adjutant to General Crook, gives the following description of these remarkable scouts:

"No soldier would fail to apprehend at a glance that the Apache was the perfect, the ideal scout of the whole world. When Lieutenant Gatewood, the officer in command, gave the short, jerky order '*Ugashe,*' 'Go.' the Apaches started as if shot from a gun, and in a minute or less had covered a space of one hundred yards front. which distance rapidly widened as they advanced. They moved with no semblance of regularity; individual fancy alone governed. Here was a clump of three; not far off two more. and scattered in every point of the compass, singly or in clusters, were these indefatigable scouts. with vision as keen as a hawk's, tread as untiring and stealthy as the panther's, and ears so sensitive that nothing escapes them. An artist, possibly, would object to many of them as undersized. but in all other respects they would satisfy every requirement of anatomical criticism. Their chests were broad. deep and full; shoulders perfectly straight; limbs well-proportioned. strong and muscular. without a suggestion of undue heaviness; hands and feet small and taper. but wiry; heads well shaped. and countenances often lit up with a pleasant. good-natured expression, which would be more constant. perhaps. were it not for the savage, untamed cast imparted by the loose. disheveled, gypsy locks of raven black. held away from the face by a broad flat band of scarlet cloth.

"The moccasins are the most important articles of Apache apparel. In a fight or on a long march, they will discard all else. but under every and any circumstance will retain the moccasins.

"Their eyes were bright, clear. and bold, frequently expressive of the greatest good-humor and satisfaction.

"The two great points of superiority of the native or savage soldier over the representative of civilized discipline are his absolute knowledge of the country and his perfect ability to take care of himself at all times and under all circumstances. He finds food, and pretty good food, too, where the Caucasian would starve. He does not read the newspapers, but the great book of nature is open to his perusal, and has been drained of much knowledge which his pale-faced brother would be glad to acquire. Every track in the trail, mark in the grass, scratch on the bark of a tree, explains itself to the untutored Apache. He can tell to an hour, almost, when the man or animal making them, passed by, and, like a hound, will keep on the scent until he catches up with the object of his pursuit.

"In the presence of strangers the Apache soldier is sedate and taciturn. Seated around his little apology for a camp-fire, in the communion of his fellows, he becomes vivacious and conversational. He is obedient to authority, but will not brook the restraints which, under our notions of discipline, change men into machines. He makes an excellent sentinel, and not a single instance can be adduced of property having been stolen from or by an Apache on guard.

"Approaching the enemy his vigilance is a curious thing to witness. He avoids appearing suddenly upon the crest of a hill, knowing that his figure, projected against the sky, can at such times be discerned from a great distance. He will carefully bind around his brow a sheaf of grass, or some other foliage, and thus disguised crawl like a snake to the summit and carefully peer about, taking in with his keen black eyes the details of the country to the front, with a rapidity and thoroughness the American or European can never acquire.

"In battle he is again the antithesis of the Caucasian. The Apache has no false ideas about courage; he would prefer to skulk like the Cayote for hours, and then kill his enemy, or capture his herd, rather than, by injudicious exposure receive a wound fatal or otherwise. But he is no coward; on the contrary, he is entitled to rank among the bravest. The precautions taken for his safety prove that he is an exceptionally skillful soldier. His first duty under fire is to jump for a rock, bush or hole, from which no enemy can drive him except with loss of life or blood. The policy of Great Britain has always been to enlist a force of auxiliaries from among the countries falling under her sway.

"The government of the United States, on the contrary, has persistently ignored the really excellent material, ready at hand, which could with scarcely an effort and at no expense, be mobilized and made to serve as a frontier police."

The expedition marched down the San Bernardino valley to the Bavispe. But for a few miserable villages this valley, once cultivated and quite populous, was deserted and overgrown with thickets of bushes and brakes and cactus, the ruined hamlets showing the disastrous effects of the Apache raids. The desolation increased with every day's march into Mexico. Footprints of the Chiricahuas were often visible, but no Mexicans were seen till the towns of Bavispe and Basaraca were reached, which were in that miserable condition of poverty and squalor

A CHIRICAHUA CAMP.

which superstition, terror, idleness and ignorance produce in the Mexican people. They received the American forces with acclamations from their wretched housetops, and kindly treated the troops that had come to deliver them from their hated foes. The next camp was made at Tesorababi twenty miles from Basaraca. This was a large dilapidated ranch, with walls of stone and adobe, and large groves of oak, mesquite, sycamore and cottonwood. On the night of May 7th, the expedition marched from Tesorababi directly for the Sierra Madre, and among the foot-hills covered with grama grass and oaks, struck the recent trail of the Chiricahuas, who were driving off cattle from the plains to their mountain camp. Hundreds of stolen ponies and cattle had evidently passed over this trail, and as the ascent became steeper their carcasses freshly slain were frequently seen, and stray animals, which had escaped their captors, were found in the woods and ravines.

The country was now extremely rugged and rocky, numerous cañons were met, in which was rapidly flowing water or deep pools. Grass was abundant. Pine and oak forests covered the sides of the ridges. The trail was marked with plunder, dropped or thrown away by the Chiricahuas. Ancient ruins were often visible, relics of extinct races. The scouts became very watchful as they approached the savage foes, zealously guarding themselves completely from surprise by pickets at night. No fires were allowed at night and rarely in the day-time.

At last the troops came to a deserted stronghold

of the Chiricahuas, where they had lived for a longer time than in their usual camps. Bones and skeletons of animals were thickly strewn about the place. The troops were in the midst of the hostile country now, and used extraordinary precautions. So difficult was the ascent that the pack-mules in a few instances tumbled over the precipices and were killed. The supply-train was finally kept a day's march behind, under a guard, and the climb up to the crest of the first high ridge made all previous difficulties of the route appear trivial. At the top were seen forty abandoned Apache lodges, and the trail led down the precipitous sides of the ridge to the headwaters of the Bavispe. These were crossed, and signs of the Chiricahuas multiplied at every step. Here were their play-grounds and dancing-places, their extinct fires, and the pits where the mescal was roasted, and acorns were ground for their food. Beyond the Bavispe the trail ascended another cliff a thousand feet above the water.

On May 11th, 150 Apache scouts under Captain Crawford and Lieutenants Gatewood and Mackey, started ahead with four days' rations and 100 rounds of ammunition, leaving the white troops in camp, to picket the three high peaks above it. At about sunset, the messenger from Captain Crawford directed where the next camp should be, with supplies of wood, water and grass. Thus the expedition with the pack-trains moved on cautiously for three days, the Indian scouts a day's march in advance. Crawford sent back word that he had reached the deserted site of ninety-eight wickyups, a Chiricahua village in these mountain fastnesses, where there were signs of great droves of horses and cattle, estrays from which were constantly met with. There was abundance of cold water in the stream of the Bavispe, which was still followed in the march, and refreshing baths were taken by the troops and animals, that would otherwise have been utterly exhausted by the steep and rugged climb in the hot hours of the day, though the nights were freezing cold on those mountain ridges.

At about noon on May 15th, nine Apache scouts reported from Captain Crawford that they were close upon the Chiricahuas, and an Apache runner, who had come in less than an hour over the mountains, reported at nearly the same time, that he was fighting them, the shots even then being heard over the hills. At dark Crawford's command came into camp, reporting that they had fallen upon bands of the chiefs Bonito and Chato, killing nine, and capturing two boys, two girls and one young woman —Bonito's daughter. They had taken from the Apaches who were killed four new Winchester rifles and one Colts' revolver. Pursuing the Chiricahuas over a very rough country, it was difficult to ascertain the number slain, but they destroyed their village of thirty wickyups, and brought in forty-seven horses and mules loaded with plunder taken from the Mexicans.

The Chiricahuas were filled with consternation by this sudden attack upon their secure stronghold by American troops and Apache scouts, who had been led to their retreat by one of their own band. They began to come in and surrender by twos and threes, and then in larger bands. General Crook sent word to the chiefs, by his prisoners, who wished to induce their relatives to surrender, that they could now return or stay and fight it out. Most of them chose to come in and to return to the reservation. General Crook had moved his camp to a small park five or six miles distant from Crawford's men, in the midst of young pine trees and where water and grass were abundant. Here he received those who wished to surrender. The women began to approach the camp, with white rags waving in their hands. One of these was Chihuahua's sister, who was soon followed by Chihuahua himself, and sixteen of his band, acknowledging his defeat and saying to General Crook that his village was destroyed and all his property lost. He received permission to go out and gather his band, to bring them in and surrender. As the scattered Apaches came in from their raids among the Mexican settlements they were amazed to find themselves in the hands of the Americans, to whom they at once surrendered. Geronimo was the last to yield, but after two or three days of parleying, he was allowed to gather up every man, woman and child of his band, with whom he followed the trail of the victorious expedition returning to San Carlos.

General Crook started on the 24th of May, with 237 captives, Chiricahuas, including three chiefs, Chato, Chihuahua, Kawtermé, Loco, Bonito, Magnus, Zelè and Nané. On the 29th, Geronimo joined the troops with his people, increasing the number of captives to 384. Thus General Crook had captured and subdued till another outbreak this most ferocious and warlike tribe of all the Apaches in the southwest. No campaign was ever undertaken against the Indians in a more difficult country. Not a single life was lost in General Crook's command. Five Mexican women in wretched plight were rescued in the mountains and restored to their people, with eight others, women and children, who had been held as hostages. But the fate of Charlie McComas was never ascertained. When the first attack was made by Crawford's scouts on Chato's camp, he was said by the Indian women to have fled into the thickets, and was never again seen by them. A violent rain the following night washed away all traces of his steps, which could never be followed.

While the warriors were gathering in the camp General Crook did not disarm them. The Apache scouts fraternized with them in their dances in sign of good will, but maintained the strictest watch upon their own weapons and the actions of the captives, well understanding their cunning and stratagems in war.

The expedition, with its long line of captives, slowly traversed the rough country cut up with ravines and cañons, and then entered the plains covered with forests, and filled with game on which the whole company subsisted after June 4th, till they crossed the National boundary on June 15th, and reached the reserve camp at Silver Springs, Arizona. The Chiricahuas, at first alarmed by reports that they were all to be hung, trusted General Crook's word, and brought to San Carlos every man, woman and child of their tribe, and were located in scattered groups among the peaceful Indians on the reservation.

The remarkable success of this campaign was due to General Crook's appreciation and use of the superior qualities of Apache warriors in fighting against those whose habits and methods in war they perfectly understood. Their caution and skill and knowledge of the country secured him from the stratagems of these wily foes, and led him to the center of their stronghold. A scout, who had been captured from Chato's band, and was by his marriage connections disinclined to join his tribe on the warpath, was the most valuable instrumentality of this campaign. Pa-nayo-tishu, or "Peaches," as the soldiers called him, was remarkable in his physical qualities and grace of movement, and on his intelligence and trustworthiness depended the unerring guidance of the expedition.

General Crook was cruelly criticised and maligned for his conduct of this campaign, which ended in such a victory over this savage tribe.

On the 17th of May, 1885, Geronimo, Chihuahua, Natches and Magnus, with forty-two men and ninety-six women and children, were again upon the warpath and raiding through western New Mexico. They were overtaken by United States cavalry in the Mogollon Mountains and pressed to a short engagement. They soon scattered into smaller bands and ravaged a country seventy-five miles square. Geronimo's band with seventeen men and

"THE ROUGH COUNTRY CUT UP WITH RAVINES AND CANONS."

forty horses, were driven through the Mimbres and Cooks Mountains, to beyond the Mexican border. The main band of hostiles was followed out of the Mogollon Mountains into the Gila country, across Steins range to the Guadalupe Mountains and thence into Mexico.

Geronimo sought to arouse the Mescalleros to join him, but his emissaries were arrested on the reservation and the movement checked. General Crook, in midsummer, organized an expedition to pursue the hostiles into Mexico, but they had there broken up into small bands, and nothing more was done than to station small scouting parties along the border from the Arizona line to Lake Palomas, to watch the return of the marauders into New Mexico.

The story of the boy captive, Santiago McKin, who was for seven months in the hands of this raiding band of Chiricahuas under Natchez and Geronimo, describes the murderous wretches in their daily experiences, while their presence carried terror to all the country through which they swiftly rode, or in which they kept their camps undisturbed by the soldiers in pursuit of them.

On the 11th of September, 1885, this boy was herding stock with his brother, fifteen years old, on the Mimbres, fifteen miles from San Lorenzo. He was but eleven years of age and was playing around the rocks when he heard a rifle shot, and saw six Indians rushing toward the place where his brother had been sitting reading a book. The frightened boy attempted to run away, but was overtaken by the Apaches, who asked him how many men were in the house. Learning that there were none, they commenced to gather up the stock, and took the lad away with them, leaving his brother shot through the shoulder and his head crushed with a stone.

The Indians traveled north along the San Lorenzo, and about evening came upon a Mexican in the road, and killed him. They traveled fast. the six bucks in the advance, and the squaws with the boy and baggage keeping a little to the rear. On the 12th, two wood-choppers were found in a cañon and one of them killed, the other hiding so well in the rocks that the Indians could not find him. As they moved along the road the Apaches would fire their rifles into the houses, all of which Santiago saw were vacant. but when any killing was to be done or there appeared to be danger, the squaws were put into a safe place, but always where they could see what was going on. Very few people were found on the way. and all that were found were killed, unless they were fortunate enough to find a hiding place.

On the second day after his capture the Indians camped in a valley a day's ride north of Cactus flat. or about twenty miles from the White House. in the Mogollons, and here rested a long time. Other Indians joined the party here, and the camp was made comfortable by the squaws. The bucks would leave the camp daily, and return with new horses and quantities of provisions, ammunition and money. The evenings they would spend in lively talk of their killings and the events of the trip, or gambling. One evening after they had been at this camp some time, he saw a party of Indians gambling to decide his fate, his life being the stake against something else. Luck favored him, Santiago said, and he was permitted to live.

After one of their trips a party returned loaded down with groceries, and a wagon load of miscellaneous goods, such as peddlers carry around in their trips to the mining camps. There was a large lot of candy in the stock, which was distributed among the women and children in such a quantity that they were all made sick for a while from a surfeit of sweetness. A French peddler had been killed on the 13th. Although the Indians remained so long in this locality and small war parties were continually arriving and going out, they appear to have been completely unmolested, no alarm having been made at any time, although during the whole time troops were riding all over the mountains, and insisting that there were no Indians in the vicinity. These Apaches must have spent two or three months within twenty miles of the White House.

After leaving this camp the Indians traveled about a great deal, making long and sometimes very hurried marches, living on horse-flesh most of the time, sometimes getting a little venison, but very seldom bread or anything else. Santiago remembered seeing several burning houses, and the party to which he belonged killed in all about twenty people from the time of his capture to the surrender.

CHAPTER XXIII.

THE CAMPAIGNS OF GENERAL MILES.

GENERAL NELSON G. MILES was assigned to command of the department of Arizona, April 2nd, 1886, with instructions to carry on ceaselessly the most vigorous operations, looking to the destruction or capture of the hostile Apaches. In his department, in a territory embracing 300,000 square miles, there were 47,000 Indians. The farms, flocks and mines of southern New Mexico and Arizona were abandoned on account of the depredations of the Chiricahua Apaches. The troops were discouraged. One hundred and forty persons had been killed by the hostiles during the year. Yet there were but comparatively few on the warpath, and they were roaming over a mountain region 600 miles long and 400 miles wide.

General Miles inspired confidence in the troops and citizens, not only by his brilliant record in

Indian campaigns, but by his judicious orders for placing the command in the most perfect condition for the difficult service before them. He employed with remarkable success the new system of heliograph telegraphing, by which the movements of the small hostile bands in this desert, rugged country were quickly communicated after discovery. Stations were established on mountain peaks from five to forty miles apart. They were often at a barometric height of from 10,000 to 14,000 feet. There were fourteen stations in Arizona, and thirteen in New Mexico. The system covered in New Mexico, 313 miles in air line. Sixty-eight operators and guards were employed in both districts, and for a period of five months 200,000 words were sent. Eight words to the minute could be maintained by the operators by these sun flashes from peak to peak, which filled the wily foe with alarm.

The military operations against Geronimo and Natchez were begun with vigor. The hostiles had made simultaneous attacks at three points in central Sonora. On the 27th of April, they broke over the line into the territory of the United States, passing down the Santa Cruz valley. Fourteen persons were killed by them. The Tenth cavalry were soon in pursuit, and overtook them thirty miles south of the American line, in the Pinito Mountains. Here an engagement displayed the bravery of the troops, but the Apaches escaped, followed continuously by the Fourth cavalry, till they were overtaken and surprised again in camp, May 15th, east of Santa Cruz. They lost twenty horses and their camp utensils.

Their trail led to the east and to the north, having divided into two bands. Those who went north crossed the Southern Pacific Railroad, and passing to the west of Fort Grant in Arizona, they were intercepted and turned south, re-crossing into Mexican territory.

These Apaches rode their horses to the limit of endurance, then abandoning them, climbed the highest mountain ranges on foot, and descended into the valleys on the other side, to steal new horses and ride away from the troops, who were obliged to send their tired animals around the mountains, following them on foot, over peaks and chasms.

The band which went west were hunted like deer by the Fourth cavalry. First fleeing north they entered Arizona east of Oro Blanco. Then they were pursued through the Santa Rita, Whetstone, Santa Catatina, and Rincon Mountains. Still pressed to the south they passed through the Patagonia range, and were forced a second time into Sonora.

Captain Lawton, whose troops had been, with other commands of the Fourth cavalry, flying from point to point on the trail of the Apaches, intercepted them once and gave them no rest night or day. He now undertook with a fresh command their continuous pursuit in the extremely rugged country of northern Sonora. The Apaches were thoroughly acquainted with this country, whose rougher portions were sought as a refuge from the operations of the troops.

"The inconceivable difficulties of this campaign in northern Sonora and Chihuahua, can not be appre-

CAPTAIN LAWTON'S ATTACK.

ciated till one stands in the plateau of the Sierra Madre, on the coast side of these mountains. From where one stands, 5,000 feet above the sea level, these peaks rise 6,000 or 7,000 feet above him. Once across the divide of the Sierra Madre, this absolute height appears in all its immensity. Down, down, down upon a rocky dangerous trail, now along a narrow divide, now a narrow side-cut into the middle of a precipice hundreds of feet high; leading one's horse for hours, riding only for minutes, looking now almost vertically into a cañon whose bottom is a mile below; and from the same point, at the ridge now thousands of feet above, the descent of the Sierra Madre is made. Mountains, rugged, rocky, barren of vegetation and of life, rise around one until hemmed in on all sides, the trail opens in front a few feet only. You feel yourself a captive indeed in an unknown and forbidden land, the topography of which is the work of forces of awful, indescribable power; forces tearing everything before them, except the granite rocks themselves, and cutting the seams of these into chasms thousands of feet deep, with sides insurmountable except in the few places where nature unwillingly, sullenly permitting, the inhabitant has made burro trails. These afford a passage for the few supplies that he must obtain from his neighbors across the mountains, whenever the river swallows up the little four-acre farm that he has laboriously scraped together, between river and the rocky terrace 200 feet away. In this land of torrid heat no glaciers ever existed to smooth the mountains, to grind away the hills, to broaden the cañons and deposit soil in the resulting valleys; no frosts to disintegrate the mountains' face, and deposit the tagus at its foot, forming grassy foothills and affording numerous easy ascents to the ridge behind them, but water, rushing, tearing, digging always at the bottom of its confines, leaving the sides towering above barren and impassable.

"Sonora is deeply cut by six parallel rivers averaging twenty miles apart, between which rise the mountains in three or four parallel ranges. The cañons between these ranges empty east and west, through which run the narrow, dangerous mule trails. On the terraces above the river are a few miserable towns, or collections of windowless adobe huts, sheltering the half-naked inhabitants, who have fled from the solitary huts, near mountain springs, in terror of the Indian raids."*

In this difficult country Captain Lawton closely pursued the Apaches, through the heat of July and August. The fugitives covered great distances with fresh horses stolen from every ranch. Some of Lawton's troops were without rations for three days at a time, from the delays of pack-trains. Their shoes were soon made useless, and their cumbersome woolen clothing had to be cast off. Only underclothing could be used. The heat was so intense, that the men could not bear their hands upon the iron-work of their guns, or on the rocks, and pack-animals were exhausted after traveling five or six miles.

The Apache camp was surprised and attacked on

* Report of Lieut. E. J. Spencer, 1886.

the Yakequi river. The hostiles lost all their horses, and scattered in all directions, but their single trails were followed up till they came together again.

During these energetic operations in the south, the whole Chiricahua tribe at Fort Apache, by the joint action of the War and Interior Departments at Washington, were safely removed under military guard by railroad to Florida. General Miles learned of the weak condition of Geronimo's camp about the first of July, and sent Lieutenant Gatewood to Geronimo, to demand his surrender. It was the 24th of August before Gatewood could reach the Apache retreat, having joined Lawton's command in the pursuit. After opening negotiations through some Mexicans and two Indian scouts, he boldly rode into Geronimo's camp, and surrounded by these savages demanded their unconditional surrender as prisoners of war. Geronimo desired first to see Captain Lawton, whose persistent pursuit had commanded his admiration. The interview was granted, and he was happy, but on the first day of conference, Geronimo refused the terms of surrender. The next day the Apaches consented to deliver themselves up to General Miles, throwing themselves on his mercy, and for eleven days Lawton's command moved north, with Geronimo and Natchez and their followers riding parallel to them and frequently camping near the troops. Geronimo sent forward his brother to General Miles as a hostage, and on the evening of September 3d, General Miles arrived at Skeleton cañon, in which transpired the closing scene of the Chiricahua Apache war.

Soon after the commanding General had joined Lawton's troops, Geronimo came into camp and dismounted. Then approaching General Miles, he recounted his grievances, and declared that he had escaped from the reservation to save his life from assassination by Chato and Mickey Free, who were encouraged in their designs by one of the officials of the reservation. Having been bravely pursued by the troops, he had not enough ammunition left to make another fight. General Miles confirmed the terms of surrender already made, but said that they as prisoners of war would not be killed, but removed with all the rest of the tribe from this country once and for all time.

Geronimo replied that he would do whatever General Miles said, obey any order and bring in his camp the next morning. This was done, and Natchez, more suspicious and wild, the succeeding day came in with his followers in company with Geronimo.

General Miles immediately started to return to Fort Bowie, sixty-five miles distant, where he arrived with Geronimo, Natchez and four other Indians the same night. Captain Lawton, three days later, came to Fort Bowie with the rest of the prisoners, except three men and three squaws, who on the last night of the march escaped toward the Mescallero reservation. The prisoners were sent under a heavy guard to Bowie Station, thence by rail transported to San Antonio, Texas, and from there to Fort Marion, Florida.

Thus the Chiricahuas, the worst of all the Apache

A NEW MEXICAN FIREPLACE.

tribes, men, women and children, were not only effectually subdued by General Miles, but removed from the country, which had for many years been cursed by their presence at Fort Apache. This measure, so strongly advocated by the commanding general, was condemned by many friends of the Indians, in the east, since it included in exile not only those who had been concerned with atrocities of every kind, but the peaceable members of the tribe, and others like Chato's band, who had been lately in the service of the United States. On the other hand, those whose friends and property and peace had suffered in the Apache raids, demanded that Geronimo, Natchez, Chato and other chiefs should be delivered to the authorities of New Mexico and Arizona, for trial and punishment, on charges of murder.

General Miles, in the controversy, vigorously defended the measure for the relief of the country and the expatriation of the Chiricahuas, claiming for these Apache chiefs the same footing and treatment by the Government which had been accorded to Red Cloud, who led the Fort Fetterman massacre — Chief Joseph, Rain-in-the-Face, Spotted Eagle, Sitting Bull and others who had burned and mutilated their victims.

The arbitrary banishment of the whole Chiricahua tribe, the education of their children at industrial schools, and the improvement of their material condition, made a salutary impression on the other Apache tribes.

The final subjection of this tribe had been accomplished by the United States troops, guided by Indian scouts. They pursued the hostiles for more than 2,000 miles among the Rocky and Sierra Madre mountains. Lawton's command marched and scouted a total of 3,041 miles in their pursuit.

The Mexican officials and Governor of Sonora co-operated in the most liberal and courteous way with the United States troops, under the terms of the compact between the two governments, in subduing the common foe. The feeling of relief was universal when this scourge of three hundred years seemed to be removed forever from the land.

PERIOD X.

AMERICAN DEVELOPMENT.

1879 TO 1890.

CHAPTER XXIV.

RAILROADS AND CIVILIZATION.

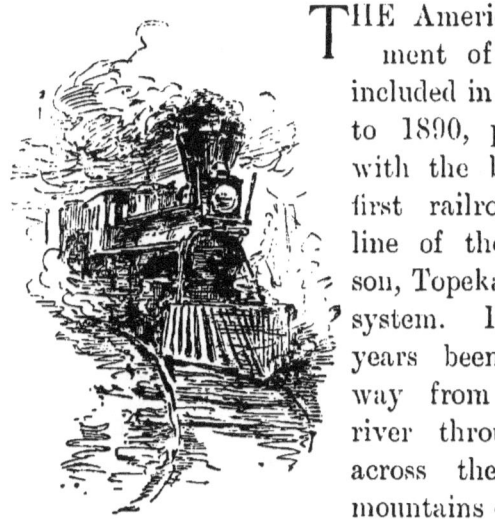

THE American development of New Mexico, included in the years 1878 to 1890, properly began with the building of its first railroad, the main line of the great Atchison, Topeka and Santa Fé system. It had for ten years been making its way from the Missouri river through Kansas, across the plains and mountains on the trail of the Santa Fé commercial wagon route, with the shores of the Pacific as its ultimate terminus.

No enterprize has had such effect on the modern history of New Mexico as the construction of this railroad, which from a single link of eighteen miles in length, in 1869, has grown to a mighty chain, with divergent parts, over 6300 miles long, under absolute control of its corporation, besides a directory of greater extent over railroads in Mexico, Arizona and California.

The distance from Atchison to Santa Fé is 1150 miles. The projectors of this road would have been satisfied with the assurance that its construction would reach that distant point within the present century. In three years it had extended eastward from Topeka to Atchison and westward to Wichita, Kansas. In 1873 it entered Colorado, and during the financial depression of three succeeding years its building was intermitted. Its ownership went into the hands of Boston people in 1875, and the same year it was pushed forward to Animas, Colorado, 531 miles from the Missouri river. A system of branch roads in Kansas was then developed, while the main line was urged on into the south-west country over the old Santa Fé trail, and in 1878 entered New Mexico, by unequalled strides in rapidity of construction. At one time 360 miles were built in 260 days in order to save its charter. On the 15th of February, 1880, the road was completed to Santa Fé, and the main line still making progress toward the south and west.

This railroad, permanently endowed with the name of the Santa Fé Route, under the energetic and sagacious administration of its President, William B. Strong, was made to traverse New Mexico by trunk line and branches a distance of 716 miles. By its Atlantic and Pacific railroad connections and California extensions it touches the Pacific. By its Mexican branch it reaches the Gulf of California at

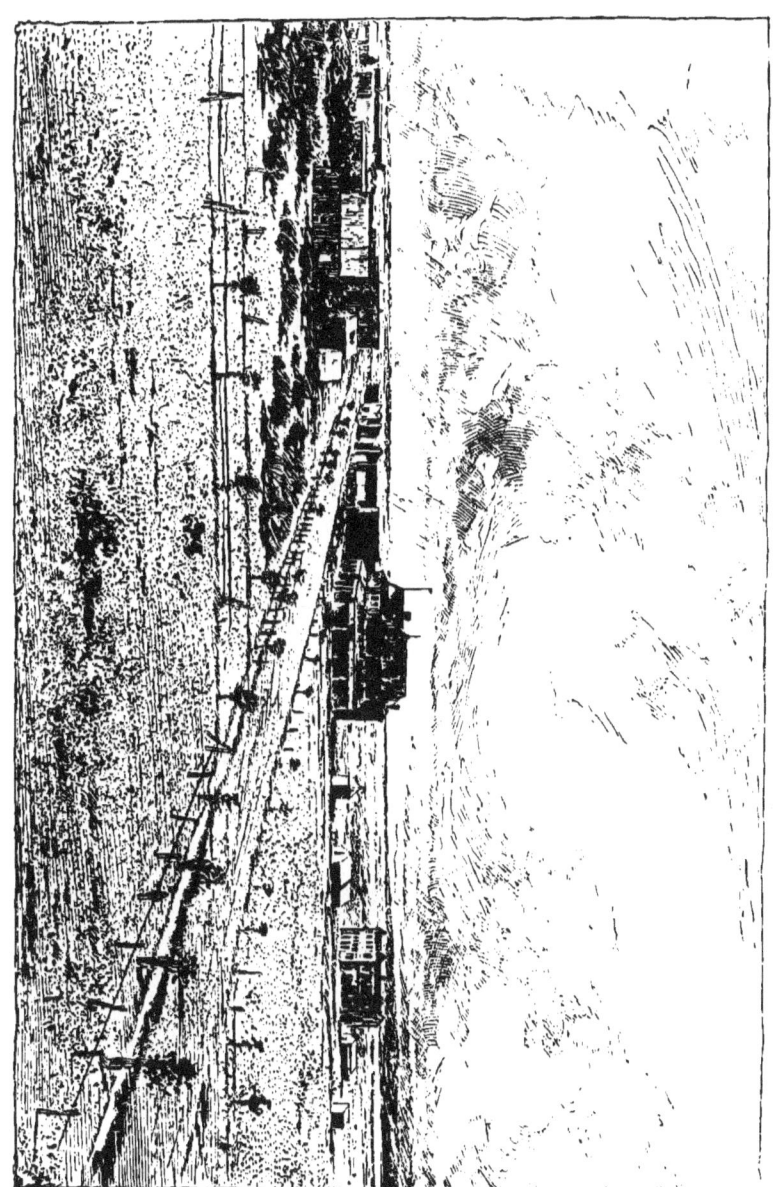

Guyamas, and over the Mexican Central it leads directly to the City of Mexico.

There are three other great railroad systems extending into and across New Mexico. On the south the Southern Pacific has 154 miles, traversing the territory in the south-west counties. On the north, the Denver and Rio Grande passes 150 miles within its borders, through mountain scenery of wonderful beauty and grandeur. The Pecos Valley Railroad connecting with the Texas Pacific system, penetrates the south-eastern portion of New Mexico, opening a short communication with the Gulf of New Mexico and with the Pacific, for the fine agricultural land along the Pecos river, and the mineral regions and vast stock ranges of Lincoln, Bernalillo and Santa Fé counties. Again, in a north and south direction runs the Denver, Texas and Fort Worth Road, extending from Trinidad north-east toward the Taos valley; and the Texas, Santa Fé and Northern Railroad is projected into the extensive Cerrillos coal fields, the San Pedro mining region and the interior counties of the territory.

The total railroad mileage of New Mexico in 1889, was 1326 miles. This was equal to one mile of railroad to 92.42 square miles of territory, and to 120.64 in the number of inhabitants. By the census of 1890, they were increased to 1400 miles, developing the immense resources of the territory with a rapidity never before equalled in its history, and giving an encouraging impetus to immigration.

CHAPTER XXV.

RELIGION AND PUBLIC EDUCATION.

FROM the first discovery, when Christianity was introduced by the Franciscan fathers, the churches, convents, institutions of charity and ecclesiastical societies have been a chief feature of the history of this territory.

In 1821, Mexico excluded all Spaniards from her borders. At this time the Spanish clergy were expelled from the Province of New Mexico, and Mexican priests succeeded to the control of religious affairs. The change was disastrous to the interests of the Church.

In 1798, the Franciscans had eighteen fathers and twenty-four missions in New Mexico. In 1805, twenty-six fathers and thirty missions maintained the religious spirit of the people. It had increased so much that when these zealous priests fled from the hatred and violence which had broken out against the corruptions and oppressions of Castilian rulers and officials, they left churches and religious services among twenty Indian pueblos and in 102 Spanish towns and rancherias. In Santa Fé, Albuquerque and Santa Cruz de la Cañada, secular priests succeeded to the places which had been filled by Franciscan friars. In the following thirty years their religious institutions were neglected. The adobe chapels and churches crumbled into unsightly ruins. The Mexican priests disappeared, and much of the property of the church was confiscated to the government, or secretly plundered through the connivance of officials.

In 1851, the most Rev. J. B. Lamy, D. D., who had been sent as the first missionary Bishop to New Mexico, under the regime of the United States, arrived in Santa Fé. There were few churches in his diocese which were not dilapidated, and he found the people both politically and religiously demoralized, through the effects of misgovernment under the Mexican Republic. Consecrated to this work as Bishop and Vicar Apostolic of New Mexico in 1850, at Cincinnati, he was destined to identify a life of undaunted courage, faith and toil for thirty years, with the progress of this south-western territory in religious and educational matters. By shipwreck in the Gulf of Mexico, sickness, hardships and perils of the overland journey, he first proved his apostolic mission. Disheartening opposition met him at the beginning of his ministry in inevitable conflicts with the authority of the Mexican Bishop of Durango, who had included New Mexico in his diocese. By a journey of 3,000 miles on horseback to Durango and return, Bishop Lamy harmonized this cause for anxiety with the prerogatives he held under his own commission. He showed great wisdom as well as zeal in the administration of the distracted diocese. Twelve times in its interest he crossed the plains from Santa Fé to Kansas City or St. Louis. In 1852, he brought back a small colony of the sisters of Loretto, two of whom perished on the journey through the wilderness. The Convent and Academy of our Lady of Light in Santa Fé, with five other convents and schools, have been the fruits of this planting amid the tears, afflictions, poverty and exile of this sisterhood.

In 1853 he appealed personally to the Pope Pius IX., at Rome, for laborers, and a company of zealous French priests and ministerial students soon returned with the Bishop across the ocean, who after a two months' journey over the plains, arrived at Santa Fé, Nov. 15, 1854. Churches in all parts of New Mexico were revived or established by their labors. The Rev. Father Eguillon, Vicar-General and parish priest of the Cathedral, one of this band, from that time became intimately associated with Bishop Lamy, and still survives him in faithful labors. He himself was sent back to France in 1859, for teachers, and in October of the same year arrived with four brothers of the Order of San Miguel, and nine priests and ecclesiastics. The present St. Michael's College at Santa Fé was then begun as a school and their first building erected in 1879. A subscription from the clergy and citizens of $5,000 was the beginning of this building, to which a still larger edifice has been added, with the increasing prosperity of the institution. It was incorporated as a College in 1883. Twenty-two Pueblo Indian youth attended this school in 1879. the first effort at systematic Indian education for these tribes; but the promised government support failed, and they returned to their villages. This beneficent effort was some years later renewed by the permanent establishment of the St. Catharine Indian school at Santa Fé. The schools of the Christian brothers in Santa Fé, Mora, Taos and Bernalillo have generally prospered, but only two now survive the changes of population and the uncertain growth of towns in a great territory like New Mexico.

Bishop Lamy enlisted the Sisters of Charity in Cincinnati in their work of founding a hospital and sanitarium which has become famous in Santa Fé, and with its extensive buildings has done immeasurable good to the sick and afflicted, and to the orphans, many hundreds of whom these sisters have nurtured and educated.

On the 15th of August, 1867, this indefatigable prelate introduced the order of the Jesuits into his diocese. Their efforts resulted in a great revival of Roman Catholic zeal and devotion throughout the territory. They founded a school at Albuquerque, and a college at Las Vegas, in 1877. They also instituted the printing of religious and educational literature for the propagation of their ideas and doctrines in the territory. Their influence and power was manifest in social movements, the control of the priesthood and the final resignation of the Archbishop Lamy and the appointment of his able successor, Archbishop Salpointe, whose installation occurred August 26th, 1885.

An enduring monument to the sacrifices and toils of Archbishop Lamy and of his priests and people, is the beautiful and massive cathedral at Santa Fé. Its corner-stone was laid July 14th, 1869. The main building, with two imposing towers, has been erected, at a cost of $130,000, and another generation will probably witness the completion of its stately and elegant design. Archbishop Lamy died in 1888, honored and loved by the people of New Mexico, of his own and other religious faiths. The influence of his life and labor in the south-west will never cease. His heroic spirit and toil were cast in with the Church in her time of depression and need, but are now her honored heritage in the history of this country which is indelibly impressed with her devotion and sacrifices. This church, when he retired from the Episcopate, consisted of one archbishop, two vicar-generals, fifty-six priests and six convents, four colleges, one hospital, three Indian schools, seven orphan asylums, three orders of sisters, one brotherhood and other ecclesiastical societies; and embraced, also, a Roman Catholic population of over 100,000, including the Pueblo Indians.

The opposition of the Jesuits to all kinds of legislation for common school education became very open, and aroused great suspicion and distrust of

VICTORIA, THE APACHE.

their society in New Mexico. They had been expelled from Mexico as a political rather than a religious society, which was hostile to the liberties of the people. The same political jealousy was also stirred against them in New Mexico, and effectually hindered an increase of their power in politics. On the 18th of January, 1878, an act to incorporate the society of the Jesuit Fathers of New Mexico was passed by the legislative assembly by a two-thirds vote over the veto of Governor S. B. Axtell, who had strenuously opposed their designs and shown the injuries which their influence would inflict upon the future welfare of the territory.

This unconstitutional act, however, was very soon annulled by the Congress of the United States. The bill as passed by the Legislature of New Mexico gave unlimited power to acquire, hold and transfer, all kinds of property, both real and personal, and the exemption from taxation of all the effects and property of said corporation. It was plainly in violation of the Revised Statutes of the United States, which declares "The legislative assemblies of the several territories shall not grant private charters or especial privileges."

The result of this effort at undue control of influence in the territory was to put an effectual check to the rapid encroachments of the Jesuit party upon the rights and privileges of American citizenship.

The Protestant Christian missionaries entered New Mexico soon after the American Conquest, but found it at first impossible to get a permanent foothold. A Baptist missionary, who was on the ground as early as 1849, began a mission school at Santa Fé, and erected the first Protestant Church in New Mexico at the capital. The Methodists also maintained a missionary there in 1850, who remained two years. The Baptist mission and church property was purchased by the Presbyterians in 1866, and their present flourishing mission school for Mexican girls was established upon this foundation. The old adobe church erected by the Baptists was demolished in 1881, and a tasteful brick edifice built upon its site by the Presbyterians.

Both the Methodist and Presbyterian denominations have planted and maintained with great perseverance, missions among the native population in many other localities. Their outlay of benevolent funds has been large. The Presbyterians had in 1888, three boarding schools for girls, and over twenty free common schools in the territory, with active churches in nearly all the important towns The Methodists have successfully maintained many native churches and several for the American population, and have begun a college at Albuquerque and an industrial college at San Juan, being one of the most progressive of the religious societies in the south-west.

The Episcopal missions were later upon the ground. The first Episcopal service was held in 1863, and a missionary diocese established in 1874, with the Right Rev. William Forbes Adams, D. D., as the first Bishop. Out of the missionary labors of this church for a number of years several churches were consecrated at important points in the territory by his successor, the lamented bishop, George K. Dunlop, D. D., whose effective service in this field ended with his death in 1887. He was succeeded by the Right Rev. J. M. Kendrick, D. D., who still holds the diocese of New Mexico and Arizona in his charge.

The Congregationalists have had the most flourishing educational institutions among the Protestants in this territory. They have academies at Las Vegas, Albuquerque and Santa Fé; ten or twelve free common schools for Mexicans, a college with its Indian Department, the Ramona school, at Santa Fé, and four or five churches in the larger towns.

The University of New Mexico, located at Santa Fé, was incorporated under their auspices, May 11th, 1881, and for seven years well occupied the ground for higher education. Its first preparatory school was opened September 11th, 1881, and the cornerstone of Whitin Hall, its first permanent building, was laid October 21st, 1882, "in the name of Christian education, in behalf of intellectual progress and improvement, in the hope and trust that it would be a stronghold of intelligence and morality, and a bulwark against ignorance and vice." Whitin Hall was completed in October, 1887, and was mainly the gift to New Mexico education of the family of John C. Whitin, Esq., of Massachusetts. The Ramona Indian Girl's school was opened April 1st, 1885, at first for the youth of the neighboring Pueblo villages, and when these were transferred to the St. Catharine school in Santa Fé, subsequently established by the Roman Catholics, the Ramona school was devoted to the education of Apache Indian youth. Under the same management of the University of New Mexico at Santa Fé, the Government Indian school in the same city had its origin, foundation and first endowment of $25,000 by Congress, with a gift of 100 acres of land from the citizens of Santa Fé. The last annual appropriation for its maintenance and enlargement was nearly three times the original appropriation.

PUBLIC EDUCATION.

Though California, like New Mexico, was a conquered Mexican province and an unpromising educational field, in twenty-five years she was one of the foremost States of the Union, in her schools and system of public education. For ten years the influences of a new American population have been likewise felt in New Mexico. In 1880, this was the most illiterate part of the Union. The Mexican and Indian population were increasing in ignorance and were mostly unable to read or write. Not ten per cent. of the youth of the whole territory were reached by any kind of school. The compulsory school law on the Statutes was wholly ineffective, and skillfully managed to collect money from property and license taxes for the benefit of unknown persons or institutions. One-fourth the territorial taxes went into the hands of irresponsible commissioners, who were not obliged to account for receipts, and never reported schools, scholars, pupils of school

APACHE BOYS, TWO WEEKS AT SCHOOL.

age, school buildings nor teachers. There were no school statistics known to territorial officials. Persons were engaged for teachers who could not read an American newspaper, others were assigned duty as sheep herders.

The legislature of 1882 passed a law by which school districts could be organized by the act of one-fifth of the voters in that district, and one-quarter of their taxes used for the support of a school. In the railroad towns two or three schools were organized and a report was given of twenty schools in Taos, as the result of this timid step forward to enjoy the most valued privilege of American citizens, the education of the common school. In a population of 120,000, there were 52,994 who could not read. It had been profitable to a few persons to keep the light of American civilization from penetrating the barrier of dense ignorance.

But a few persistent individuals had also begun the agitation of the subject of public education and never ceased to discuss it in the press, in the market place and in the legislature. A few good denominational schools, and the example of American youth coming from these schools to take a forward place in business and in society had a good effect. The native New Mexican was not slow to appreciate the increasing demand for knowledge in the conduct of ordinary business, and their religious schools were crowded by the youth of those native families whose parents could send them. Their representatives demanded in the legislature better and more numerous public schools. The school laws were improved at every session. Permanent school buildings were erected in every ambitious town, and native Mexicans were stimulated to seek for their children the same advantages which the United States Government provided for Pueblo and Apache Indian tribes, by establishing schools at the agencies and in the pueblos, and three central industrial training schools for them at Santa Fé and Albuquerque.

The total enrollment of public schools in New Mexico has reached in 1889, 14,600; the average daily attendance is 12,680. A systematic report from each county superintendent now gives reliable data on which to base the estimates of educational growth in the territory. There are public school buildings valued at about $500,000, and the property of private institutions is valued at $263,000.

By the legislature of 1888, there were established a State University at Albuquerque, a school of mines at Socorro and an agricultural school at Las Cruces, each supported by a special tax on all the assessable property of the territory. These institutions have been organized sufficiently to erect buildings and begin the preparatory educational work which will become invaluable to New Mexico as a State, whose acreage and natural resources are so vast, and whose remarkable variety of soil, climate and production will maintain the industries of millions of people.

CHAPTER XXVI.

IRRIGATION IN NEW MEXICO.

THE most remarkable feature of the American development of New Mexico was the result of utilizing the primitive ideas of its first inhabitants in their methods of agriculture in degrees characteristic of American energy and enterprise. Comprehensive systems of irrigation of great magnitude began to be devised about 1885. Legislation favorable to the forming of land and ditch companies was effected in 1886. The possession of water rights with large extents of lands through the purchase of grants and the entry of lands under the homestead and desert land acts, made the success of these companies formed on a large financial scale probable and extremely profitable. A few corporations were organized in 1887 and 1888, and in the two succeeding years about fifty organizations, with a nominal capital of $12,000,000, were incorporated for the development of the lands hitherto given up to grazing. The operations already begun by these companies brought into cultivation or into conditions suitable for it during 1890, a million acres of fruitful soil. The largest of these companies are located in the Rio Grande and Pecos valleys, and on the Maxwell land grant. The country between Raton and Springer has been changed from one of the finest pasture lands in the world, to a great wheat and fruit bearing region.

The Rio Grande valley from Wallace to the Jornada del Muerto and below the Jornada to the Texas line, has been largely devoted to the extension of canal systems, which utilize the higher benches of this great central basin. The Messilla valley has become famous for its great vineyards and orchards of peaches, pears, plums and apples, and for its rich alfalfa meadows. New towns are growing in the centers of these now fertile districts.

The most surprising development by irrigation of an uninhabited wilderness, has been well advanced in the lower Pecos valley. Its works and improvements on a grand scale of development, if more particularly described, will illustrate the probable outlays and returns in similar enterprizes in other parts of the territory.

The undertakings of the Pecos Valley Irrigation and Investment Company have been conceived and carried out by men of broad ideas, undaunted courage and great financial strength.

The remarkable river and valley of the Pecos may be regarded as divided into three distinct sections in its course through the eastern portion of New Mexico. The first division extends from the Delaware to the cañon, eight miles above Eddy, a distance of forty-two miles. It is bounded on the west by the sturdy range of the Guadalupe Mountains, and is fully sixty miles wide. Here is unquestionably what will become the richest agricultural region in the territory. It is a plain, covered with a soil of fine dark chocolate loam, from sixteen to twenty feet deep. From the Delaware to the Black river, both flowing from the west, and the latter a clear, powerful stream, the soil has more of an adobe character with considerable gypsum. It is now covered with low mesquite and greasewood, but constitutes an unbroken plain on the west of the river, as susceptible to irrigation as a garden.

On the east side of the Pecos, the ground rises by a few low hills to a similar plain, with soil of the finest quality, formed by rincons and lagoons of the ancient river bed. The country ascends from the Black river to the cañon, by a gradual slope, with a lighter and more pliable sandy soil. The cañon, formed by the ancient bluffs of the Pecos coming together, extends to Seven Rivers.

Here begins the second agricultural section of the Pecos valley, of a quite different and remarkable quality. This stretches from Seven Rivers to Roswell, still skirting on both sides of the Pecos river and broadening out into a plain, containing on the east side 50,000 acres of agricultural land. It is a country of springs and marshes, in the midst of wide, level and fertile plains. These powerful springs or lagoons, at short distances across the plain from west to east below Roswell, form deep streams with rapid flow, from thirty to sixty feet wide, constituting the Hondo river, a branch of the Pecos. This is the water supply of the upper system of canals of the Pecos Valley Corporation, which are here entirely independent of the flow of the Pecos river. The difficulties encountered in the construction of these canals have been less than in the lower system, but the land bordering upon them has been as eagerly located for cultivation and investment.

The third section of the Pecos valley extends from Fort Sumner to the mountain region north-east of Santa Fé. It is a country ill suited to agriculture by irrigation.

The Pecos river is at the bottom of this great irrigation enterprise. It runs within the limits of New Mexico fully 400 miles, but, till it reaches Roswell, its flow and volume are uncertain. From Roswell to the Delaware for sixty-five miles it is fed by springs with a natural artesian flow issuing from its deep banks or from the bed of the stream. Below Roswell the strong currents of the Hondo give a constant volume to the swift and deepened current. But for its steep, high banks, the Pecos would flood the great plain. It is in fact a series of rapids from two and one half to three feet deep, and from seventy to one hundred feet wide. This is entirely the product of springs in a dry season.

HEAD-GATE OF IRRIGATING CANAL IN THE PECOS VALLEY.

Increased by the usual mountain supply from snow and rains, the flow is ample for the canals, and the filling and replenishing of the great storage reservoirs of the system.

This portion of the Pecos valley borders on the staked plains of Texas. It has been a paradise for cattle men. Their herds by tens of thousands have fed on its rich grasses since 1870. Before that it was the domain of the Apache, and a favorite hunting ground for buffalo, antelope, deer and smaller game, that have had their range and habitation in unnumbered thousands on these plains.

Under the laws of New Mexico, Mr. C. B. Eddy, long familiar with the value of this region for agriculture, first acquired the right to use the waters of the Pecos for irrigation, and constructed in 1884 a system of ditches which should irrigate 25,000 acres on the east bank of the Pecos, above the Black river. This has been enlarged to one that will raise the Pecos valley to prominence as the most fertile region of the south-west.

As one drives up the valley toward the town of Eddy, the extent of these great hydraulic works awakens admiration. A line of reddish hue, rising above the horizon, winding in a serpentine course over the plain, first attracts the eye. It is a level rampart from twelve to fifteen feet high, constituting a perfect carriage road. The canal bed is sunk twelve feet below the ground along this huge dike. The main ditch is forty-five feet wide at the bottom, and seventy feet at the top. This continues four and a half miles from the head gates leading by a cut 500 feet long through a hill of solid limestone, to the reservoir formed by the dam, constructed of the rock thus excavated on the side of the Pecos river. From this dam the water flows back into a natural depression surrounded by grass-covered hills. The lake thus formed is six and a half miles long, and three-quarters of a mile wide, bounded by irregularly curving shores, and leaving islands to break its surface. The capacity of this reservoir is 1,000,000,000 cubic feet. When completed and filled, it will have a pressure of thirteen feet head above the water in the canal and twenty feet above its standard grade. The dam of the river requires a crest ten feet wide with a base of 115 feet in width. It stretches 1040 feet to the opposite bluff, and its crest is forty feet high from the water's edge. Its core is of limestone, rising from the bed-rock of the river, and covered with earth at a slope of two to one. Its permanency is also secured by the use of a natural draw, or outlet, five feet below the top of the dam, which will release the surplus waters of a flood. The cut which forms the entrance gate to the canal is thirty feet wide, twenty-five feet high, and 500 feet in length. This hill of solid rock can never be washed away.

The main canal diverges into two forks where the crossing of the river is made. To preserve the grade of the extension westward, a huge earthwork carries the ditch securely to the river's edge. This terreplein is an embankment 1800 feet long. Through it runs the channel, twenty-five feet wide at the bottom with banks on each side eighty feet wide. It is 169 feet wide and rises sixty feet from the water's level. It is joined by an imposing flume 475 feet long, twenty-five feet wide and eight feet high, resting on trestle work thirty-eight feet clear above the bottom of the river. Its spans are from sixteen to twenty feet apart and it is connected with another terreplein 300 feet long on the west side of the river, of the same dimensions as the other, which continues the canal to the natural bank of the river. These terrepleins were constructed of 130,000 cubic yards of packed earth from which every root and stone was zealously excluded. Timber and lumber for the flume were transported from Eastern Texas 600 miles by railroad, and over 100 miles by wagon. The excavation of the ditches occupied 1,000 laborers and 300 teams for nine months. The storage reservoir would alone supply the capacity of the canal for nineteen days.

The main canals will carry seven feet of water. The main laterals, constructed at the company's expense, will exceed 100 miles in length, with water three or four feet deep, giving draught for canal and small boats and easy transportation back and forth over these plains. The smaller ditches made by property owners, will intersect the country three times as long as the company's laterals. These will be planted by thousands of trees along these canals and over these plains; orchards and groves will soon give beauty, attract rain and thus double the fertility of the country. The northern and southern systems will make irrigable 200,000 acres of rich land in New Mexico, besides an equal amount which will be fertilized by an extension of the main ditches into Texas.

The splendid possibilities of this region thus reclaimed for habitation are demonstrated by two or three years of cultivation. Grain, fruits and vegetables common in Western and Southern States, have grown in perfection. Alfalfa, millet and sorghum have made surprising yields; fruit-trees in this equable and healthful climate have grown rapidly and borne quickly; and the most flourishing towns in New Mexico, like Eddy and Roswell, have sprung up as by magic, with modern improvements and buildings and railroad facilities in the midst of this favored region, with unquestionable financial backing. This has been furnished chiefly from Colorado and New York through the efforts of Messrs. J. J. Hagerman and Charles B. Eddy, the chief promoters of this great undertaking. These enterprises possess an unequalled stretch of fertile country to induce the immigration and settlement of progressive people, whose season of work and industry in that mild climate need never end, and whose prosperity will be identified with a wonderful progress.

CHAPTER XXVII.

CLAIMS TO STATEHOOD.

THE population of New Mexico, by the census of 1890, is 153,206, including 8,408 Pueblo Indians and 1,461 United States troops. This indicates a gain since 1880, of 32,594. It has been greatly changed in its character within ten years, but it contains quite as large a proportion of loyal citizens who spent their blood and treasure in defending the flag of the Union, as any other territory that has been lately admitted to the Union. These people have repeatedly fought against savage Indians at their own expense when the Government could not protect their homes. Yet they have been submissive to the laws of the United States for forty-three years without enjoying many advantages of citizenship.

The new population have induced the outlay of a large amount of capital in the industries of mining and cattle raising, and the modern improvements of towns, and the development of agricultural lands by irrigation corporations.

There is in New Mexico in 1890 a total taxable property of nearly $50,000,000.

Of the 77,568,640 square acres of territory in New Mexico more than one-fourth, or about 20,000,000 acres, can be made available for agriculture with the great advantage derived from irrigation. Its productive capacity, therefore, which can be increased by springs and artesian wells, is equal to that of Illinois. In 1888 New Mexico had under cultivation with wheat, corn and oats, 151,402 acres, the value of these crops being $1,973,190. During the same year Colorado had 229,208 acres under the same cultivation, with crops valued at $3,253,230.

If we deduct the total acres included in land grants, Indian and military reservations and government land entries already made by the people, which all amount to 21,822,401 acres, there is still available area of 56,551,962 acres. It is estimated that of this number, 14,125,203 acres are covered by mountains, and 3,610,793 acres are arid and barren lands. Still there remains in New Mexico 38,815,966 acres of irrigable, agricultural and grazing lands open for entry or settlement.

The agricultural lands are comprised in five sections. These include the valleys of the Rio Grande, Pecos, Canadien, Gila and Colorado and San Juan rivers. The Rio Grande has a fall of 2200 feet in a distance of 356 miles within New Mexico, and its waters can be distributed over its great valley in the heart of New Mexico, with a climate and soil remarkably adapted to the production of grains and fruit.

The country between the Taos valley and Joya is broken and mountainous and heavily wooded. Several streams with narrow bodies of fertile land enter the Rio Grande from east to west. Southward to the Puerto river the tillable land is from one to ten miles wide. At Santo Domingo it is very narrow, then widens to six or seven miles below San Felipe. Thus it contracts and expands as if a series of bays or lakes had gradually been emptied of their waters through connecting channels, and left the fine agricultural bottom lands, like those of the famed Messilla valley around Las Cruces, for the use of the numerous population that shall in the future as in the past find their homes and industrial occupation within its borders.

The upper Pecos valley, narrow above old Fort Sumner, has strips of very fertile land, but below that point from the northern extremity of the Guadalupe Mountains to the mouth of the Delaware Creek, the valley of the Pecos, except where it narrows near Seven Rivers, is one unbroken, continuous, level and fertile bottom, through which the canals of the great irrigation company extend, bringing within the possibilities of cultivation 200,000 acres. The Canadien river flows for two hundred miles through an agricultural district, watered also by its tributaries, the Little Cimmaron, Vemejo, Rayado, Ocate and Mora rivers. These streams are bordered with lands from one to six miles wide, and the main river falls gradually from an altitude of 5,000 to 3,000 feet.

The Gila and Colorado rivers, with their branches, water a belt of country from fifty to one hundred miles wide, along the whole western border of New Mexico. The San Juan river country cannot be excelled in climate or fertility of soil for the production of vegetables, grapes and other fruits. The river has three large tributaries, and the Chama valley in the great county of Rio Arriba having eight streams flowing into it with their rich lands on either side, constitutes one of the most productive portions of New Mexico.

The temperature and rainfall varies in this great territory with the elevation and latitude. In the central and moderately-elevated county of San Miguel the mean annual temperature for thirteen years has been 50.6 degrees; the coldest month, January, averaging 31 degrees above zero, and the warmest, July, 79.7 degrees. In the same county, the rainfall annually for three years, from 1886 to 1889, was 21.19 inches. Of this average, 13.85 inches fell yearly during the months of June, July, August and September of the regular rainy season.

A skilled fruit grower[*] wrote on fruit culture in New Mexico in 1889: "The abundant fruit crops of 1888 has done more to demonstrate the capabilities of the soil and climate of New Mexico for fruit production than all the years which preceded it; not only have local towns been glutted with tons of luscious fruit, but the railroads have carried our super-

[*] Arthur Boyle, Esq., of Santa Fé.

STATE CAPITOL, SANTA FÉ.

abundant harvest to distant markets. New Mexico has this year made another step in advance; she has entered the arena to compete with California as a fruit producing country, and nothing can stop her marching with giant strides to the front. All the fruit has been superior of its kind. The color, form, odor and flavor could not be surpassed, and left nothing to be desired. Strawberries, raspberries, cherries, apricots, peaches, plums, pears and apples, all in their season have been sold in open market, in competition with California and other fruit, and have invariably fetched as high or higher price than anything offered.

"But there is urgent need for more orchards. Increased product will make increased demand; shipments by the train-load will realize more profit to the grower than shipments by the car. There is not any where a better opening for the employment of capital and skilled labor than in the planting of fruit-trees in New Mexico. Fruit raising here is one of the most profitable and promising industries in the whole west."

A farmer of thirty years' experience in Iowa* thus contrasts with it his success in farming and stock raising in New Mexico: "I became disgusted with the cold winters and the stock business in Iowa, and decided to come to New Mexico. Possessing myself of improved agricultural implements in 1878, I ploughed deep about 450 acres of land, sowing about 350 acres in alfalfa, 50 acres in oats, and planted 50 acres in corn. The result was a good crop of

* Mr. M. E. Dame, of San Miguel County.

each without irrigation. I planted the corn thick, and found it made more feed, and a much better quality than the same acreage in Iowa. The corn has more foliage, is not so rank, has more ears, owing to the climatic condition; it cures better, and has more saccharine matter. The soil seems to be loaded with plant food. The winters in this part of the territory are about right for profitable feeding. My experience shows that only one-third the corn and fodder is required to fatten cattle here that is necessary in Iowa, for the reason that the feed is better, the climate is dry, clear and bracing, with almost constant sunshine. In fattening 120 head of steers last winter, I do not think there were 100 pounds of feed wasted; hogs do wonderfully well feeding with cattle, better than in the States. Of all the animals that appreciate sunshine, the hog takes the lead, they raise their young with success every month in the year. The mild, dry climate insures them a dry bed, which prevents them from piling up in sleeping and getting overheated, wet and feverish, from which throat and lung troubles proceed, very often called cholera. They take on fat wonderfully fast. I find that alfalfa will grow them to perfection with a little corn to 'top off' with to make hard, firm meat.

"The year 1888 I sowed a field of barley after the middle of July and harvested it in November. It grew rank and fine, producing from forty to sixty bushels to the acre of the best quality, very bright and heavy. I find deep fall ploughing advantageous. There is no trouble in raising two crops of oats, rye and barley, one of grain and one of hay, from one sowing on the same ground. Last week I harvested seventeen tons of fine oat hay from four acres of ground. This week I harvested a fine crop of oat hay from twenty-four acres sown in August, all without irrigation. Grain will grow and ripen any time except in winter. I am well pleased with my experience of farming in New Mexico. It is a successful stock-growing and feeding country, for the reason you can fatten cattle and hogs on about one-third the amount of food required in the States. There is no better dairy country than this. My neighbors since they have provided themselves with improved agricultural implements have made a grand success in farming, feeding from 100 to 300 head of cattle each during the fall and winter."

The extent of the mineral resources of New Mexico cannot be adequately estimated. Her coal deposits are perhaps of the greatest value, and only measured by the extent of the present workings, and prospects indicate a great future development. They are found in Colfax, Mora, Taos, Santa Fé, Bernalillo, Valencia and Socorro counties in large veins for working. The anthracite coal fields in Santa Fé county produce coal of the purest quality, and in several parts of the territory the coal possesses the finest cokeing properties.

From the four regions where coal is extensively mined in New Mexico, it is shipped to distant points: the anthracite of the Cerrillos Mines as far east as Kansas City; the bituminous coal of Raton and Cerrillos is transported to Mexico and to the

Pacific States. The coal industry already employs over 1500 men, who produce annually over 1,000,000 tons. The Monero and Amargo coal mines in the north supply in part the Denver & Rio Grande Railroad; Blossburg, Raton and Carthage coals run the locomotives of the Santa Fé and Mexican Central Railroads; Gallop mines supply the Atlantic & Pacific Railroad trains, and Cerrillos coal meets the local demand, and enters the market of distant cities.

The Cerrillos coal fields are in close proximity to deposits of iron, copper, silver, lead and zinc, and the gold bearing sands of southern Santa Fé county.

The two mining districts of Santa Fé county which have yielded the most encouraging results for large expenditures of money are at Cerrillos and San Pedro. The latter has two prominent mines, which support expensive mining operations. The most widely known belongs to the Santa Fé Copper Company, whose smelting works have built up the prosperous mining town of San Pedro, and the Lincoln Lucky Mining Company own a rich silver bearing mine proximate to the San Pedro Copper workings.

The resources of New Mexico are quite evenly distributed over its great domain. There are sixteen counties, but these would make over a hundred of ordinary size in other States.

The principal mineral bearing counties are Santa Fé, Socorro, Grant, Sierra and Doña Aña. Gold, silver, lead and copper abound in these and also in portions of Colfax, Lincoln and Bernalillo counties. There are notable mining camps at Silver City,

Kingston, Pinos Altos, Georgetown, Lordsburg, Hillsborough, Chloride, Lake Valley, Hermosa, Cerrillos, Golden, San Pedro, Kelley, Socorro, Magdalena, White Oaks, Nogal and Taos.

There are in active operation smelters, stamp mills or reduction works in most of the working camps. Some of these, as at Socorro and Silver City, are very extensive and costly mining plants. The production of a few mines like the Superior, Lady Franklin and Brush Heat, at Kingston, and two at Chloride Flats, near Silver City, have been already from $500,000 to $3,000,000 each.

The mineral output of New Mexico in 1889 was carefully figured by an experienced mining Superintendent of long residence in the territory, Mr. Walter C. Hadley, of Sierra county, to be in gold $1,136,320; in silver, $1,891,105; in copper, $642,620; in lead, $354,839, or a total value of $4,023,884. Only four States and territories in the United States exceed New Mexico in bullion product, and her resources have only been imperfectly prospected, rather than developed by careful and scientific mining.

Some of the finest pine and cedar timber in the United States is found in the Raton Mountains of Colfax county, in the Taos county ranges, in the Santa Fé Mountains and in the Tierra Amarilla table lands in Rio Arriba county; timber lies also along the head waters of the Pecos, in the Sandia Mountains near the Rio Grande, in the Sacramento Mountains in Lincoln county, in the Burro and Mimbres Mountains in Grant county, in the Black range of Sierra county, the Magollon ranges of Socorro, the San Mateo and Jemez Mountains of Bernalillo county.

The United States department of Agriculture estimates that there are in New Mexico 12,500 square miles of strictly forest area, embracing fourteen varieties of trees.

The entire territory is a fine stock range. Lincoln, Colfax, Socorro, San Miguel and Mora counties have the largest number of cattle, while the sheep and goats are most numerous in Bernalillo, San Miguel, Valencia, Rio Arriba, Santa Fé and Taos counties.

The stores of building material, besides lumber in New Mexico, are inexhaustible. Various kinds of building stone are found. There are mountains of limestone and red sandstone, and vast tracts of gypsum deposits, and cement, fire clay and slate. The sandstone of New Mexico has been regarded by contractors of superior quality. The assessed property value of New Mexico in 1890 is nearly $50,000,000, yet neither mines nor railroads nor irrigation ditches are included in this amount. The valuation of the territory in 1880 was $14,000,000. The entire indebtedness of the territory amounts to $750,000, but by an economical administration this debt is being decreased at the rate of from $60,000 to $100,000 yearly. These liabilities were incurred for the erection of the territorial Penitentiary and the Capitol building, which are of substantial and massive construction. The Capitol is creditable in design, extent, material and ornamentation, to the

A FIELD OF NEW MEXICO SUGAR CANE.

patriotism and confidence of the people of New Mexico in her future importance as a State.

Santa Fé, with a population of 6,038, still continues to be the largest town of New Mexico, and is followed in population by Las Vegas, 4,693; Albuquerque, 3.794; Las Cruces, 2,416; Silver City, 2 252; Eddy, 1,500; Lincoln, 1,000.

New Mexico has three times, by Constitutional Convention, formally applied for admission to the Union as a State. When first occupied by the American army in 1846 and by subsequent treaty obligations, she was promised all the privileges of Statehood. Her first application to Congress in 1850, when a Constitutional Convention was held and officers elected, was rejected. She was made a territory Sept. 9, 1850, and has ever since been governed by foreign officials, reaping but little advantage from her annexation to the American Republic till within the last decade. Her resources have been left undeveloped, the education and advancement of her people utterly neglected, and they have been regarded with distrust as descendants of an alien race.

It was the will of Congress to give New Mexico Statehood in 1874. The enabling act was passed by both houses by a majority of nearly three-fourths, but the failure of the House of Representatives to act upon some slight amendments passed by the Senate caused the bill to be lost. It was again passed by the Senate of the Forty-fourth Congress, March 10, 1876, but not acted upon by the House. More than half of the twenty-seven legislative assemblies have memorialized Congress for the passage of an enabling act, but without effect. In the Fiftieth Congress she has recently again strenuously sought for the recognition of her rights, and has been denied them by the Republican Senate, though the privilege of Statehood was granted to Wyoming, Idaho and Dacotah.

New Mexico, in her history, resources, population and loyalty in the Civil War, has had imperative claims upon the Government and people of the United States for her recognition with equal rights to those States that in the years of her territorial existence have been admitted to the full privilege and benefits of the Union.

Her rejection has not been from the disloyalty of her citizens, nor from her lack of wealth, the fertility and extent of her possessions, or the number of her inhabitants, but plainly from a prejudice which early gained strength against her among the people of the North.

New Mexico was conquered and afterward purchased by treaty in order to make out of her great domain several States to increase the slave power in the Union. She was conquered in an unrighteous war, waged for an unrighteous purpose, yet when the representatives of her people in convention applied for admission as a territory, they implored that slavery might be forever excluded from their domain.

The Mexican war left bitter memories of Mexican perfidy and cruelty in the hearts of the people of the United States. The New Mexicans, through their own speedy and bloody conspiracy against the United States Government, shared fully the rancor of the Americans against their nation.

The great illiteracy of the New Mexicans, who for two centuries never had public schools or hardly schools of any kind, their foreign language, customs and ideas, and religion under foreign control, have also been insuperable obstacles to fair judgment concerning their qualifications for Statehood. In 1880 New Mexico was the most illiterate of all the States and territories of the Union.

In 1878 the successful effort of the Jesuits, contrary to the laws of the United States, to control legislation for their establishment in New Mexico, was rebuked by Congress, which quickly annulled the laws that were thus made. That blow prostrated New Mexico. It strengthened the long standing prejudice against her receiving Statehood. She was thenceforth associated with Utah, as if governed by an ecclesiastical corporation hostile to free institutions, public school education and the Supreme Authority of the Constitution.

This opinion was apparently well founded, and in an address to the people the Democratic Executive, Governor Ross, in 1889 declared that her measure had been well taken by the Congress which rejected New Mexico; for while Congress was discussing her claims to admission there was being waged in the legislature of New Mexico, in session in Santa Fé during January and February, 1889, a bitter opposition to a bill establishing on effective footing a public school system; violent speeches were made against public school education by those native New Mexican legislators, whose constituents so deplorably needed the beneficent influence of such a law. The public school bill was defeated through the Roman Catholic vote, which was largely in the majority in the legislature. The door was thus effectually closed again by her own action.

The more progressive and enlightened elements of the population, however, found expression in a Constitutional convention which was authorized by the same legislature to meet in the following September.

The delegates to it were to be elected in August by a special election. The Democratic leaders refused to join in this movement, and no delegates were nominated by the party organization. The Republicans, however, elected their nominees and the convention met at Santa Fé on September 3d. After a session of nineteen days this assembly completed a Constitution embracing the most liberal and progressive ideas and provisions for education, courts of justice, civil rights and the exclusion of ecclesiastical power in the affairs of State. This Constitution was presented to the Fifty-first Congress with a new petition for Statehood, but again by partisan rulings the bill for the admission of New Mexico was defeated, though the privilege of Statehood was granted to Idaho and Wyoming. Compared with these territories New Mexico far excelled them, in the claims she presented to Congress, in her history, resources, population and loyal services to the Government, from which she sought honorable recognition and place in the Union. The Constitutional convention reassembled at Santa Fé Aug. 27th, and having revised some of the Articles of the Constitution adopted the previous year, fixed upon October 7th, as the day for this ratification by the people, by whom it was rejected.

As we look back over the strange history of New Mexico through three centuries and a half, since Europeans first trod her plains, there will be impressed upon the thoughtful mind the conviction that her people have lacked certain qualities which have quickly built up States east and north of her boundaries. In the estimation of the country at large, the position, character and history of this territory have demanded qualifications which have not been required of other territories for admission to Statehood.

New Mexico must meet these conditions, before such privileges will be readily granted to her, unless considerations of political party interests shall overlook them:

1. She needs 100,000 intelligent immigrants, untrammelled by ecclesiastical control. To these she offers the fruits of her fertile valleys and plains, the wealth of her mines and the blessings of her sunny, cheerful and healthful climate for their homes.

2. Her people must firmly establish measures of public education that shall train her youth to loyalty, independence of thought and vote, and to self-respecting industry and enterprise as citizens.

With these two conditions fulfilled New Mexico

will be welcomed to the American Union, to share the future greatness and glory of the nation, to whose possessions she will add her fair country, from whose lofty plateaus rise shining peaks like gems in the crown of the vast domain which lies between the two oceans.

THE STORY OF NEW MEXICO

IN CHRONOLOGICAL EPITOME.

PERIOD I TO A. D. 1536.

That prehistoric peoples dwelt in New Mexico is abundantly demonstrated by the relics of their habitations still in a state of remarkable preservation. Their implements of war, their pottery and even their bones hidden in lofty caves, undisturbed by beasts of prey, uncorroded by the wonderfully dry atmosphere yet, remain.

600 TO 1000.

New Mexico was the pathway of races migrating to the South. Their way-marks are left upon the rocks and are intelligently read by the archæologist.

Ethnology discovers their relation to existing tribes. The origin of these was in the northwest.

Sedentary peoples in successive or overlapping occupations of the country, built permanent habitations, first of the single detached house type, afterwards of the great communal structure plans, still seen in the houses of their descendants, the Pueblo tribes.

The roving peoples, ancestors of the various Southwest Indian tribes were later than the sedentary populations. They came from the same directions and were predatory and hostile to the peoples who sustained themselves chiefly by simple agriculture though warring among themselves and with their Athabaskan foes.

PERIOD II. 1536-1591.

SPANISH DISCOVERIES AND CONQUESTS.

1530-36. Explorations by Cabeca de Vaco and Nuno Guzman south of New Mexico.

1538. Arizona discovered by the friars, Pedro Madal and Juan de la Ascunsion. Francisco Vasquez Coronado became Governor of Culiacan.

1539. Nica's expedition set out from St. Michaels in Culiacan to reach Cibola — March 7. Cibola discovered by Nica's guide — May. Estevanico slain — (about) June 1. A few days after, Cibola was first seen by a

Spaniard, Nica, and claimed by right of discovery for the Spanish crown as the "New Kingdom of St. Francis." The official report of Marcos de Nica's expedition given to Viceroy Mendoza — September 2.

1540. Coronado's expedition set forth from Compestella — January 1. Arrived at Culiacan Easter eve. Havieu, one of the "seven cities of Cibola," taken by assault by Coronado's troops. The Colorado River discovered at its mouth by the marine division of Coronado's expedition and explored for two hundred and fifty miles. The Moqui Province (Tusayan) taken by a detachment of soldiers from Cibola under Don Pedro de Tobar. The Colorado River also discovered from Tusayan by Garciza Lopez de Cardenas.

1541. The provinces of Acoma, Tiguex, Cicuyé and Tanos captured or occupied by the Spaniards. The search for Quivera under Coronado began — May. Quivera discovered by Coronado and made part of the Spanish dominion — June 10. Return of Coronado to Tiguex — November.

1542. Coronado set out on return march to Mexico. Deaths of the Franciscan missionary, Luis, at Cicuyé, and Padilla at Quivera.

1548. Coronado deposed from office.

1581. Mission of Ruis, Lopez and Juan de Santa Maria, to New Mexico — June 6. Francisco Sanchez Chamuscado commanding their military guard.

1582. Return of Chamuscado — January. He dies before reaching Santa Barbara. Murder of Ruis, Lopez and Juan de Santa Maria. The country receives its name, New Mexico, from these friars. Expedition of Don Antonio de Espejo sets out from Santa Barbara — November 10.

1583. Espejo visits and estimates the populations of the Piros, Tanos, Queres, Jemez, Hubates, Acoma, Zuñi and Moqui-provinces.

1583. The Navajoes first encountered in New Mexico.

1590. Expedition of Gaspar de Castano de Sosa — July 27.

1593. Efforts of Bonilla and Humana to reach Quivera.

1597. Departure of Juan de Oñate for New Mexico to colonize the country.

PERIOD III. 1598-1680.

SPANISH COLONIZATION.

1598. Oñate enters New Mexico, and for the sixth time takes formal possession for the Kingdom of Spain — April 30. San Gabriel, the first Spanish town, founded between the Chama and Rio Grande rivers. First church and first convent built here in New Mexico. This town now extinct. First Conference of Pueblo tribes giving allegiance to the Spanish crown July 7. Seven religious missions of New Mexico definitely located, including the mission to the Apaches.

1601-06. Expeditions by Oñate to Quivera, to the Canadian and to the mouth of the Colorado.

1605. Capital of the colony transferred to Santa Fé.
1608-40. Pedro de Peralta replaces Oñate as governor. Increasing oppression of the natives by the Spanish military power. Concurrent missionary efforts and success by the Franciscan priests.
1630. All the Pueblos nominally Christian except Zuñi.
1642. Governor Rosas assassinated.
1650. Arguello, governor and captain-general. Forty Indians hanged for conspiracy. Another conspiracy crushed by Governor Concha.
1660-75. Frequent hostilities attempted.
1661-64. Administration of Governor de Peñalosa, and dissensions between military and missionaries.
1674. Francisco de Ayeta comes to New Mexico to be Director of Missions.

PERIOD IV. 1680-1692.

REBELLION AND NATIVE INDEPENDENCE.

1680. The conspiracy of Popé. Outbreak of the great Pueblo rebellion August 10. Attack, siege, defense and evacuation of Santa Fé by the Spaniards, under Governor Otermin. Sacking of the missions; murders of the priests; expulsion of the Spaniards from New Mexico — August 14-20.
1681. Attempted recapture of New Mexico by Otermin. Return of the expedition.
1687. Cruzate vainly attempts to subdue the Pueblos.

PERIOD V. 1692-1821.

SPANISH RULE.

1691. Diego de Vargas Zapata Lujan succeeds Cruzate as governor-general and makes an armed reconnoissance upon Santa Fé which surrenders. Taos, Piccuries and San Ildefonzo subdued without slaughter. Pecos and the Rio Grande Pueblos yield. Seventeen provinces and the Apaches offer allegiance before October 30. De Vargas returns to El Paso, after the further subjection of the Zuñi and Moqui villages — December 20.
1693. Departure of a great colonization expedition for Santa Fé and re-occupation of the country. Attack upon and capture of Santa Fé by the Spaniards — October 11.
1694. Assault upon the Mesacita de San Ildefonzo by the Spaniards and their repulse. Its final surrender — March 18. Subsequent frequent conflicts with various Pueblo tribes.
1696. Famine in New Mexico. Distress of the colonists. The last rebellion and massacre by the Pueblo Indians.

1700-1800. Slow progress of the colony.

1780. The four centers of trade with Chihuahua and Mexico were Santa Fé, Albuquerque, La Cañada and El Paso.

1798. There were eighteen Franciscan priests and twenty-four missions in New Mexico.

1805. There were twenty-six Franciscan priests and thirty missions in the Province. First American, James Pursley, arrives in New Mexico.

1806. Lieutenant Zebulon Montgomery Pike with remnants of his exploring expedition captured and taken to Santa Fé — March 3, 1807.

PERIOD VI. 1821-1846.

NEW MEXICO UNDER THE MEXICAN CONFEDERATION.

1821. Iturbide declared emperor of Mexico — February. Abdicated — March. All Spaniards excluded from Mexico by the decree of the Government.

1823. The Mexican Republic created — November 19.

1824. Iturbide returns from exile and is executed — July 19. Bartolomé Baca appointed first governor of New Mexico under the Republic.

1837. New Mexico created a Department. Governor Albino Perez assassinated by Pueblo Indians — August 9.

1838. Josié Gonzales rebel governor executed by Manuel Armigo, who was recognized as governor at Mexico and continued in office from 1838 to 1846.

1840. Population of New Mexico forty-five thousand.

1841. Texan Santa Fé Expedition arrested on their way to Santa Fé from Anton Chico — September 15.

PERIOD VII. 1846-1862.

THE AMERICAN OCCUPATION.

1846. Departure of the Army of the West from Fort Leavenworth, Kansas, for New Mexico — June 26. Doniphan's expedition. Arrival at Fort Bent — July 30. A flag of truce from General Kearney reaches Santa Fé inviting New Mexico to accept annexation with the United States, which was declined — August 12. Santa Fé occupied and New Mexico formally declared a part of the United States — August 22. General Kearney's Expedition down the valley of the Rio Grande — September 2. Fort Marcey constructed at Santa Fé. Charles Bent of Taos appointed governor. Colonel Sterling Price arrives with one thousand and two hundred men and artillery at Santa Fé — September 28. General Kearney marches overland to California. Col. Doniphan sets out to subjugate the Navajoes — October 26. Returns and marches into Mexico — December.

1847. Insurrection of the inhabitants of New Mexico against the United States — January 22. Governor Bent and six officials of the territory assassinated on their way to Taos. Col. Price attacks and defeats the insurgents at Cañada — January. And at Taos and Embudo — February. The insurgents also defeated at Mora.

PERIOD VIII. 1862-1865.

NEW MEXICO IN THE CIVIL WAR OF THE UNITED STATES.

1862. Invasion by the troops of the Southern Confederacy in the months of February, March and April. Arrival of Texan troops near Fort Craig — February 7. Armed reconnoissance under General Sibley (Confederate) upon Fort Craig — February 16. Crossing of the Rio Grande by the Confederates — February 20. Battle of Valverde — February 21. Evacuation of Albuquerque by Federal troops — March 1. Evacuation of Santa Fé by Federal troops — March 4. Occupation of the capital by Confederates. Engagement between Texan and Colorado troops at Apache Cañon — March 26. Battle of Glorietta Cañon between Texan troops and Federal forces and retreat of the latter — March 27. Junction of Colorado and New Mexico volunteers and U. S. Regulars at Pecos church — March 28. Capture of Confederate wagon train by Colorado troops near Johnson's Ranch — March 28. Confederate evacuation of Santa Fé — April 12. Retreat of the Texans down the Rio Grande Valley, and artillery battle at Peralta — April 13. Subsequent escape of Confederates into Texas.

PERIOD IX. 1865-1878.

AMERICAN RULE. — NAVAJO AND APACHE WARS.

1849-1865. Thirty million dollars expended by United States Government in the subjugation of Indians in New Mexico and Arizona.

1849. Expedition into Navajo country under Colonel Washington.

1851. Expedition against the Navajoes under command of General Sumner.

1851-1859. Indians comparatively quiet.

1859. Navajoes again at war with the United States troops.

1860. Navajoes attack Fort Defiance. Summer campaign of General Canby.

1861. Hostilies cease — March.

1862. General James H. Carleton succeeds General Canby — September 18. Kit Carson sent against the Mescalleroes and Navajoes near Fort Stanton. The Apaches subdued and removed to Bosque Redondo. Fort Wingate established — December.

1863. Expedition against the Gila Apaches. Magnus Colorado captured — January. Navajoes ordered to remove to Bosque Redondo reservation till July 20. War of extermination begins on all Navajoes who do not surrender and remove to reservation at Bosque Redondo.

1864. Three thousand Navajoes reported captured or removed — February 29. War of extermination continued in the Navajo country. Two thousand and four hundred Navajoes removed — April. Seven thousand Navajoes at Bosque Redondo.

1865. Colonel Kit Carson sent on an expedition into Navajo country to Cañon de Chelly. Conference with Chief Manuelito — February.

1867. Indian Peace Commission appointed by President Grant consisting of Gen. W. T. Sherman and others.

1868. Report of Indian Peace Commission. Signing of treaty with the Navajoes by the Peace Commissioners — June 1. Return of the Navajoes to their country. Removal of the Chiricahua Apaches to Ojo Caliente reservation under Chief Victoria.

1879. Chief Victoria takes the war path against the United States government.

1879-83. Apache Wars under Chiefs Victoria and Geronimo.

1883. Death of Victoria and his followers. General George Crook resumes command and makes a campaign against the Apaches. Chiricahua Apache raid under Chato, near Silver City. Judge McComas and wife killed. Capture of Charlie McComas — March. Expedition of General Crook into Sonora in pursuit of Apaches — April. Captain Crawford and Lieutenants Gatewood and Mackey overtake Apaches — May 15. Capture of Chihuahua and other chiefs with their followers — May 15-24.

1885. Apache raid under Geronimo and other chiefs — May 17.

1886. General Nelson G. Miles assigned to command of the Department of Arizona — April 2. Apache raid into Santa Cruz Valley — April 27. Engagement with United States Cavalry — May 15. Pursued into Sonora and Chihuahua by Captain Lawton's command — July and August. Apaches overtaken by Lieutenant Gatewood — August 24. Surrender of Geronimo to General Miles at Skeleton Cañon — September 3.

PERIOD X. 1879-1890.

AMERICAN DEVELOPMENT. — MATERIAL.

1878. Entrance of the Atchison, Topeka and Santa Fé railroad.
1880. Completion of this railroad to Santa Fé — February 15.
1886. Legislation favorable to irrigation companies.
1889. Beginning of the Pecos Valley Irrigation and Investment Company's great system.

RELIGIOUS AND EDUCATIONAL DEVELOPMENT. — ROMAN CATHOLIC.

1851. Arrival of Bishop Lamy at Santa Fé.
1852. Arrival of colony of the Sisters of Loretto.

1854. Arrival of French Priests — November 15.

1859. The order of San Miguel enter New Mexico and begin the school afterwards (1883) incorporated as St. Michael's College in Santa Fé.

1867. Introduction of the order of Jesuits.

1878. Act of incorporation of Jesuit Society by the New Mexico legislature vetoed by Gov. S. B. Axtell.

PROTESTANT.

1849. First Baptist Missionary in New Mexico at Santa Fé.

1850. First Methodist Missionary.

1863. First Episcopal service in New Mexico, at Santa Fé.

1866. Presbyterians purchase Baptist Mission property at Santa Fé.

1874. Establishment of the Episcopal Missionary Diocese.

1879. Congregationalists established academies at Santa Fé, Las Vegas and Albuquerque.

1881. University of New Mexico incorporated under Congregational direction — May 11. Opened — September 11.

1885. Ramona Indian School of University of New Mexico opened — April 1. United States Government Indian School at Santa Fé receives first appropriation from Congress of twenty-five thousand dollars, and one hundred acres of land from citizens of Santa Fé.

1887. Whitin Hall, University of New Mexico, building began — October 21, 1882. Completed — October, 1887.

1889. Extensive buildings erected at Santa Fé for government Indian school.

POLITICAL.

1850. First application of New Mexico to Congress for Statehood.

1882. Improved Public School law passed by New Mexico legislature authorizing the organization of school districts and support of schools.

1888. Establishment by Legislature of a State University at Albuquerque, a school of mines at Socorro, and an agricultural school at Las Cruces.

1889. Constitutional Convention at Santa Fé — September 3. Adopted Constitution.

1890. Reassembled — August 27. Revised Constitution, which was defeated by vote of the people on ratification — October 7.

www.ingramcontent.com/pod-product-compliance
Lightning Source LLC
Chambersburg PA
CBHW022059300426
44117CB00007B/515